THE BEAVER HILLS COUNTRY

THE BEAVER HILLS COUNTRY

A History of Land and Life

Graham A. MacDonald

AU PRESS

© 2009 Graham A. MacDonald

Published by AU Press, Athabasca University
1200, 10011 – 109 Street
Edmonton, AB T5J 3S8

Library and Archives Canada Cataloguing in Publication

MacDonald, Graham A. (Graham Alexander), 1944–
The Beaver Hills country: a history of land and life/Graham A. MacDonald.

Includes index.
Also available in electronic format (978-1-897425-38-1)
ISBN 978-1-897425-37-4

1. Strathcona (Alta.: County) – History. 2. Strathcona (Alta.: County) –
Biography. I. Title.

FC3695.B43M33 2009   971.23'3   C2009-901824-1

Cover design by Valentino Gerard
Book design by Infoscan Collette, Québec
Back cover photo: LAC. C-030279
Front and back cover skies: Photos.com

Printed and bound in Canada by Marquis Book Printing

 This book was funded in part by the Alberta Historical
Resources Foundation.

CONTENTS

ACKNOWLEDGMENTS

This book developed out of an earlier enquiry into the history of the bison conservation story at Elk Island National Park undertaken for Parks Canada. The broader natural, social and economic history of the Beaver Hills seemed to invite scrutiny. The post-1880 years are the richest in a documentary sense, but there is great time depth to the hills and an effort has been made to outline the shifting character of the hills since glacial times. I must first thank for unrecorded discussions and assistance the many colleagues who encouraged this line of enquiry. Thanks are also owing to many individuals who shared stories and to organizations which shared information and photography. To all those known and anonymous editors and contributors who laboured to produce the many large and profusely illustrated local histories pertaining to central Alberta, I owe a great debt. Special thanks to Don Wetherell and Don Purich for their reading of earlier versions of the manuscript. At AU Press, I am grateful to Walter Hildebrandt, Erna Dominey and Carol Woo for their encouragement and disciplined interest in seeing the manuscript through to publication.

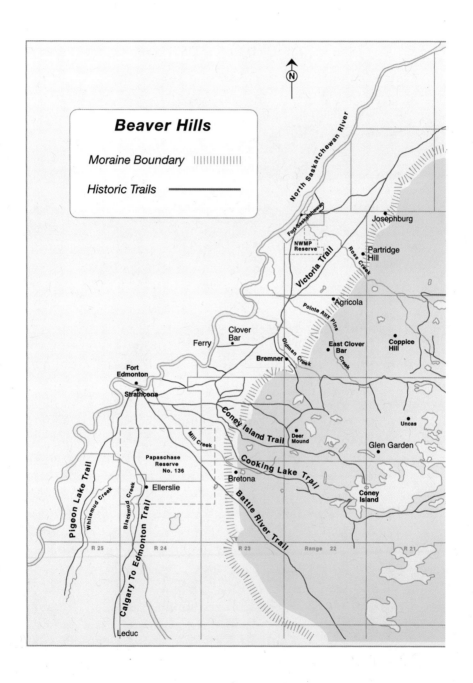

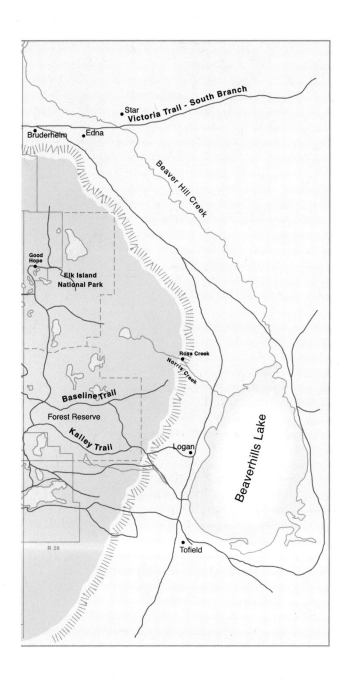

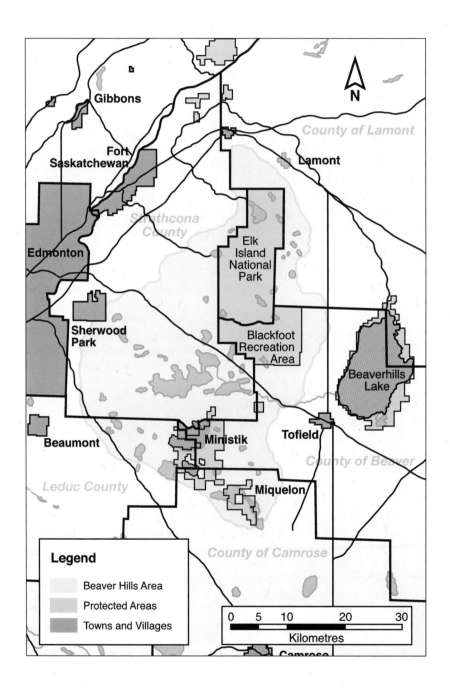

INTRODUCTION

On the Name "Beaver Hills"

The Beaver Hills rise subtly out of a hospitable and moist mixed-farming region identified with the Aspen Parkland, a web of grasslands and trees running in a broad swath from south-central Manitoba towards Edmonton. Trees characteristic of this region include the Trembling Aspen and the Balsam Poplar, along with willows. Manitoba Maple and Burr Oak appear in the eastern portions of the range south of the Qu'Appelle River. A variety of other species are found, some associated with the Boreal Forest to the north and others with more southerly climes that favour deciduous growth. Thus, in the Beaver Hills one can find the Paper Birch, White and Black Spruce and Tamarack.

This Aspen Parkland belt is one of the distinctive Canadian landscapes, for many centuries providing favoured wintering areas for the great herds of bison. The groves of trees were a source of shelter from the bitter prairie winds while much-needed grass could also be found for winter forage. It is a genuinely transitional type of landscape, embodying elements of the somewhat more uniform features which lie to the north and south of the belt.[1] These diverse qualities have made the uplands an important place of resort for many generations of Native peoples.

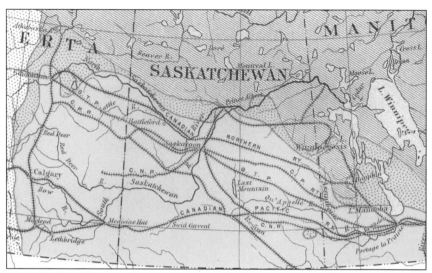

Aspen Parkland Belt, 1915 The Aspen Parkland in Western Canada, shown in mottled pattern, runs in a northwest direction from the Red River Valley of Manitoba, across Saskatchewan and into central Alberta where it then follows a line south along the edge of the foothills.

Representations of these gentle hills have appeared in European cartography since the mid-eighteenth century. On a map prepared in 1760 under the sponsorship of Moses Norton, Chief Factor for the Hudson's Bay Company at Churchill Fort, what is clearly the North Saskatchewan River is identified as the Beaver River. The map shows "Beaver Mount" from which there is a trail route described as "Ye track to Henday's tent." The chart was, Norton claimed, "Laid Down on Ind'n Inform'n" gathered no doubt with the assistance of Attickasish, "that trusty leader" who had con-ducted Anthony Henday in his Journey inland to the Earchithinues country in 1754–55.[2] The identification of "Beaver Mount" is prob-ably an early intimation of the Rocky Mountains, the presumed source of the Saskatchewan River. On Norton's map, however, only the presence of a river flowing from this western quarter was known, for "ye river Kish-stock-ewen" is misconceived and appears on his chart as the river flowing east in to Baker Lake, far to the north. By 1774, however, a map produced by Andrew Graham demonstrated a fairly modern understanding of the course of the Saskatchewan River.[3]

In 1793, Hudson's Bay Company cartographer and explorer Peter Fidler made rough reference sketches of the Beaver Hills on a number of occasions. Beaver Hills Lake appears prominently on David Thompson's great final map of western North America of 1814. Thompson remarked upon the hills, along with their currency in Native parlance, indicating that they were an area of resort amongst several of the major tribes, especially the Cree and Sarcee.[4] For the Cree the hills were known as the *a-misk-wa-chi*, which captures the notion of a place rich in beaver. Among the Stoney they were called the *chaba hei*. To the Blackfoot they were the *kaghghik-stak-etomo*. Beaver Hills Lake was called by the Blackfoot the "*Kakghikstakiskway* – the place where the beaver cut the wood."[5]

John Palliser's British-sponsored scientific expedition of the late 1850s entered the hills from the eastern side. On the published maps accompanying Palliser's Report, the hills appear a little more boldly than today's atlas makers would probably render them. The hills had registered on Palliser's men with some force. In late 1857, James Hector's segment of the party, moving westerly and south of the North Saskatchewan River, "soon came in sight of the Beaver Hills, a low blue line to the S.W. of us, evidently thickly wooded." About a year later Hector gave a more detailed account of his impression of the land on the eastern edge of the hills through to the western side:

> I crossed the Egg Hills which are 300 feet above the plain and to the south-west of which lies a large lake of the same name. Its margins are very swampy, and it was swarming with ducks, geese, swans, and other wild fowl at this season. From the north end of the lake we struck through dense poplar thickets, which continue all the way to the northwest angle of the Beaver Hills, where we again fell on the Edmonton Track.

About the possibilities inherent in this area, Hector stated: "I was much struck with the admirable pasture which is to be found

even at this season all over this extensive tract of country, and of
that kind which is most valuable for the support of animals during the
winter." The poplar thickets "affording shelter surround and enclose

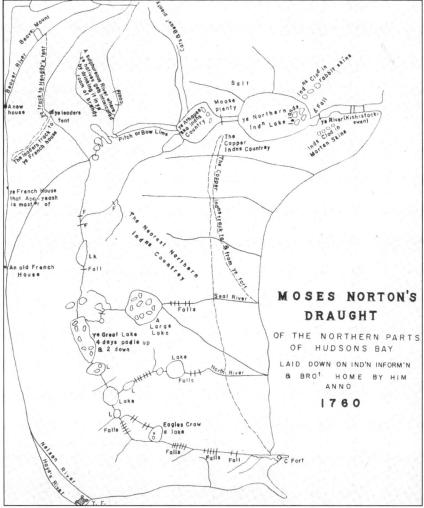

Moses Norton's Draught of the Northern Parts of Hudson's Bay (1760)
This Hudson's Bay Company map was compiled on the basis of reports from other
traders and guides. Redrawn in this version by Richard Ruggles, it identifies, very
imperfectly, some of the main features of Western Canada and the Rocky Mountain
barrier in the vicinity of the source of the Saskatchewan River.

limited prairies that yield a rich growth of vetches and nutritious grass of sufficient growth to bear up the snow and keep it loose, so that horses and cattle can scrape their food from under it at least until the later spring months, when in some winters, the crust might be a serious obstacle." Hector noted spots "where there is a deep rich soil admirably adapted to agriculture" and which are "to be found in every direction."[6]

In the mid-1880s, the ubiquitous Joseph B. Tyrrell of the Geological Survey of Canada remarked upon the hills which he found lying east of the Calgary-Edmonton Trail: "there is apparently high and thickly wooded country which goes by the name of Amisk-wachi or Beaver Hills." Of this country "little could be learned even among those who were living in the immediate vicinity, and it has been left as a hunting ground for the Indians who yearly kill a large number of moose in the deep recesses of its forests." Having gained some firsthand acquaintance of the terrain, he remarked upon their "most striking feature" which was "the absence of the rough hill character which this name would lead one to expect." In fact, the "country is found to be simply low ridges or sandy knobs, often thickly covered with large balsam, poplar and spruce separated by valleys drained by numbrous small streams." The hills were apparently well named, for "these streams have everywhere been dammed back by beaver giving rise to extensive meadows." Some of these were "impassable marshes" but others where beaver dams had been broken down "are again drained by the creeks and form beautiful and wide alluvial tracts covered in long grass" sufficient to provide hay for "large herds of cattle and horses."[7]

A few years later, some of the first Irish settlers at Deville, near Hastings Lake, confirmed the presence of Native hunting grounds of both ancient and recent vintage. Stone tools, arrowheads and other projectile points, as well as "pemmican balls" were regularly turned up in the new fields.[8] A formal beginning on the ethnology of the area was commenced in 1892 by that rambling and literate veteran of the Hudson's Bay Company, Isaac Cowie. At the request of the eminent scholar, Franz Boas, he saw to the collecting and safekeeping of a substantial amount of Cree artifacts drawn mainly from the Bear Hills area of the Battle River Valley, near Wetaskiwin.[9]

Some 35 years after Tyrrell's observations, Alex McCauley, the Mayor of Tofield, gave an address in which he recalled the hills in earlier times:

> The large lake at our door was called Beaverhills Lake and the country for over twenty miles west of this lake was called the Beaver Hills, owing to the large number of beaver being found here. Amisk Creek, a few miles east of Town was given its name for the same reason, "Amisk" being the Cree word for

Isaac Cowie (1848-1917)   This veteran Hudson's Bay Company trader had a literary bent and an interest in Native cultures. He made a collection of Cree artifacts and material culture items from central Alberta for the American anthropologist, Franz Boas. The materials are now in the Field Museum of Natural History in Chicago.

beaver. Like the evergreen island you can see from Cooking Lake Station, these hills were covered with jackpine, spruce and tamerac, and the depressions between the hills with water. In this forest were to be found buffalo, bear, moose, deer, as well as beaver and on the lake swam geese, ducks, pelicans and all kinds of waterfowl by the thousands. During the first part of the nineties fire destroyed this great forest.[10]

Over the years there have been many references to the hills, to their reputation as a traditional hunting ground for beaver, and as a well-watered haven for birds and wildlife. While the place name has persisted, Mayor McCauley's testimony reinforced a tradition of commentary which began around the turn of the century. This body of opinion suggested that the hills had undergone radical changes in the early settlement period, particularly through the agency of fire. This tradition was still alive in the 1960s when questions concerning the ideal character of the hills became points of departure for naturalists and parks and lands administrators then seeking to develop a more coherent and reasonable policy for human use of the hills. "If it could only talk, what stories Beaverhills Lake could tell!" exclaimed a local historian at Tofield.[11] The following chapters will attempt to relate some of those stories and to see the hills when they were part of more distant theatres of human action.

CHAPTER ONE

The Character of the Beaver Hills

As a place name, the Beaver Hills has a long history both in common parlance and through the mapmaker's art. Despite long standing popular use of the name Beaver Hills, a cooler and more scientific designation for them also exists: the Cooking Lake Moraine. In this designation the inherent glacial origin of the hills is acknowledged. The key to their present surface forms may be found in local glacial history. While many of the landforms around Edmonton were created through the draining actions of the great Glacial Lake Edmonton and its associated spillway channels, the Cooking Lake Moraine has been described as a "spectacular exception" to this process. The moraine was formed on high ground along a broad front "where the ice sheet stagnated and melted away."[1] The absolute position of the hills, before they were hills, was along the main edge and contact zone between two great clashing systems of ice: the mountain glaciers which flowed out of the Rockies and the great ice sheet which covered the plains and Canadian Shield, having advanced from the northeast. At the glacial maximum, some 21,000 years ago, only the odd elevation on the prairies, such as the Cypress Hills, poked heads above the great ice sheet. Such unglaciated aspects, or "nunataks," were not present in the Beaver Hills, for these uplands were themselves formed only as the outcome of late glacial erosion and melting. As the ice receded, what was left, in Roger Morton's words, was "a drastically modified landscape, bearing the erosive scars of glaciation and littered with the debris of destruction." Around Cooking Lake, for example, great "slices of bedrock were bulldozed out and dumped by the ice." Where no hills had been before, there was now deposited a confused and jumbled base.[2]

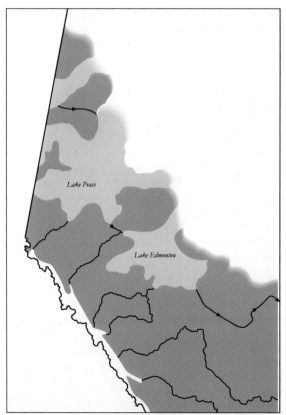

Glacial Lake Edmonton   As the ice of the last glaciation receded, large temporary lakes were formed at the edge, such as Glacial Lakes Peace and Edmonton. The latter had an important influence on the final arrangement of soils and lakes in the Beaver Hills.

When the glaciers started to lose their punch about 12,000 years ago, melting actions left behind some large archaic lakes, such as Glacial Lake Edmonton, a lake that was quite short lived. Its gradual drainage left extensive secondary deposits composed of finer material atop some of the uprooted and tumbled layers of bedrock, producing distinctive landscapes such as the Cooking Lake Moraine. The "hummocky" nature of the hills was described by local naturalist Deirdre Griffiths as a classic example of what geographers call "knob and kettle topography" terrain. Such landforms indicate that there had been large, slow-melting chunks of glacial ice embedded in the moraines during the early phases of glacial recession.[3] In the Beaver Hills many small, sometimes land-locked ponds gradually developed in the depressions, the product of the subsurface melting of these large chunks of buried glacier ice. The pattern of these wetlands is still visible today.

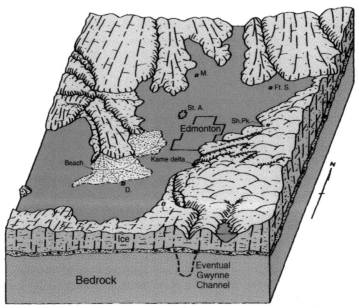

Decline of Ice in the Edmonton Area   This block diagram by J.D. Godfrey, superimposes the future locations of Fort Saskatchewan and Edmonton on the chaos of the melting glacier. Ice is still shown over the Beaver Hills area.

Elk Island Golf Course   At the golf course near Lake Astotin, players get a view
of the nature of moraine topography.

In the nine millennia since, belts of primary vegetation slowly
developed across western North America. On a grand scale this
involved the gradual configuration of boreal forest to the north
and grasslands to the south. These two large classes were divided
only by the broad area of ecological compromise called the Aspen
Parkland belt. This great arc of trees intermixed with grass defines
a transition vegetation zone between the true prairie to the south
and the boreal zones to the north. The unique dynamics of the
Aspen Parkland are driven by a combination of fire and moisture
availability, and together these produce substantial tree growth with
a successional cycle ideally terminating in spruce growth. Since
the fifteenth century, climatic conditions on the prairies have been
relatively unchanged, with the pattern of short-and tall-grass
prairies and the Aspen Parkland stabilized in a pattern generally
similar to the one we see today.[4]

The boundaries of these belts have never been absolute and
instead have been subject to movements north or south in keeping
with long-term shifts in climate. At times, as in the 1930s, periods

of drought set in. If such drought conditions persisted the vegetation patterns adjusted accordingly, producing this boundary-shift phenomenon. So severe was the prairie drought in the period from 1200 to 1400 A.D. that some have argued for a general abandonment by both human and animal in much of the lands to the east of the central and southern Rocky Mountains. This particular drought was no ordinary one, but was brought on by the movement of the winds somewhat to the north of their normal latitude of operation. In the resulting rain shadow that developed east of the mountains, little lived, or so it would seem.[5]

Conclusions such as these are more by way of impressions gained by modern environmental scientists; but archaeologists can sometimes confirm these suspicions at selected sites, if only imperfectly. Addressing the questions arising out of a knowledge of such broad shifts in climatic and vegetation conditions has become an important driver of post-war archaeological enquiry. The archaeologist seeks an understanding of the ways in which people adapted to such fundamental changes. While many tools of ancient Albertans have been found and examined since the 1960s, the reconstruction of the environmental contexts of such finds is the other task of the modern archaeologist.[6] With the assistance of that profession, it is here and there possible to follow in the footprints of a succession of different peoples, all of whom undertook activities shaped by their own contemporary relationships with land and life.[7]

The Aspen Parkland belt was of great significance to those who frequented the high plains in earlier periods. The open prairie in pre-horse times was a hostile environment. Use of tree-lined water courses, the uplands, or the relative shelter of the Aspen Parkland were central requirements in the relatively sedentary life of pre-eighteenth century times. Nomadism was certainly a reality, but communities were also rooted in localities; people only picked up and moved when necessary. The home base was significant for the opportunities it afforded for collecting plants, herbs, and berries. Hunting forays could depart from such a base camp in a familiar territory. In the treed portions of the Parkland, groups of hunters

Aerial view of the Beaver Hills, Elk Island National Park vicinity

drove the bison into a pound, which operated rather like both a trap and a corral.[8]

At its far western limit the parkland belt curves through Edmonton and Wetaskiwin, then moves south along the foothills towards Calgary and on to the American border, the tree roots benefiting from the river systems and sufficient localized rainfall. Nestled in the inner edge of the arc where the parkland turns south, lying between the North Saskatchewan and the Battle River, are the Beaver Hills.

During fur trade times, the hills became identified with the early fur posts of the Edmonton area. Later, along with the adjacent plains, they provided the initial settlement frontier for a large numbers of pioneers, including many of Ukrainian origin. These pioneers started to arrive in the early 1890s and many found that wresting a living from this topsy-turvy landscape was not always easy or rewarding. It is appropriate that one of the closest students of this post-glacial landscape was the geologist Luboslaw Bayrock (1930–1989), a post-war immigrant to Alberta from Ukraine. His surveys and map work did much to fathom the character of the geological forces which had shaped the river valleys, rolling hills and prairies of central Alberta, the same lands which many of his compatriots had worked so hard to tame in the years after 1897.[9]

It will be helpful to keep in mind the rather unusual circumstances of vegetation history in the hills as we make the journey from past to present. The vegetation cover indicates that while the Beaver Hills are *in* the parkland belt they are not quite *of* it. This was the conclusion of S.C. Zoltai, an authority on forest history, who closely studied the internal composition of the Aspen Parkland and its regional variants. He found a strong aspect of the Boreal Forest in the northern fringes of the belt, particularly in the Beaver Hills.[10] For this reason, the unique qualities of the hills have been described as follows: "Elk Island and the Beaver Hills are elevated above the Aspen Parkland that surrounds the hills" and are considered to be "part of the Boreal Mixedwood Forest."[11] That is, the hills seem to partake somewhat more of the northern forest than southern plains. The significance of this particular suggestion, we will see later, came to be debated at some length by park administrators and research scientists at Elk Island National Park in the 1960s. The supposed transitional features of the landscape have become somewhat blurred by historic land use practices and fire suppression, but they may still be noticed during a north to south tour of the hills. The northern aspect reveals a thicker forest tending towards spruce, while in the south the character is more towards open Aspen stands punctuated by extensive grasslands.[12]

Such rolling country, along with the well-wooded river valleys which coursed through it, was naturally recognized and used by generations of ancient Aboriginal folk. The ultimate identities of the most distant inhabitants remain obscure; but it is certain that various peoples came and went during the many centuries prior to the coming of the horse to the northern plains in the first half of the eighteenth century.[13]

Before the horse, life was more localized for residents of this quarter, and the dog was of great importance. During what archaeologist Jack Brink calls "dog days on the prairies," individual or group transportation was a more laborious undertaking, for it lacked the convenience and efficiency occasioned by the horse.[14] The arrival of the horse had great consequences for the taking of that great mainstay of prairie life: the bison. Since time immemorial, the bison had been the "staff of life" but unlike artist images of nineteenth-century mounted hunters, the bison's taking throughout most of human time has been a matter of communal strategies. Well-defined escarpment features were often an important component in the seasonal round of group hunting. Relict features can be seen today by visitors to various ancient "buffalo jump" sites on the prairies where bison were known to have been systematically driven over cliff edges as a hunting procedure.[15]

Head-Smashed-In UNESCO Historic Site   Prominent escarpment features such as found at the Head-Smashed-In Buffalo Jump near Lethbridge, Alberta, are not found in the Beaver Hills. The strategies for taking bison in the hills were more dependent on driving the animals into "pounds" rather than over cliffs.

Use of such dramatic headland jump sites was not a feature of life in the Beaver Hills. The required type of cliff relief was not present. In pre-horse times, the group hunting methods used here were akin to those of ancient caribou hunters further north in the Boreal Forest and on the tundra.[16] Native peoples perfected techniques of the woodland "buffalo pound" in the Beaver Hills in the pre-horse era, aided by a certain assurance that the bison would seek out the shelter of the hills in winter when winds blew hard across the more open prairies to the south.

Over the centuries the parkland gradually took on a role as a kind of cultural "half-way house" for peoples who kept one foot in the forest and one on the prairie. The long east-to-west belt of the Aspen Parkland with its interlocking zones of trees and grass provided the lookout from which various Algonkian and Siouan speaking peoples came to master the possibilities of survival in the adjoining prairie landscapes. At that crucial stage in their group histories when the horse started to alter economic prospects on the northern plains, the peoples of the parkland started to range more widely. Some groups, such as the Blackfoot, left their compatriots behind entirely for a life on the open prairie. Trade and ancient ties tended to bind the old parkland residents together on more or less good terms until the last decade of the eighteenth century, when economic relations became strained in the heat of British-American competition for both land and furs. Good memories were replaced by bad along the marches of the prairie and parkland. When Henday visited this part of the country in the 1750s, the name "Battle River" did not appear to be in use, indicating the still amicable nature of Blackfoot-Cree relations. By 1793 this had changed, for Peter Fidler recorded in March of that year his arrival at "the Battle or Fighting River." As a recognized place name, Battle River was in use at least by 1802, when it appeared on one of the Arrowsmith Firm's maps. The subsequent nineteenth-century "time of troubles" which often pitted the Cree, Assiniboine and Saulteux against the Blackfoot Confederacy, appears, then, to be recent in origin.[17]

Bison in Parkland, Elk Island National Park The interplay of grassland and aspen trees made the hills a good winter retreat for bison.

Fire, both natural and induced, was another factor that assisted the ancients of the parkland and plains in their quest for the bison. Students of anthropology and archaeology have been considering the place of fire in earlier Native cultures for some time.[18] Somewhat naive notions about how the pre-European community was in some general way "in harmony" with nature have given way to more critical inspections and appreciations of how given groups actually proceeded to make a living and how they were assisted by vegetation – and wildlife-management techniques. Human-induced fire played an important role in Alberta's Boreal Forest Native communities, according to an intricate and well-ordered pattern of burnings executed within a seasonal round of land use.[19] Fire-use methods for stampeding and corralling animals, or for stimulating vegetation favourable to the increased genesis of certain species, were all part of evolving Aboriginal tool kits.

Albert Tate, a Beaver Hills fur trader, left a striking memoir of one of the last great buffalo hunts in the Battle River valley in the winter of 1867–68. It was conducted during that period when the last of the bison herds were disappearing ever further south. Food was short, and the various elements of the community came together for this hunt. "The white men and half-breeds conceded to the request of the Indians who had inferior guns and horses, to build a 'pound' or *Pee-tee-quahan* – and drive the buffalo in, and each share up alike."[20] On this occasion "buffalo pound" hunting methods were employed. The combination of strategically placed hunters on foot, horse-back riders and erected barriers were all used to good effect. The event revealed how in the nineteenth century the overall scale and possibilities of this ancient technique had increased.

The decline of the bison induced an important shift in the frequency and scale of prairie fires. Widespread and frequent fires before this decline were long matters of historic and artistic record.[21] In 1846 the artist Paul Kane was at Fort Edmonton, where he witnessed a vast fire spreading across the Beaver Hills. He produced a remarkable painting of the occurrence. Some years later, explorer and geologist Henry Youle Hind reconfirmed the regular nature of fire on the prairies. He reported "a vast conflagration, extending for one thousand miles in length and several hundred in breadth." These "annual fires prevent the willows and aspens from covering the country."[22]

With the decline of the bison and the progressive measurement of the land into standard homestead plots, public reserves and Indian reserves, the traditional reasons for stimulating the great seasonal fires on the prairie commons disappeared. Historian J.G. MacGregor has drawn attention to a side effect of the bison's disappearance. The large herds of the past had done much to keep the prairie grasses short. The disappearance of these great and gregarious grazers now allowed for a period in which the grasses grew waist-high. In dry conditions these large tracts were much more fire-prone: "almost any spark could touch off a conflagration that might rage far and wide for miles."[23]

Based on the evidence, any notion that fire-swept landscapes were only a product of post-1880 settler influence cannot be sustained. There was, however, a decided qualitative difference in the

sources of many of the post-1880 fires, and when these combined
with the vulnerability of ungrazed prairie grasses, it is not surprising
that the years from 1880 to 1920 have taken on a certain reputation
as years of destruction. The role of railways, agricultural clearing
and forest enterprise on fire occurrence was certainly very great
in the pioneer settlement period. By 1920, according to many accounts,
the ancient character of the Beaver Hills had been distinctly altered
owing to indiscriminate use of fire in the land-clearing process.[24]
This was a significant accusation, for in many centuries previous,
the Beaver Hills consistently acted as a kind of oasis and holding
area in which the intricate pattern of lake and streams guaranteed
a permanent land cover. People had settled there seasonally, or
perhaps for longer periods, but never altered the local landscape
except in minor ways. This was no longer the case in the 1890s.
Consider the words of the editorialist in the *Edmonton Bulletin* in
the spring of 1895, aimed at the indiscriminate use of fire in the
pioneer ranges of the Beaver Hills: "there is the greatest objection
to the destruction of 100 or 1,000 acres, as the case may be, of
good wood for the sake of the settler having greater ease in bringing
ten, twenty, fifty or even one hundred acres of land under crop."[25]

The years around 1880 defined a hard line of land-use change
in the Beaver Hills, brought on by new social and economic pressures.
Owing to the post-1890 establishment of certain special land reserves
in the Beaver Hills, some of the old order remains to provide echoes
of a social and economic world which has by and large disappeared.
These reserves had particular significance for the conservation of
threatened species such as elk and bison.

The hills have many stories to tell drawn from the decades on
either side of 1900. Turning the hills towards agriculture has long
been an enterprise of frustration and only partial success, ultimately
keyed to the uneven nature of the soil and the unpredictable subsurface
conditions. Before considering such relatively recent history, it is
proper to enquire into those who frequented the lands between
the Battle and the North Saskatchewan Rivers in much earlier
times. The modern themes of drought and moisture; fire and

its control; wildlife scarcity and abundance; the frustration or advance of transportation; the advent and shifting of settlement frontiers, all of these topics have their counterparts in earlier times. The particular ways in which these themes have been at play in the Beaver Hills region is the main subject of this book.

CHAPTER TWO

Ancient Ways Between Two Rivers

The Beaver Hills started to attain elements of their present character between 10,000 and 12,000 years ago. This came about as part of the general series of adjustments made by the western landscape to the retreating glaciers. In time, water courses and lakes took on a certain stability, including the main channels of the North Saskatchewan and Battle Rivers. During those distant millennia many of the ancient faunas of glacial times started to disappear, including a large form of Pleistocene bison. These vanishing stocks were gradually replaced by other forms, and under progressive conditions of warming, the modern species of bison gradually came to dominate the new grasslands. Some 9,000 years ago buffalo pounds, jumps and traps were already in use.[1]

Piecing together a picture of ancient human life in Alberta has been largely a post-war enterprise. In the 1950s, archaeologist Richard G. Forbis and his associates analyzed many local collections, some of which related to the Beaver Hills. Included in the analysis were assemblages gathered from farms around Bruderheim, Pakan, Skaro and Sedgewick.[2] For the earliest reaches of human time in the Beaver Hills, these local collections provided evidence of big-game

hunters who employed thrusting spears. Such spears were tipped
by variations of the long fluted or parallel flaked points first associated
with the famous Clovis site in the south-western United States.
Points known as Cody are common and a number have been found
in ploughed fields in the Beaver Hills region. A spear point of the
Agate Basin variety was found in the hills directly north of today's
Elk Island National Park. This particular kind of point enjoys a
wide distribution and has been found in eastern Wyoming and far
to the north at Acosta Lake in the North West Territories. These sites
all represent occupation sites active between 10,000 and 7,500 years
ago.[3] Knowledge of the region's prehistory advanced in the 1970s
when the Strathcona site on the western flanks of the hills, close to
the North Saskatchewan River, was inspected by archaeologists.[4]

Following an extended period of Atlantic warming (sometimes
called the "Altithermal" climatic period), extending roughly from
7,500 to 5,000 years ago, the vegetation belts of the prairies and

This type of large spearhead point has been found in the Beaver Hills. Characteristic of
the early Prehistoric period, eight to nine thousand years before the present, it was often
placed on the Atlatl.

In this reconstruction of an early Prehistoric period hunt of the now extinct *Bison Occidentalis*, an Atlatl is being used armed with a large "fluted" point. The two-part lance, secured by a thong at the elbow, provided highly leveraged throwing power.

parkland assumed an identity somewhat similar to the patterns in place today. Towards the end of this great warming time a notable trend appears in the archaeological record. A shift occurred towards the use of smaller side-notched and stemmed spear points. These were used in various ways, but most remarkably in a spear-throwing device called the atlatl. This device, already long in use, was able to maximize throwing power and could be used with great accuracy. The appearance of such sites in the lands just south of the Battle River, at Buffalo Lake for example, suggests that there was a slow accommodation being made to the more varied terrain of the parkland and a growing reliance on smaller game and waterfowl, as well as on bison.[5]

Over the next two and a half millennia, many other technological and social adjustments were made in plains society. The identification of the widespread Besant culture by archaeologists revealed the importance which the bison had come to assume in the economy of many groups. Here was a bison hunting culture and its members appear to have introduced a version of the bison pound to the conditions of the open prairie.[6]

There were still other bearers of culture entering the prairie scene. Archaeologists are generally agreed that significant changes took place on the high plains around the time of the early common era. In those times both pottery and the bow and arrow came into use. The Avonlea peoples, named for a site in southern Saskatchewan where remains of their culture were first described, introduced or adapted from elsewhere the use of the bow and arrow.[7]

How did these advances come about? Debates centre upon the nature and extent of influences originating from very different directions, particularly from the Columbia Plateau across the mountains to the west, from the eastern woodlands, and from the southern Missouri River basin. While it is difficult to keep all of the balls of post-war Plains archaeology in the air at once, some have made efforts to synthesize the evidence.[8] Reeves has argued that in the high plains region of some 1,800 years ago, "the bow and arrow was adopted by the Tunaxa cultural tradition from Salishan tribes of the mountainous west." The new technology "rapidly replaced the spear thrower for killing buffalo." In addition, pottery "was also adopted from neighbouring cultures to the east."[9] The conclusion was that peoples ancestral to historically known tribes, such as the Blackfoot and Assiniboine, have long been resident on the plains and parkland. Their manners of arrival, their earlier hearths, and the nature of their interconnections as groups take on greater obscurity as one moves back in time. Piecing together these lines of connection has been one of the main tasks of North American archaeology.

Systematic survey work in the parkland belt did not really begin until the 1960s, usually in provincial and national park settings. Of interest to professional archaeologists were the many locally gathered private collections, such as that of Mary Dunn Tiedemann of Deville, near Cooking Lake. A collector since youth, she developed a small museum on the family property in 1962 and shared the results with students and archaeologists.[10]

One focus for survey work was Elk Island National Park in the very heart of the Beaver Hills. Ian Wilson and Thomas Head undertook a formal archaeological survey in 1977 and located some 150 prehistoric sites, mainly oriented towards the water bodies and rivers of Elk Island. These were frequently sites of a quarry or campsite nature, and together they reflected a "wide range of human activities in the prehistoric past." Subsequent work has amplified knowledge indicating that, in temporal terms, peoples have made use of the Beaver Hills for at least the last 8,000 years and that "seasonal rounds" of resource use have been of a longstanding order. That is to say, over the span of a given year, diverse peoples were accustomed to use the hills for different purposes, depending on the season and according to their requirements. The seasonal round was at the very core of nomadic and semi-nomadic economic life. Elk Island archaeologists noted that the number of sites encountered was "far greater than anticipated" and that they provided sufficient evidence to suggest that "the area was not a peripheral area

Archaeologist Rob Bonnichsen discussing Beaver Hills artifacts with collector Mary Tiedemann of Deville in the late 1960s.

or a prehistoric frontier zone" but was instead "a centre of activities."[11] Ancient ceramics were also found and while they were first considered to be of uncertain origin, new thinking on the distribution of Avonlea sites has suggested that bearers of that culture occupied not just the more open prairies but also the parklands.[12]

The forces driving these changes may have ultimately originated in the area of the Upper Saskatchewan and Missouri and adjacent Rocky Mountains perhaps with certain bison-hunting peoples "ancestral to the western Algonkian and Kutenai tribes." In the distinctive language of archaeology, Reeves drew a line of connection between these ancient hearths and some of the more familiar social groupings of recent times. Thus, the "Old Woman's Phase" the "archaeological representative of the three Blackfoot tribes," is said to have developed out of Avonlea "around 1,000 years ago." Extending the observation to the local level, he notes that "distinctive Old Woman's phase pottery has been found in Elk Island National Park."[13] In such passages do archaeologists abridge and unfold the centuries.

In the following half-millennium leading up to 1500 C.E., grassland and parkland groups continued to perfect these ceramic traditions. While refinements may have had their origins in the organized villages of agriculturalists further south and east along the middle Missouri, the ceramic traditions of the Beaver Hills may also reflect the northern forest origins of at least some of these folk. It was variants of the Algonkian languages of the north-eastern forests which were spoken by the historic Cree and Blackfoot peoples resident in the parkland belt, the people first encountered by European traders in the late seventeenth century.

The presence of fur traders on Hudson Bay after 1670 slowly changed the ways in which at least some Algonkian Cree peoples viewed their life at the fringe of the forest belt. When the Hudson's Bay Company traders arrived, the Cree were a widely distributed people extending in a great arc across the boreal forest from Labrador to central Alberta.[14] There were variations within this great patchwork of related peoples. The groups close in to James and Hudson

Bay quickly took on a favoured position in the prosecution of the fur trade, enjoying as they did the sudden benefits of trade goods such as guns. The Cree close to Hudson Bay derived an economic advantage as knowledge of these new goods reverberated down the line, causing groups to move, to alter their territorial ambitions, and enter into new diplomatic and trade relationships. Some have seen in this process the origins of an "invasion" by the Cree of the plains in an effort to extend the interests of the Hudson's Bay Company. More recently, this undeniable southward movement of the Cree has been viewed as more of a self-directed adjustment by which select groups took to the prairies out of economic self-interest.[15] Certainly adjustments did not always involve a direct thrust of people from the Bay regions down and out onto the prairies. There were many nuances of time and place. Some Algonkians had long been frequenters of the parkland zone, and only slowly mediated an expanded sphere of influence onto the prairies. Bands would have kept a foot firmly planted in the forest until the coming of

Artist John Innes illustrated a comparison of the dog and horse travois showing the relative load capacity of each.

the horse, at which point some committed more firmly to a prairie way of life, becoming the full Plains Cree.[16]

Fur trader Henry Kelsey witnessed the last vestiges of "dog days" – the ancient pre-horse world – when he came to the prairies from York Factory in the early 1690s. If the grasslands represented one great "commons," then the sheltered and well-watered uplands were certainly recognized in somewhat similar terms by those who dwelled in the parkland belt. The gradual shift to horse use was not straightforward or always permanent. Alison Landals has noticed that the care, feeding and use of horses posed a wide range of new problems as opposed to the tasks required with dogs.[17] Nevertheless, much changed in the 50 years after Kelsey's visit with respect to mobility and extended tribal ranges.

When Pierre de La Vérendrye of Trois Rivières, Quebec, started to explore the plains in the 1730s, he was doing so on the very eve of the arrival of the horse among the northern tribes.[18] In the centuries before 1730, mobility on the plains was measured and divided into the categories of the seasonal round in which knowledge of the movements of the bison was central and in which the strategy of the laborious communal hunt was important.[19] The vagaries of climate meant that predictability of animal movements was, at best, very general. Frank Roe contended that it was "not the buffalo, but the Indian himself [who] was the architect of the Indian trails on the North American continent."[20] Those living in river valley settings were naturally more sedentary. The villages of the Mandan, Manitaries and Arikaries visited by La Vérendrye in the 1730s suggest longstanding occupancy by gardening peoples in the well-watered portions of the Middle Missouri such as the Knife River Valley. In time, the combination of gun and horse soon turned the northern prairie and parklands into landscapes in motion.[21] The Mandan villages disappeared in the process, victims of the new mobility that unwittingly aided in the deadly spread of contagion, affecting even more strongly those who were clustered in higher density and more fixed abodes.

For centuries the Beaver Hills had been something of a resource frontier for peoples of diverse backgrounds but limited geographic range. This had not come about by chance, but was instead a reflection of the rather unique position of the hills as a boreal outlier in the Parkland belt. As such, it provided a series of windows – north, south, east and west – onto landscapes which the diverse residents had, by degree, either left behind or were reluctant to enter. Within the bounds of the hills were to be found an amalgam of boreal, parkland and prairie resources, providing the best of all previously known worlds. After 1730 the possibilities inherent in increased mobility had wider day-to-day business implications. By 1800, international and cultural circumstances had conspired to pit some of the peoples of this old resource commons against each other more consistently. Thus, between the Battle and Saskatchewan Rivers, a sequence of hill regions traversing central Alberta and Saskatchewan, including the Neutral Hills, came to define a kind of rough dividing line between the newly mounted cultures of the Cree and Blackfoot, so much so that several traditions exist concerning the origins of this boundary.[22]

In the nineteenth century, we shall see that the Beaver Hills, traditionally something of a "no-man's land," took on increased definition as specific tribal territory associated with the Cree and their allies. Such shifts in regional identity did not take place overnight, but were spread over a period of some 70 years.[23] The Cree, having gained access to European goods and technology and having fostered many kin relationships, gradually forced an evacuation of the Hills by the Sarcee and Blackfoot, establishing more firmly their own identity as the "Beaver Hills People" or the "Upstream People."[24] Many events, legends and tales recorded in memoirs and historical accounts stress the dramatic and bloodthirsty aspects of those adjustments, although for centuries the Beaver Hills had been less a battle ground, more an uncontested resource commons.

CHAPTER THREE

Traders, Horses, and Bison, 1730–1870

In 1730 the tribes of the northern plains were starting to learn the possibilities inherent in horse culture. The cumulative effect was to put groups in touch with each other more regularly, for travel in the dog days had been slower. The arrival of the horse also acted to increase hunting, trade and war opportunities, and to expand or shift traditional residential ranges, often in an overlapping pattern.[1] Areas of natural abundance played an important role in this period of expanded awareness and simultaneously became important as resource centres for more people. For centuries, plant and tree succession had helped keep water levels high in the Beaver Hills. Culturally induced prairie fires at the peripheries were less frequent with the result that spruce extended further south, and the hills themselves were less prairie-like. They were a refuge for wildlife, with good hunting and fishing opportunities, a place to find berry crops, and shelter for settlements, particularly in the harsh winters.

The northern plains were becoming a more fluid place in terms of social arrangements after 1730. This tendency was reinforced by the unseen presence of Europeans who had introduced exotic trade items into the equation. The horse, the gun, disease and trade goods all served to mix peoples in ways which were unfamiliar and by no means perfectly understood today.[2] It was as though the heat was being slowly turned up under the pot of prairie society. By the 1870s it had come to a boil and the lid lifted. Almost simultaneously, the pot ran dry, as the great fuel, the bison, vanished. This chapter provides glimpses of how forces of change were at work and of how they imparted a distinctive character to the Beaver Hills by the particular circumstances of local land and life.

Henry Kelsey had a glimpse of the prairies in 1690–92, but only in the 1730s did French traders begin to gain a systematic insight into the character of Canada's western interior. This view was gained more in the hope of finding a route to the elusive *"Mer ∂' l'Ouest"* – the way to the western sea and the orient.[3] The river the Bay men had earlier called the "Keskachewan" appears as *Rivière Poskaiao* on La Vérendrye's 1750 map, and *Rivière Poskoiac* on another. It is the *R. ∂e Poskoyac* on Philippe Buache's map of 1754. The Montreal-based trader Alexander Henry the Elder stated in 1775: "We gained the mouth of the River de Bourbon, Pasquayah, or Saskatchiwanine." The general significance of the name, James Bain tells us, was Cree, for "swift-flowing and "derived from *Paskquaw*, a prairie or desert, as its course is through the great plain to the east of the Rocky Mountains."[4]

In early 1755 another trader, Anthony Henday, journeyed onto the plains from York Factory via the Saskatchewan. He travelled the length of the Battle River valley, during which time he reported on presumed Blackfoot peoples at *Earchithinue Sokohegan* (Blackfoot Lake) northeast of present day Leduc. Henday appears to have explored the area and hunted in the Beaver Hills. In his time, then, the Blackfoot were frequenting lands well north of the Battle River The sketchy nature of his memoirs has been a frustration to later chroniclers. For the next twenty years the English traders on the prairies were represented only by their Cree middlemen, who undertook the main tasks associated with extending the fur trade to their Blackfoot allies, bringing them into the Hudson's Bay

Company trade ring. Fur traders from the English bay-side posts established permanent footholds along the Saskatchewan River only in the years after 1774.[5]

In the same years that the bay-side traders were gaining a sketchy view of the interior plains, there were also French Canadian trade interests trying to bring the central prairies into perspective. The Sieur de La Vérendrye's parties had not penetrated as far as the upper Saskatchewan country when the imperial crisis between France and England came to a head in the mid 1750s. The result was that the fur trade initiative from old Quebec rapidly declined, despite many achievements. The French Canadian traders had established posts as far west as Fort St. Louis (Fort à la Corne) some distance below the forks of the North and South Saskatchewan. The great game was up however, and control now shifted to English and Scottish traders from Montreal.

The focus of the fur trade soon became the distant Athabasca country, far to the north of the Saskatchewan River, and it was there that the HBC and the newly forming, if shifting, alliances of "Nor'westers" pressed each other hard, sometimes violently. The Saskatchewan River Valley was by no means neglected and through the journals and accounts of the competing traders of this quarter, new views of the plains and parkland became available. William Pink made four trips into the country between 1766 and 1770, his accounts being notable for leaving the first good account of the workings of a bison pound. In his trip of 1768–9 he appears to have wintered somewhere between modern Vegreville and the Beaver Hills.[6]

At York Factory, the brevity of the reports received from the traders sent inland, such as Pink, proved something of a frustration to Chief Factor Andrew Graham. His solution was to send young Matthew Cocking to the prairies in 1772, with results that were not disappointing. While Cocking does not appear to have wintered further west than the Eagle and Bear Hills near Saskatoon, his Journal gives new insights into the activities of the so-called Beaver

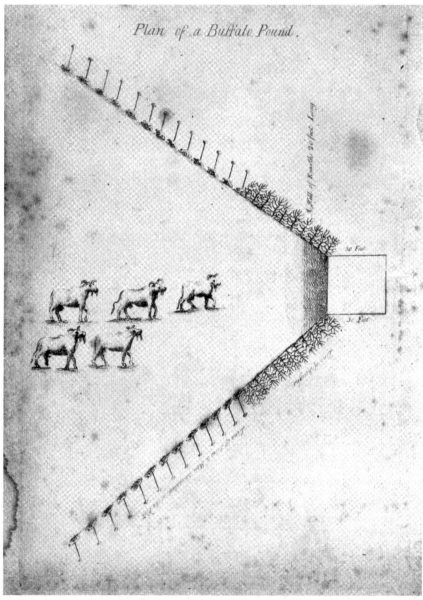

Buffalo Pound   In his book *The Present State of Hudson Bay* (1790) fur trader Edward Umfreville included a diagram to illustrate the principles of the working of a "Buffalo Pound."

Indians of the upper Saskatchewan River, and this would have included those resident in the Beaver Hills area.[7]

The upshot of Cocking's report was "to thoroughly awaken the Hudson's Bay Company from the dream of a peaceful and comfortable monopoly of the fur trade." Action inland was required, for while the French had been cast out of the western fur trade, they were being replaced by others.[8] The response by the HBC was the establishment of Cumberland House in 1774. That very same year had marked the arrival on the Saskatchewan of a large number of free-trading "pedlars" from Quebec, including Alexander Henry the Elder. From that time on, the competing interests built fur posts in a matching pattern as they rushed ever further west, each seeking to give close rivalry to the other. The "pedlars" were quick to take the lead, but so disruptive were their tactics in certain quarters that the entire conditions of the trade were threatened by 1780. Some of the posts on the Saskatchewan and Assiniboine River systems were spared from destruction only by the coincidental outbreak of the great smallpox epidemic of 1781–82.[9]

One of the earliest notices of the Native residents of the Beaver Hills area was contained in a reference to this great tragedy of plains life. The Cumberland House Journals of William Tomison and William Walker provide insights into the terrible effects of the plague.[10] Historian Frank G. Roe has referred to the desperate nature of life in the hills at that time when, contrary to traditional dietary and social customs, the Beaver Hills Cree were driven to eat their dogs and horses out of sheer need.[11] The effects of such deprivation were then compounded by the conquest in 1782 of the English posts on the Bay by the French commander La Pérouse. The effect was to disrupt trade in both directions and to cut off the inward flow of much-needed supplies of all kinds.[12] By the mid-1780s the fur trade had recovered.

The Hudson's Bay Company had, in the interim, founded Manchester House on an island in the North Saskatchewan near contemporary Maidstone. In 1786 James Gaddy took the young

David Thompson with him on a trip to winter with the Peigan of the plains, a journey that led them south-west through the Battle River watershed.[13] By 1792 the Nor'Westers had built Fort George and the HBC erected Buckingham House in the vicinity of Elk Point on the North Saskatchewan. A year later, Peter Fidler and his associates found themselves busy surveying the prospects for a new HBC post even further up the river. They selected the site of the first post in the Edmonton area at the mouth of the Sturgeon River near today's Fort Saskatchewan. Fidler was not entirely sold on the virtues of the site: "The Sturgeon or Tea River is the end of our Journey, but not a proper place to build at owing to the small woods that are here." A post appears to have come about nonetheless, for he later reported that "in the year 1795 Edmonton House was built which was about one mile higher up the Saskatchewan river than the mouth of this river." A tradition developed among the local tribes in which the new post was referred to as "Beaver Hills House" and this tradition persisted in some quarters down to the 1860s.[14]

Down river, Duncan McGillivray, clerk at the North West Company's Fort George, followed reports of this initiative with the usual keen interest. About the vicinity of the proposed new post he noted in his diary: "This is described to be a rich and plentiful country abounding with all kinds of animals, especially Beaver and Otters, which are said to be so numerous that the Women and Children kill them with sticks and hatchets." The Nor'Westers naturally responded with great haste, establishing Fort Augustus in the same vicinity. Duncan McGillivray left us a glimpse of one of the Cree Chiefs of that quarter:[15]

> "The Grand Sateau" a Cree Chief, arrived from the Beaver Hills. His nation amused themselves by driving buffalo into a pound–a very unfavourable circumstance for our returns. Gave him a few articles to the value of fifteen beaver which will be charged to him in case he gives his spring hunt to the English which we think he intends.

Fort Edmonton, or "Beaver Hills House," c. 1900

McGillivray had further dealings with trappers in 1795:[16]

> Goweke and three young men arrived from Beaver Hills with about two hundred beavers which they traded for rum, ammunition and tobacco. The extraordinary amount of snow prevents the natives from pouring in upon as at this time which is the usual custom.

These first years of trading appear to have been productive but activity had dropped off significantly by 1800. The fur trade records for the Edmonton district posts between 1800 and 1806 have not survived, but it appears that during that interval, decisions were taken by both companies to relocate their forts to the vicinity of modern Edmonton. In time the vestiges of the old Sturgeon Creek posts deteriorated and then were eventually burned by the local Natives.[17]

Other impressions of the local peoples can be learned from Fidler's Journal. For January 27 of 1793, he wrote: "Several more tents of our Indians moved toward the Bad river. The 12 tents of

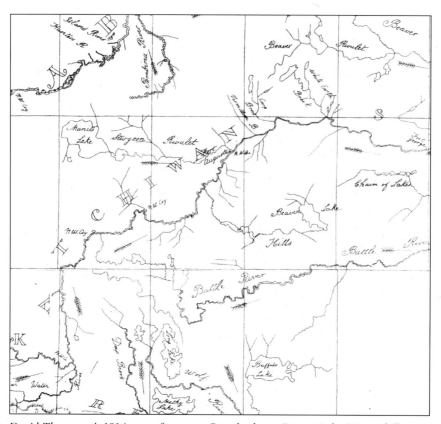

David Thompson's 1814 map of western Canada shows Beaver Lake [Beaverhills Lake] in proximity to the North Saskatchewan River.

Sessewa [i.e. Sarcee, or Tsuu'Tina] also pitched away for the upper Beaver hills in the vicinity of the Saskatchewan River."[18] The following month he saw "what these Indians call the South Eastern most end of the Beaver Hills, in the vicinity of the Saskatchewan River."[19] An entry in the Edmonton House Journals for 1797 reported that eight men finally had arrived at Buckingham House after having been lost "in the little Beaver Hills" for two days.[20]

As mentioned, the coming of the horse had dramatically extended the traditional tribal ranges. There was no absolute fixity

of place for the prairie tribes, although there were undoubtedly
heartlands of some duration. The extending ranges are revealed
in the social makeup of the various tribes trading at Edmonton
House. A description from 1799 includes a reference to "a small
band of Fall Indians" (presumably the Gros Ventre) on March 21.
These "brought nothing but provisions, which they traded and
went off again and a few Sussew Indians arrived, also three
Assinepoiet Indians. The following day, other Sussew and Stone
Indians traded and went away, the former brought seven skins and
the latter twenty-four made beavers; also several Indians arrived
from the Beaver Hills, brought a few beaver and martens." In 1811,
Alexander Henry the Younger commented on the differences
between the Sarcee and the Assiniboines, although both groups
were resident in the vicinity: "The environs of the Beaver Hills is
generally their station."[21]

Clearly, the hills were being frequented by a number of different Native groups in these years. In light of the heavy fur returns
in the last years of the eighteenth century, the hills were undoubtedly rich in wildlife and water bodies supporting the beaver. The
capacity for traders to get lost in them suggests that they also
represented something of a *terra incognita*. A decade or so later, the
hills were still very productive of beaver. In July 1810, Alexander
Henry the Younger reported on returns taken from French Métis
trappers: "Letendre and family arrived from Beaver Hills on south
side, bringing upwards to a hundred beaver skins" but he had "seen
no Indians." A week later he recorded that "La Boucone arrived,
and his Indian, a hunter from Beaver Hills, where he and Marion
are working on the beaver."[22]

About this time, relations between the Blackfoot and the other
main residents of the hills began to change. Mention of the normal
residency of the Blackfoot starts to disappear, replaced steadily by
reports of hostilities. Earlier, the Blackfoot and Sarcee traditional
home range lay well into the Aspen Parkland belt and extended
north of the Saskatchewan River, betraying perhaps their earlier

connection with the woodlands. This had not been exclusively their territory however, as Cree, Assiniboine and Saulteux peoples also frequented the lands north and south of the river, and continued to do so as the eighteenth century unfolded.[23] Despite nineteenth- and twentieth-century reports concerning long-standing traditional Blackfoot-Cree hostility, later writers suggest that this hostile tra- dition was in fact rather a post-1810 development, issuing out of altered ecological and economic conditions and shifting alliances.[24] With the perfection of horse-riding skills, the Blackfoot Confederacy came into being, and the various components of this loose fede- ration opted increasingly for a life on the open prairie and along the southern foothills. As a response to this shift in lifeways, the Cree and their allies came to gradually dominate the Beaver Hills. Place names associated with this shift started to come into use around 1800.

Population numbers for the hills remain impressionistic, but a report for Edmonton House for 1822–23 indicates that the Beaver Hills Cree consisted of thirty tents or about 120 fighting men. This does not clarify the larger regional relationships, or say anything about the ways in which groups may have come together and then dissolved on a seasonal basis. For example, Palliser in the late 1850s plotted on one of his expedition maps some three hundred tents of Cree along the southern edge of the hills. Indeed, Palliser described the Prairie Cree of his time as favouring camps "of two to four hundred tents." As geographer Robert Scace observed, these large camp concentrations undoubtedly reflected the benefits of the hills, offering seasonal advantages for the bison hunt from the Aspen Parkland edge and access to the thicker wooded centre of the hills. In the mid-1850s, fur trader Henry Moberly reported that the hills people still provided a great deal of meat to Fort Edmonton.[25] Up to 1860, then, there was a strong continuity between contemporary and older populations in terms of economy; but there was also a defensive aspect, implied by the mounting concentration of people in the hills.

Beaver Hills Society and the Coming of the Missions

Settlements in the northwest in the years after 1790 took other forms besides fur trade posts and Native camps. Métis settlements and mission stations were grafted on to older centres or defined a more stable presence at customary gathering places. In the 1790s a distinctive Métis settlement started to form around Lac La Biche, the gateway to the Athabasca country. Two factors helped foster later Métis settlements in the Saskatchewan River Valley: the first was the Red River Hunt, the annual quest which took large groups of Métis hunters and their families far out onto the plains, west from Fort Garry, in search of bison.[26] Over time, some of the participants in these hunts never returned, but stayed in settlements of their own at favourable locations. The second element came about as the long-term effect of the first great "downsizing" operation in Canadian history. In the aftermath of the amalgamation of the Hudson's Bay Company with the North West Company in 1821, many in the traditional labour force lost their jobs. By 1838 a considerable number of Métis had settled around Fort Edmonton and elsewhere, in the hope of making a new life. The attendant growth in demand for social institutions complicated the work routines of the local Chief Factor, John Rowand.[27]

Religious and educational needs were foremost. There were pressures within the Church of England to respond to this need from the Methodists. The latter were particularly anxious to cater not just to the needs of settled fur trade communities but also to the Native populations. The Protestants were the first on the ground in the Fort Edmonton area. Hudson's Bay Company Governor George Simpson had his reasons for preferring missionaries from the Wesleyan Methodists instead of from the Anglican Church Missionary Society. Simpson was not much interested in educational extension activities to the Native peoples or in preachers who wanted to conduct most of their work from the forts. He felt the latter practice was inclined to attract Indians in off the land, thereby encouraging only "idleness." As a man who

The Rev. Robert Rundle and Mrs. Rundle, following their marriage in 1854

wanted to visit the camps, Robert Rundle was Simpson's ideal candidate, although Simpson later had some concerns.[28] Rundle, a product of the evangelical Wesleyan tradition, arrived at Fort Edmonton in 1840. He impressed the Roman Catholic Chief Factor with the fact that he was a good man although perhaps, thought John Rowand, he was "too young" for his job. Rowand was inclined to view missionaries as busybodies, but the two men got on well enough over the next eight years. Rundle's Journal is full of expressions of gratitude for the assistance given to him by the veteran fur trader.[29]

From a landscape-perception point of view, Rundle's Journal provides us with some excellent pen pictures of the Beaver Hills, an area he visited regularly with a view to making converts. He described the satisfactory game provisioning qualities of the hills during one trip. Having set out from Fort Edmonton at seven in the evening in a dog cariole driven by one John Cunningham, in order "to pay a visit to the Hunter's Camp near Beaver Lake" they stopped at a camp at about one o'clock in the morning, where they were hosted by two men from the fort. Afterwards "we proceeded until abt. sunrise when we again halted on the Beaver Hills."

> The Beaver Hills extend for a long distance & are generally covered with trees & bushes, interspersed with small lakes. The scenery in summer must be very splendid but I saw only the rude ravages of winter in the woods & ice covered the lakes & snow mantled the ground. In the afternoon a herd of buffalo appeared on a small lake, but partially covered with snow, which rendered travelling over it very difficult. The consequence was that one of the buffalo, a cow, fell on the ice & was soon dispatched by one of the party.[30]

Rundle noted the effects of the prevailing cold on the butchering of game. The "carcass was at once cut up & lodged under the snow against our return" but the "cold was so severe" that "the blood froze about the instrument employed in cutting up the animal."

The hunter using it "was obliged to soak it 2 or 3 times in the warm blood lodged in the carcass."[31] Two days later we find Rundle visiting a "Buffalo Pond" [i.e. pound] which was close to the camp. This was one of the great traps long employed by prairie peoples to herd bison into an enclosure for the take. "The pond was strewn with half-devoured carcasses" and these fragments "afforded a fine feast for the wolves which came during the night seasons & gorged themselves at their pleasure." The missionary had "hoped to witness the capture of buffaloes by the method of decoying them" but "was doomed to be disappointed" for while two or three herds "were driven near the entrance" they all "escaped by rushing off in a contrary direction to that of the mouth of the pond."[32] Through this account, we come to understand that bison pounding work was time consuming, labour intensive and not always successful.

Rundle's attempt to capture Native souls was not so successful on this occasion either. Having "Addressed them in the morning on Jesus Christ" he frankly admitted that "attendance bad, several of the Souteaux Indians left in the morning to hunt buffaloes because I had preached the previous evening against their idolatries."[33] The missionary was back in the Beaver Hills in August of 1842, at which time he contacted a sizable camp of Cree and Assiniboine Indians of "45 tents" and where he "held service that evening in the open air."[34] He then rode to Battle River where he thought a Mission station would have been useful, but concluded that "the country here is in too unsettled a state to permit anything of the kind being established," a reference no doubt to the tense conditions then existing between Blackfoot, Cree and Assiniboine.[35] By 1844 Rundle had yet made some progress in establishing church relations in the Beaver Hills. We find him in February of that year staying at Kisenak's tent near the buffalo pound and that "services were well attended & I was encouraged."[36]

Rundle's tenure at Fort Edmonton coincided with the climax years of what climatologists often call the "little ice age." This may have been the coldest extended period of reduced annual temperatures since the retreat of the glaciers.[37] There is much in the missionary's notes to confirm that winters were of unusual severity. In early 1841, when he accompanied Rowand and Peter Ogden to the hills, his record for January 14th states that it was "so dreadfully cold that I could scarcely get any rest" and that "Mr Ogden informed me that the cold at this time was as intense as ever he knew it in the country."[38] The missionary tended to be sickly for much of his tenure, and the cold was often a matter of comment. In April, 1843 he complained: "What a terrible winter we have just gone thro' & how cheering is the approach of spring. The Ther. was 39 degrees below zero one morning at the Beaver Hills."[39]

In 1848, a tired and physically run down Robert Rundle returned for good to his native Cornwall in the British Isles. By that time the Methodist missions had taken root, particularly at Pigeon Lake to the south-west at the headwaters of the Battle River. The arrival of an assistant from Norway House, Benjamin Sinclair, helped ensure that Christian influence continued to grow among the Cree and Stoney of that quarter over the next two decades.

In the same years that Rundle had been getting to know the tribes of the Edmonton region, the Roman Catholic Church was also mounting a response to requests from the faithful. Rowand, among others, was anxious for priests to "leap the 600 mile gap from Le Pas to Fort Edmonton" on behalf of the many adherents in the fur trade and in Métis communities.[40] Rowand appealed to the Bishop of St. Boniface, at Red River. Bishop Provencher did not ignore his request, nor a letter written by Alexis Piché, the Quebec-born guide who had escorted Rundle on some of his earliest proselytizing tours. In response, the Bishop sent Father J.B. Thibault to Fort Edmonton in 1842. He founded a mission station at Lac Ste. Anne shortly thereafter. Subsequently, Roman Catholic influence along the North Saskatchewan increased steadily.[41]

In the wake of Rundle's departure, his Methodist successors, first under the Rev. George McDougall's leadership in Red River, continued to make progress along the North Saskatchewan, starting at Victoria (Pakan) directly north of the Beaver Hills. The new mission, built in 1863, was close to where the Hudson's Bay Company

established a post a year later, in an effort to counter the appearance of numbers of free traders along the Saskatchewan. The
"probable reason for building at this spot was that it intersected a
trail leading to the old Smoking Lake mission to the north and a trail
to the south paralleling Egg Creek onto the parkland plains."[42]

It was into this scene of nascent missionary activity that Peter
Erasmus (1833–1931) appeared, becoming one of the great wit-
nesses to western Canadian events in the last half of the nineteenth
century. He was born at Red River of a Danish father (alleged to
be a veteran of the Battle of Waterloo) and a mixed-blood mother,
related to Matthew Cocking. Peter Erasmus Sr. had come to
Rupert's Land to enter service with the Hudson's Bay Company,
following which he turned to river-lot farming. Peter Jr. leaned
much Native lore and tradition at his mother's knee but as a young
man showed little inclination to follow in his father's agricultural
footsteps. In 1851 he was sent to The Pas to work with his uncle,
Henry Budd, a Church of England catechist working with the Rev.
Robert Hunter at Christ Church Mission. Here he commenced a
study of classical and Native languages that would later place him
in constant demand by persons associated with prairie exploration
and political life. His systematic training in Native tongues started
with his assistance to Budd in the translation of the Bible and portions of the Prayer Book into Cree. In 1854, he departed for Fort
à la Corne on the Saskatchewan River, but then returned to Red
River for further studies at St. John's School, apparently intending
to join the ministry. His interests altered, however, and he accepted
an offer from the HBC to go to the upper Saskatchewan and work
for a Methodist, the Rev. Thomas Woolsey. His job was to act as
"hunter, guide, interpreter and general assistant." The two men
met for the first time at Fort Pitt in September, 1856, from which
they departed for Fort Edmonton. Their course took them through
the northern reaches of the Beaver Hills. "The old trail passed
through what was later called Hairy Hill, Whitford, Andrew, Star,
Bruderheim, and thence to Fort Saskatchewan, where there was
a good crossing."[43] In 1858, Dr. James Hector observed that

"Mr. Woolsey's mission station is properly out at Pigeon Lake...
where the Thickwood Crees and Stoneys have made a few attempts
at agriculture."[44]

The Great Land Appraisal: The Palliser Expedition and the Beaver Hills

The 1850s were years of marked anxiety for the proprietors of the
ancient fur company which had for so long held sway in its great
commercial fiefdom of Rupert's Land. The only control that seemed
to apply to the Hudson's Bay company was that every so often its
licence came up for renewal. Now, however, the worm of international politics had very much turned. The pace of American settlement south of the 49th parallel, criticism of the company monopoly
at home and abroad, and the difficulties of controlling pressures
from free traders, all signalled the coming of the end. In 1857, the
tabling in the British House of Commons of a voluminous select
committee report into the actions of the company marked the
beginning of a political process which ended with the transfer of
Rupert's Land to the new Dominion of Canada in 1869.[45]

Political hints favouring limitations on HBC control of the
subarctic and western lands of British North America were already
quite noticeable in 1857. These included survey projects broadly
appraising land and resources and investigating the practicalities
of transportation routes across the mountains. James Hector's presence at Fort Edmonton was owing to his participation in John
Palliser's exploration of western British North America. Palliser's
party assembled at Lower Fort Garry in July, 1857 and then
worked its way across the plains, arriving in early 1858 at Fort
Edmonton. Little escaped James Hector's eye. In February he
wrote that "Some Indians arrived to-day from the Beaver Hills,
where they have killed six moose-deer within 10 to 20 miles from
the fort. At one time they were very common in this district, and
formed a sure source of food for the traders, but for many years
they have almost disappeared."[46]

Before the expedition's advance on the mountain country, guides and packers had to be retained. On March 7, 1858 Hector recorded: "This morning I started with a guide and Peter Erasmus, the Rev. Mr. Woolsey's interpreter, to endeavour to engage men for the Expedition from among the band of 'freemen' that are at present travelling in from the plains to Lake St. Ann's settlement." Searching them out became the occasion for some exploration of the country east of Fort Edmonton. "After crossing the Saskatchewan River on the ice, our course was at first easterly over the Beaver Hills. After ten miles we turned to the south-east, and commenced to traverse very inviting country...hitherto we had passed over swampy ground, but now the surface was dry and undulating, and in the hollows are lakes, some of which are of good size." Then in the afternoon "we got into some open country, and travelling briskly reached the tents of the freemen's camp about an hour after dark, having travelled forty miles from the fort. The tents were pitched beside Hay Lake which is a few miles in extent and within four hours ride of Battle River." It seems that only "half of the party had got thus far on their return, as they were heavily loaded with the proceeds of their hunt, but the rest were expected to pass this place next day, so we resolved to wait before beginning negotiations."[47]

The following day at about 11 o'clock "the rest of the band arrived, forming a motley troop with loaded horses and dogs, and travelling in a style hardly different from Indians." The day "was spent in winning the good will of their old chief Gabriel Dumont who has repeatedly crossed the Rocky Mountains, and can also talk Blackfoot." Hector was relieved for "when I succeeded in getting him to consent to act as guide for the Expedition, I had no difficulty in filling up my complement from among the young men."[48]

The final reports of the Palliser Expedition reveal that the members took a keen interest in trying to assess the population and distribution of the Native peoples they encountered. The last recorded summary listed the peoples of the Beaver Hills at that time as being mainly of the Plains Cree according to the following chart which accounted for them by lodges:[49]

Plains Cree Bands	No. of Lodges
Moose Mountain	100
Moose Jaw	120
Coteau de Prairie	400
Eagle Hills	200
Moose Woods	200
Jackfish Lake	200
Vermilion River	300
Snake River/Lac La Biche	100
Beaver Hills	300

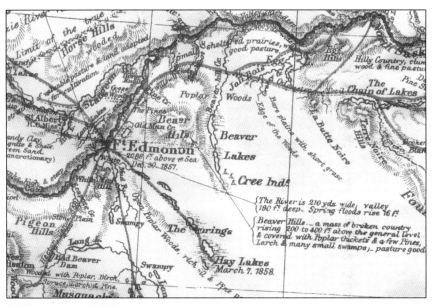

Palliser's map of 1860

Rev. George McDougall (1821–1876)
In 1863, McDougall returned to Pakan
to found the Methodist Mission (Victoria)
on the North Saskatchewan River. He
founded several other missions in the
foothills country of Alberta.

Elizabeth Chantler McDougall
(1823–1904)   At her husband's missions, Elizabeth had a busy life of child
rearing, nursing and teaching. Eight of
her children survived, including John,
who followed in his father's footsteps.

Victoria Mission   Also known as Pakan in recognition of the name of leader of the
local Cree, this community on the North Saskatchewan River became the economic
and spiritual focus of the area north of the Beaver Hills after 1862.

The Beaver Hills group was clearly one of the larger concentrations of Plains Cree at the time of the expedition, and the hills, with their reputation as a source of beaver, would have long been a significant source of the local fur trade.

Personalities remain obscure in the historical record, but the efforts of the churchmen had clearly borne fruit. Hugh Dempsey noted that "Lapotac, a leading Chief of the Beaver Hills Cree until his death in 1861, had become a convert to Methodism, as had one of the lesser Chiefs, Broken Arm, or Maskepetoon." It was part of the context into which the Methodist, George McDougall, introduced himself in 1862 in order to found the Victoria Settlement some 50 miles east of Fort Edmonton. The mission was initiated with a view to softening the inevitable effects which departure of the HBC would have on Native populations. The location, shared with the Hudson's Bay Company, had some advantages over the mission station at Smoky Lake, some miles to the north, which it now replaced.[50] According to John Maclean, the Victoria Mission house was the setting for the advent of European-style education west of Red River with the training of nine students in 1863.[51] The Indians themselves had thus become involved in mission field politics. Similarly, near Buffalo Lake "the warlike Chief Bobtail supported the Oblates," perhaps because his father, Alexis Piché, "had been instrumental in bringing the first Catholic Clergy to the region twenty years earlier."[52]

In the early 1920s such events were still within memory's reach. Tofield's Mayor, A.J. McCauley, recalled: "Mr William Rowland...told me stories of the buffalo hunting days." During the sixties, he was "a chief trader for the Hudson's Bay Company" and "The Chief Factor sent him out periodically to trade with the Indians at Beaver Hill Lake." According to this reminiscence, a wide zone of tension and conflict between the Blackfoot, Stoney and Cree Indians lay along the Battle River for about 20 miles between today's Ponoka and Wainwright. The Blackfeet, with their Sarcee allies, were proving very troublesome to the Cree of this quarter and had "commenced to make raids around the south end of Beaver Hills Lake" between 1860 and 1862. In order not to lose this great hunting ground the Crees "persuaded Chief Ketchamoot" of the Fort Pitt area to "come up with 400 braves." This he did and over several days his "small army" was joined by others in the Beaver Hills. They made up provisions and then headed south-west to meet the Blackfeet in battle south of Wetaskiwin where the victory fell to the Cree. Ketchamoot spent his remaining years in the hills and is commemorated by the name "Ketchmoot Creek," which empties into Beaverhills Lake.[53] According to Erasmus's biographer, Henry Thompson, this battle "under the leadership of Ketchamoot, won the Crees an initial victory" but was also the "means of rendering the whole area unsafe for any Cree for a number of years afterward."[54] This view of a prevailing general turmoil is supported by the writings of a Fort Edmonton fur trader and in the Journal of John Sellar, one of the "Overlanders" who arrived at Fort Pitt in 1862.[55] By the following year relations between the Cree and Blackfoot had improved somewhat, according to the account of those observant tourist-adventurers, Milton and Cheadle, who were at Fort Pitt in the spring of 1863. They contended that a peace treaty, albeit of somewhat uncertain substance, had been concluded between the warring tribes.[56] It is of interest that after interviews with the Dumont family in 1925, the veteran naturalist of the Beaver Hills, Frank Farley, maintained that Meeting Creek in the Battle River Valley was something of a traditional border line between the Cree and Blackfoot, a place where they would meet for joint bison hunts.[57]

Shortly after, Milton and Cheadle departed for Fort Edmonton. Having crossed to the south side of the Saskatchewan River near Egg Lake, they eventually skirted the northern edge of the Beaver Hills. Guided by a veteran Métis of the plains, Louis Battenotte, (known as "The Assiniboine") the party arrived just in time to experience one of the great spring fires. "When we gained the level plain above, dense clouds of smoke on every hand told that the prairie was on fire, and we soon reached the blackened ground which the fires had passed over. The only pasture we found for our horses was a large marsh, where we encamped for the night."[58]

Fort Edmonton was the administrative centre for the upper Saskatchewan region during the Hudson's Bay Company's declining years of authority between 1850 and 1870. The name "Edmonton House" can be linked to some of the old fur trade families who lingered on in the Beaver Hills long after the HBC relinquished its monopoly position in Rupert's Land in 1869. They helped preserve memories of the passing order and also represented the first transitional generation attracted by the possibilities of settlement. One of these families was that of John Peter Pruden.

Pruden was born in England in a district of the great city of London known as Edmonton. After joining the "Great Company" in 1791, he had worked his way to the position of Chief Trader by the time of the amalgamation of 1821. Much of his time after 1795 was spent in helping develop a post north of the Beaver Hills on the Saskatchewan River. Following its abandonment and burning, he helped William Tomison establish the new "Edmonton" post, erected near the present Provincial Legislative grounds. One tradition is

John Peter Pruden (1778–1868) An experienced fur trader with the Hudson's Bay Company, Pruden was at Fort Edmonton in its earliest days. Buried at Red River, many of his descendants remained in the Edmonton area, including his son, James, who was buried in a pioneer cemetery near Tofield.

that Tomison suggested the name for "Edmonton House" in honour
of Hudson's Bay Company official William Lake. It is coincidental
that this district appears also to have been the home of Pruden.
The name certainly was in use by 1795.[59]

Pruden was active at a number of other posts during the 1820s
and 1830s, including Carlton House. It was his mixed blessing to
receive notice in Governor George Simpson's notorious "Character
Book" of 1832. While Simpson found Pruden to be "a man of good
conduct and character" he also considered him "weak minded vain
& silly." He was "Over fond of good living" although he "Speaks
Cree, and is a tolerable 'Plain Indian' trader." Furthermore, Pruden
was "by no means bright" and was "attached to old customs, an
Enemy to all innovations" and "ought to consider himself fortunate
in having obtained his present situation."[60] Pruden must have had
some commendable diplomatic and business skills nonetheless,
since a year before he retired in 1837, he had risen yet higher in
the organization, to Chief Factor.[61] Upon retiring to the Red River
Settlement he served on the Council of Assiniboia, and on a number
of other civic bodies. He died there in 1868.

Peter Pruden had a large family by Nancy, whom he married
à la façon du pays (according to the custom of the country). Nancy's
identity remains obscure. She died prematurely and was buried at
Red River in 1839. Pruden then remarried an English school
governess, Ann Armstrong.[62] One of Pruden's sons, James, participated in the great 1854 expedition from Red River to the Oregon
country led by James Sinclair. He later returned to the Beaver
Hills and took up land in the Tofield area, being one of the earliest
settlers of that quarter in the 1880s. He was buried in 1902 in one
of the hidden historic places in the hills, the small pioneer cemetery
at Logan, west of Beaver Hills Lake.[63]

Another of the local fur trade veterans was William Rowland
(1826–1910). According to Albert Tate, he was born at Cumberland
House and during his early years worked the northern routes from
Churchill to Fort Chipewyan. Between 1860 and 1875 he held not
only "the important post of special trader and interpreter to the

great, war-like tribe of Blackfeet" but also attempted to mediate between the Cree and Blackfoot "to see that there was no open rupture between these enemies, at least within the horizon of the H.B. Co."[64] During his travels of the early 1870s, the Earl of Southesk encountered Rowland and his father, the latter whom he described as "an Orkney man of forty years service with the Company, and celebrated for breeding fine horses." About the son, William, he said he was "considered about the best light weight rider in the district."[65]

One of Rowland's neighbours, Robert Logan (c. 1844–1909), had served with the HBC at Edmonton House and also at Pakan between 1864 and 1874. He eventually took out land on the west side of Beaver Hills Lake in 1886 where he ran a small trading operation.[66] His place took on sufficient identity that on an 1894 survey map the community of "Logan" appears.[67] His landholdings were considerable and became the basis of the Trent Ranch after 1910.[68] In 1886, his property also became the setting of the pioneer cemetery mentioned above, for which he donated the land. Families such as these represented the last vestiges of a plains way of life which had been undergoing adjustments for several decades.

Outside the control of the fur companies, in addition to the Natives living on the land, were the holdings of small Métis communities that had formed across the prairies and in the parkland from the 1840s.[69] They were an outgrowth of the traditions of the Red River Hunt initiated in the 1820s by which English, Scottish and French mixed-blood buffalo hunters seasonally moved west out of the Red River Valley in pursuit of the herds.[70] In time, the price of bison robes rose, and with it, the numbers taking part in the hunt. Some chose to remain permanently in various enclaves in Saskatchewan and Alberta rather than return to Red River. When ramblers Milton and Cheadle arrived at Fort Edmonton in 1863, they remarked on this process with reference to the St. Alban's community of "freemen" and the even "more ancient colony" of St. Ann's "of similar character but with more numerous inhabitants."[71] *The Nor'Wester*, Red River's early newspaper, reported in 1864 that twenty-five French Métis families were departing for Lac La Biche.[72] Some Métis sank roots at other more obscure enclaves from which they farmed and pursued the last remnants of the great bison herds. Their presence also reflects the fact that establishments such as Edmonton House had, by mid-century, long ceased to be mere emporiums of trade.[73] Even in the early years of the century, however, the Saskatchewan forts had played a role in provisioning the more northerly posts, an important aspect of that function being the coordination of the taking and preparation of bison meat. By 1870, with the great herds disappearing, much of the regular basis of organized life in the west also disappeared. Those already on the land, of whatever background, had to consider the prospects of change brought on by this crisis. Over the next 30 years the Beaver Hills, as a place of common and communal refuge, changed radically under conditions of pioneer settlement and animal domestication.

CHAPTER FOUR

Visions of the Promised Land, 1870–1905

"When a person is hungry, pride is forgotten."

Joseph F. Dion, Cree Elder

Following the sale and transfer of the Hudson's Bay Company lands to Canada in 1869, the government in Ottawa moved to consolidate its new western empire, with memorable results. The spark igniting Riel's rebellion at Red River was struck by what was locally perceived as the premature appearance of government surveyors in the vicinity of Fort Garry.[1] The man who led the civil resistance, Louis Riel, survived its military suppression and became the "father" of Manitoba in 1870. The first western prairie province was born well ahead of the schedule that Ottawa politicians had projected. Outside the boundaries of this new "postage stamp" province, however, there remained a need to exercise some kind of minimum territorial government until the proper conditions of settlement prevailed, conditions strongly contingent upon success-ful railway building. In turn, railway building was premised upon the achievement of satisfactory land settlements with the resident Native peoples. A sense of impending crisis about their ancient lands had not escaped the notice of the old residents for they could well see mounting chaos all around them: the bison's disappear-ance, intruding adventurers, the appearance of survey parties, and

Chief Bobtail and son, c. 1885   Chief Bobtail (Kiskayo) frequented the Beaver Hills and signed an adhesion to Treaty 6 in 1877. He resisted the land settlement provisions until 1885 when he finally approved survey of a reserve northeast of Ponoka.

information about the fate of tribes south of the 49th parallel, caught up in warfare on the ever advancing mining and ranching frontiers. These events all served to focus the collective Aboriginal mind after the transfer of Rupert's Land to Canada.

There were other complications in the late 1860s. As in the previous century, disease again swept across the northern prairies, carrying away large numbers and reducing the collective stamina of the tribes.[2] If this visitation was not the total disaster of the small pox outbreak of 1781–82, caution still guided the actions of the more prudent, such as Beaver Hills Cree leader, Chief Bobtail (Kiskayo). The son of Hudson's Bay Company factor, Philip Tate, noted that smallpox had been moving through his part of the country in the early 1870s. A portion of Chief Bobtail's Cree "acting on the advice of their friend and pastor" had been camped around the outlet of Beaverhills Lake. They had "isolated themselves from the other bands and made for the then more wooded part of the country," which was to say the "north and north-west sides of the lake toward the hills." While the hunt had been very good during the past winter, these Cree decided not to approach Victoria Fort but instead sent for the "Oukeyma or his agent to come to them and their furs." Young Tate was pleased when his father suggested that he accompany him to "visit the Indians in their camp near Beaver Lake."[3]

> It was a good and wise custom for friendship and policy that each official of the H.B. Co. should have a "Quay-may" of namesake or a "Chewam" or brother, or uncle, or nephew, as the case may be, in every camp where one was recognized as the chief or head man.

Upon arriving in the camp, father and son were greeted by Philip Tate's *chewam*, Chief Bobtail, who would later be one of the signatories of an adhesion to Treaty 6.[4] In the camp "there was nothing too good for us" for all the "known delicacies of the times were placed at our feet – moose noses, beaver tails, buffalo 'boss', or bump, ducks, geese, eggs, and will you believe it – good maple sugar, made in their camp. Dainty maple syrup in skin vessels, or properly speaking, bladders."[5] These were some of the obvious reasons for maple trees, which used to prosper in the Beaver Hills, to have remained in young Tate's memory.

It was an idyllic recollection, but even in the days of Tate's youth forces of change were afoot. News of the troubles in Red River trickled west and it fell to missionaries such as George McDougall to try and calm local feeling. Circulating among the tribes of Bobtail, Sweetgrass, Pakan and others, McDougall recalled that he "would stop for days" having gone "from lodge to lodge" to hold meetings and give talks and these were sometimes "packed full of English history and Canadian experience and fair play, justice and liberty." Such confident rhetoric, in Christian guise, rang of the nineteenth century British faith in progress, the more convincing because of the sincerity of its expression. Some, such as Chief Big Bear, were capable of resisting the confident arguments of the theologians, but others were swayed, or at least confused enough to be uncertain: "Even Sweetgrass was having his head turned by the priests, as were Kehiwin and Bobtail."[6]

Leadership among the Cree of the Beaver Hills began to crystallize around a few individuals. In the pre-treaty period, the band members of Papaschase (the Woodpecker) were steady users of the hills. His people had often teamed up with the St. Albert Métis for the bison hunt. Some were aware that the "business as usual" approach to life was a delusion and a snare. Big Bear, more than many of the leaders, was quite certain of the magnitude of the crisis facing Native peoples and was aggressive in seeking to limit the activities of the Europeans in favour of a land policy which might work to conserve a significant range for the bison. According to Hugh Dempsey, "Big Bear had proved to be such an effective leader that many families were gradually drifting to his camp." Indeed, his following surpassed that of the peaceable Sweetgrass, although Big Bear still remained loyal to him, despite the former's conversion to Christianity. Big Bear's Cree following in the upper Saskatchewan region was exceeded now only by that of the great warrior Bobtail. Chief Bobtail and his people, rich in horses, traditionally occupied land south of Edmonton where, from the Peace Hills to Buffalo Lake, they guarded the frontier against the Sarcee and Blackfoot. During the smallpox epidemic of 1869–1870, his people had fared somewhat better than their enemies.[7]

The growing dominance of the Cree of the Beaver Hills by 1870 was in part owing to the distracting influences of the American free traders from Fort Benton in Montana who had moved into the Cypress Hills.[8] The wolfers and whiskey traders in the border zone were in many respects a social off-shoot of the ever-shifting mining frontier of the Pacific slope, the effects of which were being felt even at Fort Edmonton by the mid-1860s.[9] As had happened in the earlier part of the century, the Blackfoot and Sarcee were once again drawn away from Fort Edmonton in favour of opportunities provided by southern traders.[10] There were other factors. The smallpox epidemic outbreak of 1869–70 was serious enough, but that was only the first disaster to descend upon the Native peoples in these transition years. Cree historian Joseph F. Dion reported on the "starvation of the next two winters" – the famine years of 1871–72. It was a time of the re-emergence of the awesome *Witigo* – that fearful psychological bogeyman of the Algonkian world which for many centuries had stalked the winter landscapes in times of want. Cannibalism, in other words, had been the undoing of many families trapped without food in the icy grip of winter. It was still not unknown in the Edmonton area in the later 1870s.[11]

A glimpse of the prevailing scarcity, even in the seasons before the first winter of famine, was left in the account of Michael Sandy Cardinal of the Saddle Lake country. There was clearly a connection with the rising wave of hide hunters then so active on the prairies. Cardinal's hunting party had crossed the South Saskatchewan from the north at Brosseau Crossing, east of Victoria Post, and headed south. "We had gone a comparatively short distance south of the river when we noticed where other parties had already done their work of slaughtering the buffalo." Whole carcasses "lay scattered all over the prairie." The hunters had "taken only the hides and all the good meat was left to rot, or was partly eaten by wolves and other flesh eating animals."[12] The party returned to Saddle Lake but in the fall another hunt was planned, this time in concert with Chipewyans from the north. In October, they headed south again in search of the bison but were quickly stalled by an early winter storm. "The Chipewyans decided to return north but the Crees kept going south." Travel was rendered difficult by the crusting of the snow. The party moved past "what was then known as Big Forest Mountain near the present town of Vegreville." On the counsel of an elder, Shandro, the party decided to winter over in Big Forest Mountain. Based on the location and description, this place name undoubtedly specified the Beaver Hills:[13]

> The snow, although very deep, was not so hard in the bush. There were several fair-sized sloughs in the vicinity where our horses found enough to keep them alive. Rabbits were quite plentiful: besides there were deer, elk and a few moose. There

were several good hunters in the camp and so we never suffered from want of food.

Towards early spring word reached this party, still sheltered in the hills, that a starving band of Plains Cree was headed its way from the south. Some of the hunters and their families departed for Saddle Lake, but some remained to assist this devastated party of about fifty persons.[14] As in the Cypress Hills country in the early 1870s, the crisis in the bison supply was forcing people to resort en masse to more thickly wooded wildlife haunts in order to find reliable sources of food. The "boreal" aspect of the Beaver Hills provided a wider variety of species than was to be found in the surrounding prairie and parkland. By 1879, however, the possibilities were bleak on the prairies. From Fort Pitt, Willie Traill wrote to his mother about the position of the Indians, that he did not "know how they are to be tided over the winter for there are no buffalo and government cannot afford to feed them all on flour & beef."[15]

As if the recent experience of disease and famine were not sufficient, the greater prairie social equilibrium started to deteriorate. A "massacre" in the Cypress Hills of some Assiniboine Indians

Detachment of North West Mounted Police moving along a corduroy road in the Beaver Hills, c. 1905.

Fort Saskatchewan, c. 1905 Sergeant-Major Sam Steele was a central figure at this post on the south bank of the North Saskatchewan River in 1875.

by American wolfers in May, 1873, reinforced the perception in Canadian government circles that there was a need for clear and disciplined action and for "treating" with the Indians. The Liberal government of Alexander Mackenzie was returned to office later that year and it moved as quickly as possible to dispatch members of the newly established North West Mounted Police to the South Saskatchewan country. Members of the new force arrived at Fort Macleod in 1874.[16]

Organization of the western territory for police administration was then hurriedly undertaken. "A" Division was sent to Fort Edmonton in August, 1874, where it wintered. After a long and exhausting trip, a contingent of police arrived at Victoria Post in October. The following year "A" Division moved to the old fur trade post site at Fort Saskatchewan, which served as headquarters for the Edmonton District until 1911. The main objectives for the force were to contain the liquor trade, enforce basic laws and assist in extinguishing Native title to the land as a preliminary to any systematic surveys and settlement.[17]

Dealing with the implications and nature of aboriginal title on the upper Saskatchewan was viewed as an urgent task of diplomacy for

Alexander Morris, resident Governor of the North West Territories. He initiated negotiations to allay fears among the Indians brought on by the appearance of railway, telegraph and geological survey crews in the lands west of Battleford. Treaty 6, which included the Beaver Hills country within its boundaries, was signed at Fort Carlton and Fort Pitt in 1876.[18] In this treaty process, Peter Erasmus played an important role. He was the paid interpreter for the Indians, acting independently of the Government party.

Chief Bobtail was not present at the original treaty discussions at Fort Pitt, but he signed an adhesion to the treaty in 1877. Under this treaty his people were assigned lands straddling the Battle River to the north of present-day Ponoka along the Calgary-Edmonton Trail. Only in 1885 however, did Bobtail finally consent to have the formal surveys made in accordance with the agreed-upon formula of one square mile for every five Indians. Dissatisfaction then arose on the part of Bobtail and many of his followers, some of whom withdrew from treaty in 1886, opting instead for land scrip – vouchers given to individuals that might be used in the future as a claim on certain specified units of land. Many preferred to adhere to the original treaty arrangements. Much of the Bobtail reserve land remained vacant during the 1890s and its history became further confused by the assignment of some of the land to a group of Cree in Montana who had fled south in the aftermath of the 1885 conflict.[19] This decision was in part a consequence of the early days of the Riel rebellion when Bobtail, along with a number of other Chiefs in the Edmonton area, gave some support to the resistors at Batoche. Following this partial flight to Montana, the vacated lands, (under the Hobbema Agency) then became subject to various pressures for surrender and development from members of the new pioneer class and other parties inside and outside of government. These pressures were however, generally resisted by the Commissioner of Indian Affairs, David Laird.[20]

More confusing is the history of the band under Papaschase, who had signed an adhesion to Treaty 6 for a large block of land south of Edmonton in 1878.[21] While Papaschase maintained the

Papaschase (1838–1921) A signatory to an adhesion to Treaty 6 in 1878, Papaschase and his band briefly occupied a reserve in what is today south Edmonton. Under pressures from the new settler class, the reserve was consigned back to Canada by 1889, after which it was opened to settlement under current regulations.

peace in 1885, he had to contend with Frank Oliver, long aggressive in his editorials, who wanted to see Native reserve lands located further from Edmonton. In the aftermath of the rebellion and under pressure with respect to the location of the new Calgary-Edmonton railway route, most followers of Papaschase took scrip and moved to the Enoch Reserve. When the last families agreed to leave in 1889, the lands were consigned back to Canada, leaving the lands open for public sale. The manner of the disposition of the reserve in favour of scrip provisions has been a matter of controversy ever

Chief Samson (Battle River), Chief Pakan (Whitefish Lake), Jonas Bigstone (Morley), 1886   These Chiefs were influenced by the Methodist Missions and maintained peaceful relations with the new settlers and Government authorities.

since. As late as 2008, the Supreme Court of Canada ruled against further consideration of land claims being made with respect to the old reserve.[22]

Reserve boundaries drawn on the ground may seem to be objective symbols of some kind of intended fairness in dealing, but the loss of old traditions of mobility remained firm in the memories of the descendants of those who had to repeatedly adjust to new Canadian dispositions of land. The life of Elizabeth Brass Donald illustrates the many dilemmas facing the people of the country. She was listed in 1879 as no. 82 on the Papaschase Band List. A descendant has summarized her biography: "Betsy was born in the 1830s near the Hudson's Bay Company post at Fort Pelly." Her family and community, "a mixture of Cree and Saulteux" eventually agreed to the Terms of Treaty 4 of 1875 and then settled "on the Key Reserve" in south-eastern Saskatchewan. Later she married George Donald, a Métis who was employed by the HBC as a carpenter and blacksmith. According to information on Betsy's 1885 scrip document, George had worked in Red River before the couple's marriage in 1853. The couple moved to Fort Pitt in 1855 and then to Fort Edmonton in 1864. As the fur trade declined and the Edmonton community grew, confusion developed over the river lot held by George and Betsy owing to their inclusion as members of the Papaschase Band. Reduced to increasing poverty through the abandonment of the reserve in 1889 and scrip arrangements, the Donald extended family removed to the Cooking Lake area in the Beaver Hills, where there were long-standing Métis settlements.[23] Such were the complications facing just one family.

From his base at Whitefish Lake, Peter Erasmus continued to keep an eye out for the needs of his Indian friends. In 1884 Chief James Seenum (Pakan) asked Erasmus to go to Regina with him to talk with the Governor in an attempt sort out unresolved details of the lands Seenum felt were owed to his people in the vicinity of Whitefish and Goodfish Lakes. Many of the issues were resolved, more or less satisfactorily, although Seenum grumbled to Erasmus on the way home that "promises by government people were like

Peter Erasmus (1833–1931)   In his old age, this great witness to prairie life and social change, recounted his remarkable memoirs to Henry Thompson, later published as *Buffalo Days and Nights*.

the clouds—always changing."[24] It seems that Native peoples had their own peculiar understanding of the term "The Promised Land." Erasmus explained the slowness of government dealings to Seenum as best he could, and tried to convince him that having certain lands closed off from settlement was the most important aspect. James Seenum was of the Christianized Methodist connection at

Victoria, and of peaceful disposition and counsel; but the delays and frustrations confronting him were characteristic of wider unresolved conditions, and not all leaders were as patient as Seenum.[25] Treaty 6 had been signed, but by 1885 there was still much to be worked out concerning legal surveys and the refinement of arrangements with Native and Métis peoples.

Changing Nature of the Population in the Beaver Hills

Since the troubles in Red River in 1870, an increasing number of Métis had moved out onto the prairies and into the parkland. A census of the Red River Colony in 1871 indicated that there were about 9,800 people of mixed-blood heritage. By 1878 the most politically refined centre of Métis influence on the prairies was St. Laurent, located between the branches of the North and South Saskatchewan, even though the St. Albert settlement near Edmonton

Gabriel Dumont (1837–1906) Descended from Montreal trader Jean-Baptiste Dumont and a Sarcee woman, Josette "Sarcisse," Dumont played an important role in 1885 as Riel's military commander. Many of the large Dumont clan lived in the Beaver Hills area.

was somewhat older. At least 750 people resided at St. Laurent,
politically organized under Gabriel Dumont. While the Métis were
well known for their abilities in the bison hunt, other more sedentary activities had steadily become just as important to their way
of life. The maintenance of river lot or lakeside farms, grazing of
stock, and seasonal engagements in the fur trade and transport
were all important aspects of Métis economy. Hence, small communities appeared across the prairies after 1870. These were first
the settlements of the "hivernants," those who "wintered over" but
no longer returned to Red River after the seasonal hunts.[26]

The decline of the bison induced changes in Métis attitudes towards
the land and re-selection of home bases. James MacGregor noted
that in the 1870s "the Métis who so recently had made the Boss
Hill echo with the laughter of their feasting, had moved to new
homes." Of such new settlements, one was along the southern rim
of Beaverhills Lake, and another further south at Laboucan or
Battle River Crossing. According to local historians at Duhamel,
the recent settlers at Laboucan were actually old residents of the
country from Lac Ste. Anne. They included the Dumonts, who
arrived in 1875. Gabriel Dumont later achieved fame in several
capacities, most notably during the 1885 troubles when he served
as Riel's military commander. In 1876 François Dumont, based at
Battle River Crossing, became the first agent hired to pay out
annual treaty monies to the Native peoples of that quarter.[27]

Other early Métis residents included the six Laboucane brothers
who hailed from the Whitehorse Plains near Portage La Prairie.
They were described as having "recently settled" along the Battle
River about 1878. This fur trade family name may possibly be
connected with that same "La Boucone" who had dealings with
Alexander Henry the Younger in 1810, then in charge of the
Nor'Westers at Fort Augustus.[28] The Laboucanes had been pre-
ceded by Abraham Salois and his sons, who established a river lot
farm at this location before 1875.[29] On the south and western edges
of Beaverhills Lake, the Whitfords, Mackenzies, Prudens and
others were also starting to congregate.[30] Charles Whitford made

some preliminary efforts at settling as early as 1865, his daughter contending that he was "the first man other than the Indians to make his home on the shore of Beaverhill Lake."[31] This was only his latest base of operations, for his origins were also in Red River. Peter Erasmus worked with many members of the family after 1858.[32] For some time they occupied lands on what is now known as Whitford Lake to the north-east of the Beaver Hills.[33]

A grand gathering appears to have taken place on the southern shore of Beaverhills Lake in 1868. Métis hunters from Edmonton, St. Albert and Lac Ste. Anne and from Victoria, Whitefish Lake and Lac La Biche all met "to make plans for hunting buffalo during the summer." According to this account Chief Factor Hardisty and the Rev. George McDougall were present at the gathering.[34] Such coordinated assemblies were clearly part of the final push for the bison, which were steadily disappearing to the south. Such events help explain some of the movement of Métis hunters from more northerly enclaves into the southern fringes of the parkland belt. Erasmus participated in such a hunt in 1870, one in which John Whitford was nominated as hunt leader.[35]

From the 1840s a Métis presence in the Beaver Hills area had gradually been grafted onto older patterns of traditional Native use. The fusion of European with Native did not always issue in the breaking-off of a splinter group and the setting up of a new settlement. Fur trader Louis Piché, originally of Terrebonne, Quebec, had "gone native" in the 1820s, fusing his social identity with the Cree. Two of his sons, Bobtail and Ermineskin, later gained recognition as traditional Cree Chiefs of high standing. These men absorbed some of the ways of their father, and indeed, were the first envoys to the Bishop of St. Boniface in 1842, requesting Roman Catholic missionaries for the Fort Edmonton area. Their later interest in the details of land settlement and a certain inclination towards the interests of the Métis during the 1885 troubles, are explainable in terms of long affinity with and their ability to move knowledgeably in the worlds of the European fur trader, the Native and the Métis.[36]

The Year 1885 in the Beaver Hills

By kin and circumstance, diverse peoples of the old fur trade society had jelled reasonably well along the upper Saskatchewan Valley during the 1870s, but by the mid-1880s all was not well in many of these communities. The railway was creeping west and there remained outstanding land issues. To the peoples of this region, it was not certain what rules were in place when the veteran interpreter Peter Erasmus and his party arrived back home at Whitefish Lake in the spring of 1885. "Big Louis came forward to greet us" and it quickly transpired that news had reached the settlements of the beginnings of the second resistance led by Louis Riel. Frank Oliver's *Edmonton Bulletin* proclaimed in April that "There appears to be plenty of ammunition among the Indians at Bears' Hill and plenty of Winchester rifles."[37]

All the military engagements were in Saskatchewan as far as could be told, "and only their echoes reached Edmonton" noted historian James MacGregor. They tended to be "echoes true or distorted by distance, and always two weeks old." Fort Edmonton became the bastion of the alarmed settlers in the area. Superintendent Griesbach of the North West Mounted Police sent word to Calgary to mobilize the Alberta Field Force. A traveller reported that Bobtail and his son Coyote were the mischief makers south of Edmonton, their men robbing a freighter of his goods and executing a raid on the Hudson's Bay Company post at Battle River Crossing.[38] In July, Henry G. Tyrrell, while undertaking a reconnaissance of the Battle River valley, encountered a Methodist missionary to the Stoney Indians, John Nelson, who was rebuilding his mission. Nelson related that he had "only left a few hours with his family for a place of safety when Bobtail's band came down, pillaged his house, drove his horses and cattle away and, after exhausting their means of destruction, rode off, leaving the place a total wreck."[39]

There was probably little agreement on the issues within either the Native or the Métis communities. There was a considerable difference in outlook marking the Métis around St. Albert and Lac

Ste. Anne and those on the middle Saskatchewan. Many of the former had been born on the land and possessed little knowledge of Red River or of the particular grievances of the St. Laurent people.[40] A general result of this second Riel resistance was to encourage a substantial number of Métis from Saskatchewan to move further west into the older established settlements around Lac Ste. Anne, Lac La Biche and St. Albert, or else to take lands on a "scrip" basis at such places as pleased them.[41]

This general dynamic had some influence on the settlement patterns in the Beaver Hills. Edo Nyland suggested that in 1885 a migration took place. "During that summer a large number of Métis left the South Branch of the Saskatchewan River, and settled at the Battle River" while a "smaller group" entered on the west side of Beaver Hills Lake.[42] Some of these destinations were already established centres such as Laboucan, Salvais, Victoria, and perhaps others along the western and southern edge of the lake. In the course of his geological surveys, J.B. Tyrrell passed through the Battle River country and was at Salvais Crossing in 1886, where he found a settlement of forty Métis families in "substantial log homes."[43] On the south-western edges of the hills, there were other Métis and Native peoples such as the Auguste Gladue family and "Black Jack" Sanderson at Hastings Lake. The latter was of Lakota Sioux background and had been active as a guide with the forces which moved against Riel in 1885.[44] The identities of some of these old settlements were soon reinforced by the cartographer's chart. Some pre-1883 river lots are still evident on maps today. They are particularly visible in the case of the Victoria Settlement, where the sizeable country-born population had settled along the North Saskatchewan in the deep, narrow lot pattern characteristic of Quebec and the Red River Valley.[45]

With the 1885 troubles put to rest, militarily at least, the residents of the hills set about adjusting to the new order. Chief Bobtail reluctantly authorized the surveyors to proceed on his lands in 1886.[46] The way was now clear for a wide-scale redefinition of many western Canadian prairie lands.

In eastern Canada, the worst abuses of institutionalized private land-owning privilege had been curtailed by virtue of the British North America Act of 1867, the founding document of the new nation.[47] In western Canada no official landed class became entrenched except with respect to certain corporate bodies, such as the Hudson's Bay Company, the Canadian Pacific Railway and the church. The first two would continue to profit from land sales during the settlement period, but for the intending settler there was the sweet knowledge that once land had been "proved up" by their sweat and paid for, any corporate landlord would be out of his hair.[48] Resentment against the large corporate interests naturally became a bond of commonality between the immigrant and the older settler. This bond had been foreshadowed as long ago as 1849 by none other than Louis Riel's father, who helped bring to an end the Hudson's Bay Company's ability to constrain private trade in Rupert's Land. Owing to the subsequent drama which came to surround the personality of Louis Riel after the resistance of 1869–70, it is sometimes forgotten how unified the entire community at Red River was in terms of objecting to what many considered to be unilateral and arbitrary administrative actions exercised by a new foreign power called Canada. The lure of almost free or cheap land, however, was sufficient to foster much forbearance in the more recent pioneering classes.[49]

New Arrivals in Central Alberta

As a social frontier, the Beaver Hills were remarkable for the sheer diversity of national and religious groupings that settled along their fringes in the years between 1890 and 1920. A limited pioneer advance began somewhat ahead of the transportation improvements and federal policies that accelerated the process after 1896. The forerunners were adventurers and colonizers who had entered the territory around Edmonton shortly after the completion of Treaty 6 in 1876. Excluding small wandering groups of miners criss-crossing the foothills regions in the 1860s, the earliest to homestead east of

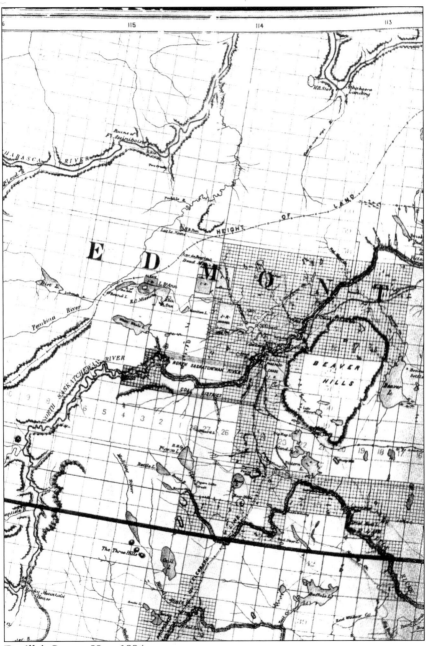

Deville's Survey Map. 1884

old Fort Edmonton were four Ontario men. Tired of working the mines and boats of Lake Superior, they came to the Northwest in 1881. Among them was Philip Ottewell, who brought with him a keg of Red Fife wheat seed with a view to testing the soils of the Saskatchewan River Valley. On the west side of the Beaver Hills, in the Clover Bar area close to the south branch of the Victoria Trail, he and three associates became the first new pioneers.[50]

Clover Bar was at the centre of a proposed unit of land speculation being promoted by surveyor George A. Simpson. With the transcontinental railway proposed to run through Edmonton, Simpson speculated that a land boom would unfold. He formed the Edmonton and Saskatchewan Land Company and "secured four townships for settlement and town site under an ambitious plan." This land block commenced on the western slope of the Beaver Hills and ran west across the Saskatchewan River to the boundary of the large Hudson's Bay Company land reserve now attached to Fort Edmonton. With Ottawa's decision to abandon the "Yellowhead Route" and run the railway through Calgary instead of Edmonton, Clover Bar was suddenly left to grow on its own. Between 1882 and 1885, not all was smooth among the early settlers of the Edmonton region, as certain gaps in land law made for confusion and alleged land claim "jumping" by new arrivals. These difficulties were ironed out but many of the first settlers to the area, now without the promise of railway-based prosperity, had to become pragmatic, some combining homesteading with gold-panning on the Saskatchewan River.[51] Even more remote on the eastern shore of Beaver Hills Lake were Richard and Geoffrey Steele, who had pioneered land in 1881. Such independent-minded settlers were still quite rare at this time, most preferring, and being encouraged, to wait for the official process of survey to be completed. In 1887 the Land Commissioner for the Hudson's Bay Company noted the struggles of the new Clover Bar settlers, owing to frost.[52]

The Canadian Pacific Railway, meanwhile, had reached Calgary in 1884. This allowed a few sturdy groups of German-speaking settlers to enter the country north of the Red Deer River well before the completion of the Calgary-Edmonton Railway. Some trekked north into the Beaver Hills proper. German speakers from Austrian Galicia, largely of Lutheran background, established themselves as early as 1891 at Josephburg, a short distance southeast of Fort Saskatchewan. In the spring of that year some forty families reached the end of steel at Red Deer, then went by cart along the rough route north known as the Edmonton Trail.[53] A chronicler of the movement has recorded that among the arrivals those "of the Reformed denomination with some 'Old Lutherans'... took homesteads southeast of Fort Saskatchewan" and that "they registered the name Josephburg as their school district in 1893."[54]

The experience of George Becker illustrates the origins of this early wave. In Austria, a rush for naphtha oil in the east Carpathian Mountains in the early 1880s had attracted the speculative financial resources of Becker and many of his fellow citizens in Josephburg and Brigadau. When the rush failed, Becker was counted among the disappointed. Despite advancing years, he decided to strike

The Schmidt Farm, c. 1895   This staged photograph, taken by C.W. Mathers, is remarkably complete with respect to the details of early farm life as practiced by the early German settlers in the Josephburg area.

out and gamble on the free lands in western Canada which had come to his notice. He and his party departed for Halifax. Their arrival on the North Saskatchewan would be round-about, taking a number of years. They first attempted to work lands in southern Saskatchewan and Alberta, but finding those soils unsuitable for homesteading, they then sought out the cooler and moister regimes of the Parkland belt between Red Deer and Edmonton.[55] This willingness to shop around, even in advance of improved transportation, indicates that some early pioneers understood very well the value of a disciplined land appraisal and the interplay of soil and moisture. Robert Scace observed that many homesteaders after having filed "on a piece of land which proved unsuccessful or undesirable" would then "simply leave and file on another quarter elsewhere." This was a useful frontier convention by which one might cut one's losses, even though a year or two of labour might have to be written off. Progress in land clearing in the interior Beaver Hills was slow going owing to the nature of the soils, the heavier timber conditions, and the frequency of water courses. Grazing was therefore a more popular mode of land use for the new settlers.[56] Progress there was, however. In 1893, the *Edmonton Bulletin* reported that in the Josephburg district there were some 390 people and 1,000 acres under cultivation.[57] The quality and well-tailored appearance of some of these early homesteads was well illustrated at the Schmidt property.[58]

The arrival of steel at the south bank of the North Saskatchewan River at Strathcona in the fall of 1891 opened the door to more systematic settlement of the central parts of Alberta, including the Beaver Hills. Despite previous, if modest, indications of pioneer interest, the last years of the long federal Conservative regime of Sir John A. Macdonald had been somewhat halting in terms of agricultural promotion of the West. Correction of this situation had become a regular editorial theme for "Honest" Frank Oliver at the *Edmonton Bulletin*. In public office or out, Oliver relished his role as "gadfly of the administration."[59]

More promising was the year 1892 which saw movement into the Beaver Hills by a group of colonists from Magnetawan in the Parry Sound District of Ontario. Responding to the silver-tongued arguments of CPR colonization agent, D.L. Caven, they arrived at Strathcona by rail to take up lands reserved for them in advance. "Nearly all of these people settled in what is known as the Beaver Hills and Beaver Creek District, at and around the old Northwest Mounted Police post at Fort Saskatchewan."[60] The Rye family was an exception, settling north of the Saskatchewan River, but maintaining ties with their fellow colonists.[61] The Pollards were among the second contingent of the Parry Sounders of 1894, composing "an additional 200 families" that had set out from Sundridge. The first two years had not been easy for the first group. W.C. Pollard recalled the day of his arrival: "the sight of most of the members of the first colony was somewhat dampened by the fact that they were clad mostly in the homespun that they had taken with them two years before." Indeed, the "hardness of the water and scarcity of soap had changed many a bright countenance to such a degree that they were hardly recognizable." Some of the men "had not even the luxury of a shave since they had left Parry Sound" and "adorned with their tattered fur coats" they looked like "the wildman referred to in Daniel Defoe's Robinson Crusoe." These Parry Sounders, in the interests of primary survival, had resorted to many of the solutions which the first Ukrainian pioneers would employ a few years later to get through their first years. "The people lived in small houses, for the most part built with logs and sod roofs."[62]

Pollard's memoir confirms later perceptions about the extensive nature of human alteration of the hills in the wake of pioneer settlement. "The prairie fires were aglow, and the whole country seemed either to be burning or have been burned. Fires were seen in the distance, and at twilight the flames would rage higher and higher."[63] With a view to controlling the water sheds of the Beaver Hills, the federal Department of the Interior had withdrawn a number of townships from settlement in 1892, prior to this first

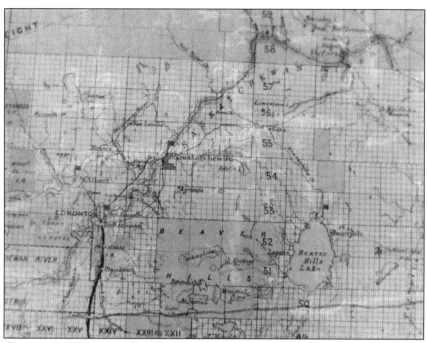

Forestry Map. Beaver Hills, 1894

wave of settlement, thus establishing a land base for what was formally established in 1899 as the Cooking Lake Forest Reserve.[64]

A parallel invasion of the hills was being made by settlers of Scandinavian origin who arrived on the southern flanks in the Wetaskiwin and Camrose districts. Some came directly from northern Europe and others from Massachusetts or from Crookston in the Red River Valley of Minnesota. There, "a Canadian immigration agent had recently opened an office" and was able to provide official propaganda to prospective immigrants such as Nels Jevning and Martin Finseth. The Hay Lakes district became a favoured location for Swedes and Germans, while the Bardo area, a short distance south of Beaverhills Lake, was preferred by Norwegians. The Kingman and Ryley districts, south-east of the hills, continued to absorb many more Nordic people after 1910.[65]

People of Norwegian stock had been working the Minnesota country since the mid-1870s, but like the Josephburg pioneers, they kept an eye out for new possibilities. In response to the promptings of the Canadian agent an advance party of about twenty left Polk County in 1894 to look over the lands in Alberta. Southern Manitoba, Saskatchewan and Alberta struck them as being too similar to their own Red River Valley, but upon reaching the Red Deer area they started to become interested, especially by the added advantages of a local coal supply. It was the Beaver Hills country that really sold them. Game, timber and water were to be had close at hand, along with good-looking soil on the borders of the hills. Martin Finseth and his associates encountered a seasoned settler, Edmund Thompson. When he took them to Beaver Hills Lake, with its fishery, they became convinced:

> This is the place we have been looking for. Here is a wonderful soil for raising crops; in the hills to the west we have trees for building. The prairie openings in the parkland with a luxuriant growth of grass will be fine for stock-raising. And now a lake with fish in it. What more can a Norwegian ask for?[66]

Edmond Thompson was retained for future land selections by intending settlers from the Crookston area and settlement on Amisk Creek, a southern tributary to Beaver Hills Lake, commenced in earnest. The name Bardo was given to the settlement in 1904, recalling the locality of Bardu in Northern Norway, from whence many others immigrated to the Beaver Hills.[67] The settlement was at the very centre of a Nordic belt which would develop from Wetaskiwin on the west through the Hay Lakes area and Skandia colony at Bittern Lake, to Camrose, Trondheim (Round Hill) and east to Viking.[68]

These trends all received some notice in the promotional writings of the former Hudson's Bay Company trader and artifact collector, Isaac Cowie, who arrived in Edmonton in 1892 and became the main voice of the Edmonton Board of Trade.[69] He saw Edmonton as the key to the development of the greater northwest and the Yukon, imperial ventures which he promoted in distinctly British terms. The opportunities were aimed at patriots with ambition. Cowie provided information for "Railway and other Capitalists, Tourists, Sportsmen, Big Game Hunters, Scientific Explorers and other seeking fresh fields for their energies, UNDER THE FLAG."[70] His works were characteristic of frontier boosterism all across the North American west. Cowie spent a good deal of time analyzing the results of a questionnaire circulated to local farmers in 1896 by the Edmonton branch of the Western Canada Immigration Association. The fifty-two respondents provide a glimpse of local settlement to date and on the very eve of the great influx of immigrants from central Europe about to be facilitated under Clifford Sifton's new policies.[71]

The largest and steadiest stream of settlers into the area was that of Ukrainians from Bukovyna and Galicia. After 1891, for the next three decades, they defined new settlements in a broad band to the north and east of the Beaver Hills.[72] Institutional development started to take place among the Ukrainians after 1900, as it did among the other diverse peoples who had entered the region. A certain geographic sifting took place along lines of past association and kinship, but these were not hard and fast.

The links forged back in Europe within distinctive groups were sometimes very strong. Two of the important early pioneers in the Beaver Hills, John Krebs for the Josephburg Germans, and Ivan Pylypow for the Ukrainians at Star, were childhood friends in Nebilew in Galicia. Each man in his own way had worked to encourage their compatriots to take a chance on the new world and eventually the two men joined hands in this effort. Pylypow was an indifferent student, but while attending school in Stanyslaviv he learned several languages and befriended the young German, John Krebs. Pylypow benefited from his contact with the Prosvita Society, founded at Lemberg in 1868, which sought to promote general enlightenment among farmers and workers all over Ukraine. The society's local institutes became a model for the National Halls later built in many a Ukrainian community in Canada. Dr. Joseph

Oleskow, the great promoter of Ukrainian settlement in North America, was associated with the Prosvita movement.[73]

By 1890, Ivan Pylypow was not successful financially and turned to the local Prosvita group for advice on emigration. Unimpressed with eastern Russia as a prospect, he decided to find out where Krebs had gone. He eventually heard from his friend, who was already in Alberta, in the Medicine Hat area. Krebs advised him to come and bring others, but he also hinted that his group was thinking of going north to Edmonton in search of better land. In September of 1891, Pylypow set out with Wasyl Eleniak to inspect conditions first-hand, initiating what was to become a steady stream of settlement from western Ukraine. Upon his return to Galicia, Pylypow had to pay an unexpected penalty to the Austro-Hungarian authorities. They were not amused by his attempt to siphon off their working population to Canada. This was too late, however, for predictably, the publicity occasioned by the Vienna trial of Pylypow and Panishchak only furthered the cause of immigration. "No one," says Hall, "could have devised better propaganda than this turned out to be." Pylypow arrived in Canada again, and his homestead near Star was close to many of his countrymen, including his old school chum, John Krebs, who lived just to the southwest near Josephburg.[74]

Immigrants of Polish background also arrived in the vicinity. Father Francis Olszewski established the first Polish parish in Alberta not far from Mundare, in 1899. He proposed "the name of Krakow to remind the people" that as that place represented "the heart of Poland" so too would this be the place "from which Religious life" would "emanate to all Polish settlements" in Alberta. Olszewksi took his Roman Catholic missions to Slovaks, Poles and Ukrainians as far south as the coal mines of Canmore and Bankhead, and also initiated a convent school staffed by a teaching order of nuns. Following a destructive fire in 1910, the centre of Polish cultural activity shifted from Krakow to Skaro, where Catholic Ukrainians and Poles mixed easily, many having come from the same regions of Galicia.[75]

Many settlers in the Beaver Hills, be they from the United States, the British Isles or Europe, had undertaken the trauma of emigration largely on economic grounds. Others, however, had uprooted themselves with religious motives foremost. The link between politics and religion in Europe was close in the nineteenth century, and for some it was virtually coincident. This was true for many Mennonites, Hutterites and Moravians. A historical difficulty for such groups with deep roots in the dissenting traditions of Anabaptism was that the necessary holy protector or prince they found supportive in one generation might not remain so in the next.[76]

Among the communal or pacifist religious foundations, one of the earliest to appear in the Beaver Hills was that of the Moravians. As with the Mennonite tradition, the Moravian outlook may be traced back to the earliest stirrings of reform in the European Christian Church in Bohemia, well before Luther's time. The Moravians trace their religious origins to the fifteenth century when followers of Jan Hus founded the *Jednota Brakrska*, later known as the *Unitas Fratrum*. The reformers congregated east of Prague at Kunvald, there "to pursue a pietistic mode of life in which purity of morals and conduct was stressed over and above doctrinal uniqueness."[77] With the protective assistance of dissenting European lords and princes, they held their own as a group until the Thirty Years War. After the decisive Battle of the White Mountain in 1620, the Moravians were forced underground, retreating before the powerful forces of resurgent Catholicism in the Hapsburg Empire.[78] The search for a suitable protector prince had to begin all over again.

One was found in the Austrian nobleman, Count Nicholas Ludwig Von Zinzendorf of Saxony, a pietist who in the 1720s gave refuge to a group of dissenters from Bohemia in the hope of converting them to his own brand of belief. As it turned out, Zinzendorf was converted by his own guests, and he is credited with leading the revival of the Moravian Church. This new church, based at Herrnhutt, then suffered from success. By 1736 it was suppressed by the Government of Saxony, which forced Zinzendorf into exile.

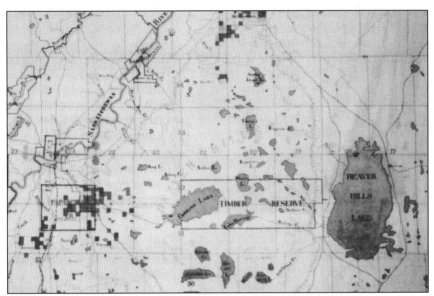

Beaver Hills Area, 1898   Bishop Clement Hoyler, the spiritual leader of the
Moravian settlers, prepared this map in 1898. It includes the outline of the Papaschase
Reserve south of Edmonton, on the northeastern edge of which the Moravian settlement
of Bruderfeld would eventually develop.

He took the opportunity to join the English Methodist, George
Whitfield, and together they went to Pennsylvania with momentous
results for both of those church movements in North America.[79]
The European membership survived in parts of Poland and the
eastern Austrian provinces of Bukovyna and Galicia. In the 1880s,
however, reacting to new forces of suppression and frustrated by
the changing political situation, many Moravians started to look
further afield. In 1894 word was had in Russian Volhynia that relief
might be found in the far-off Canadian Northwest. Subsequently
"a number of families prepared to dispose of their possessions"
before departing for the New World.[80]

Moravians settled at two locations in the Edmonton area: at
Bruderheim east of Fort Saskatchewan, and in the Colchester area
to the south, where lands previously set aside as the Papaschase
Indian Reserve came available for sale.[81] The latter location became

Bishop Hoyler and Mrs. Hoyler

known as Bruderfeld. Thrift was a tenet of Moravian life, so despite the difficulties of travel and unfamiliar economic conditions, many were still able to purchase land and equipment. An "Old Timer" noted that the little "sod-covered shacks in which the Bruderheim pioneers spent their first winters were of the same general pattern, but all had individual characteristics." The most "striking feature of their construction" was the "old country method of building in which wooden pegs and plugs took the place of nails." The "pioneer cabins had only one room. There was a row of supporting posts under the gable, which also carried the framework for a loft." In one corner of the room "there often would be a chicken-pen, in which birds were confined at night. During the day, they had the run of the room." Fire prevention was a constant cause for vigilance in these early cabins, particularly as it might be transmitted from stove to sod roof. "These same sod roofs were a sight to behold after a wet spell in the spring or summer. Grain, grass and weeds would spout profusely to give a verdant effect."[82] The communal ties fostered by the *Unitas Fratrum* were sufficient to counter periodic domestic disasters associated with fire or to enable the less prudential to get through their first years. By 1895, a congregation had been established at Bruderheim under Andreas Lilge.[83]

Land hunger and social disruption in late nineteenth century Europe was sufficiently severe and widespread to motivate a number of pioneer groups to seek out the Canadian Northwest in advance of regional transportation improvements, civic organization or government assistance. During the 1890s, the practical requirements of settlers were eased somewhat as a result of new federal policies.

Distant Diasporas and Immigration to Western Canada

With the coming to power in Ottawa of the Liberal Laurier administration in 1896, Clifford Sifton of Brandon, Manitoba, was appointed Minister of the Interior. He was not impressed with the statistics on immigration to Canada under his immediate predecessors. He could only conclude that more people had left Canada over the last fifteen years than had arrived.[84] His main achievement over the next ten years was to reverse this trend by means of a thorough revamping of national recruitment policy and by advertising the merits of western Canada abroad. One of his initial tasks was to address the mess in settlement policy occasioned by the rules which allowed the CPR to defer selection of the blocks of land committed to it by the original railway building contract with Canada. By refusing to select lands, it escaped paying taxes, but created an on-going delay in land selection by intending settlers. Other properties were tied up by land companies and speculators who also did little to encourage settlement in the short term. It took Sifton a few years, but by 1903 he had remedied most of these abuses.[85]

Sifton was aggressive in his attempts to attract new immigrants to the country. Advertising in the United States was not difficult and he managed to attract a substantial number of experienced American agriculturalists across the border, including a number of expatriate Canadians. Europe was more problematic as governments were often hostile to immigration schemes. In a press address of 1896 he outlined his thinking: "experience has shown that those who make the best settlers are those whose condition in the land from which they come is not too rosy, and who are content in coming here to get along in a humble way at first."[86] Sifton's officials made arrangements, usually in private, with individual shipping agents placed at strategic places in Europe. He then engaged W.T.R. Preston "a former Liberal organizer of malodorous reputation" to organize the European recruiting effort. Preston was instrumental in the formation of the North Atlantic Trading Company, an organization of European shipping agents that D.J. Hall has described as "clandestine" but which succeeded in increasing the numbers of agricultural settlers destined for Canada.[87]

Having cast his net broadly in the United States and among the land-hungry of Europe and western Russia, Sifton offered terms and conditions for land which many could not refuse. There was no shortage of Europeans and Russians willing to compete with the more advantageously placed applicants from the British Isles and North America.[88] Helping to move the lukewarm to action were the racial and nationalist policies afoot in many parts of Europe, the result of both ancient and contemporary disaffection. "Diasporas" of diverse peoples, grouped along religious and ethnic lines, were being stimulated by various ideologies and discriminatory pieces of legislation.[89] Sifton's ambitious programme for settlement of western Canada was a success although it induced "nativist" reactions to immigration policy in many quarters, including among some of his colleagues such as Frank Oliver.[90] From Sifton's point of view, the results were quite satisfactory.

Peoples from Western Ukraine were strongly attracted by the possibilities of the prairies. The late nineteenth-century political and economic context of most Ukrainians residing in the eastern reaches of the old Austro-Hungarian Empire was summed up by Myrna Kostash:[91]

Squeezed between the Polish Landlords and the Austrian Army, reduced to a strip of land that could support fewer and fewer people, denied literacy and cultural self-expression, consigned to high taxes and low wages, suspicious of the priest's compromised position within a state financed church and harassed by personal debts piling up at the tavern, the Ukrainian peasant was at his wit's end precisely when the Canadian government opened the North-west Territories for settlement.

People with such an outlook had little to lose and much to gain. This was confirmed by the memoirs of a Rumanian pioneer who had come up against similar exasperating economic limits of family land subdivision in the old country: "How could he hope to raise a family on this meagre bit of land?" In 1898 therefore, the Kokotailo family relocated from Boian, Rumania, to the Whitford Lake area northeast of the Beaver Hills.[92] The interest was greatest among Ukrainians, who were encouraged and induced to come to the bloc settlements of east-central Alberta, where they joined, or were joined by, Germans, Poles, Hungarians, Scandinavians, Rumanians, Russians, and others seeking a new beginning.[93] They were not joined by interested Doukhobors, whose representatives had inspected and shown interest in lands around Beaverhills Lake in 1898. Frank Oliver, M.P. was opposed to this group on the grounds of their social values and he persuaded Sifton to redirect them to Saskatchewan.[94]

It is not unexpected, perhaps, that there was a tendency for Old World settlers to bond together for reasons of religion and language. Upon arrival in the West, immigrants found that the complexities of land-appraisal were many, but social considerations were often more important elements in site selection. Land choice was much driven by the desire to be close to one's own kind, where one might travel the path of least resistance, already slashed out by previously arrived compatriots. Thus, on the lands surrounding the Beaver Hills, the results of Sifton's shake-up of immigration are etched on the ground in the form of place names revealing past communal connections, names such as Bruderheim, Lamont, Krakow,

Bardo, Wostok, and Skaro. These names indicate the mix of peoples who sought to put old worlds behind them, but not without some sense of recollection.

Old worlds die hard however, and for the next forty years, the cultural landscapes of the Beaver Hills took on a certain mosaic quality in which religion and ancient sentiments drew people clannishly together in order to keep out various forms of economic and social cold. The history of one community on the eastern edge of the Beaver Hills illustrates the process. "The road to Mundare" was a long and complicated one in historical terms. To be sure, the actual origin of the place name Mundare is not certain. The first name for this community was Beaver Lake, the place where the Ukrainian Basilian order first located its institutions.[95] Their arrival was the outcome of an appeal made in 1899 by the Ukrainian pioneers themselves. A letter had been sent from Winnipeg to the Basilian Monastery at Zolkwa in western Ukraine making a case for their consideration:[96]

> Worst of all the small children will fall into delinquency for they will not attain any learning in the catechism. There are even those who having been born in Canada will not know anything about the church or education, and they will not wish to obey their fathers or mothers if they will not have any church teaching.

Basilian Fathers and Teaching Sisters arrived in Edmonton in late 1902, temporarily hosted there by French-speaking Oblates. The vitality of this ancient monastic movement was brought to bear on the eastern edge of the hills where the order first established a monastery then took a leading role in the educational history of the region's new settlements.

Historically, the road to Mundare commenced construction in fourth-century Caesaria on the east Mediterranean coast. There, a brilliant young Christian scholar made his repeated mark, somewhat to the discomfort of the venerable church father, Eusebius. The western half of the Roman Empire was on its last legs and the "Eastern way" of Christendom, based at Constantinople, started to make its great mark on church history. The young man at

Caesaria eventually became St. Basil the Great (A.D. 329–79), the founder of a monastic, but non-reclusive, tradition of service which, over time, came to have a great influence in both Kiev and Moscow.[97] The tradition grew strong and lasted down the centuries. With the arrival of St. Basil's ancient order in the hills in the early twentieth century, Mundare started to take on an identity as a centre of Ukrainian-Canadian cultural and religious life.[98]

The Changing Face of the Beaver Hills

> Altogether, it was a most satisfactory fall, but they did have a series of prairie fires. Although not as severe as the one of the previous year, they were still capable of endangering life and property. A daily concern in all the settlements around Beaver Lake was to be on the lookout for fire.
>
> – Magda Hendrickson
> *This Land is Our Land* (1972)

By 1905 the pioneer generation which had seen the last of the prairie world of the bison and fur trade in the Beaver Hills was itself growing old and prone to recollection. This generation had witnessed some striking changes in the local land cover and ways of life. A 1907 issue of the *Tofield Standard* contained a lengthy letter penned by the son of Philip Tate, the latter for many years the Hudson's Bay Company factor at Victoria Post. Signed as "Son of the Blackhead" the letter reflected upon the role of fire over the past forty years and on the changed character of the hills:[99]

> The destruction and wanton waste caused by prairie fires are incalculable. Beautiful groves, timber, wild fruit trees, the young wild animals, with thousands of duck eggs and prairie chicken eggs, are swallowed up by the indispensable friend and relentless foe. First, not having seen Beaver Lake or neighbourhood since I was a boy in the early seventies, it was with a genuine feeling of regret that I noted the total absence of maple trees during a recent tour of your beautiful Lake so changed from those early days.

The 1890s were, indeed, the occasion for a number of fires in the hills, the one of 1895 reputedly being very destructive. In a report on the Cooking Lake Reserve for 1907, the Superintendent of Forestry stated: "This reserve has probably suffered more from fire than any of the other reserves and there is at present hardly a square mile of virgin timber left." According to the report "the original stand was spruce, larch, aspen, balm, birch with some jack pine and balsam" but now "the conifers have almost all disappeared and only an odd old spruce or larch which has been protected by a muskeg or a hill remains to show that there was once a coniferous forest on these hills." While aspen and balsam were at the time "coming up thickly over almost all of the reserve" nevertheless "some of it has been burned over three or four times and is now

Recreation at South Cooking Lake. c. 1896

beginning to lose its vigour. In these places it will be necessary to replant it if the forest is to be maintained."[100]

Altered fire regimes in the hills had other sources unrelated to the first wave of pioneers. J.G. MacGregor observed that the sources of fire in the years after the decline of the bison were the long prairie grasses which could now grow waist high in the absence of natural grazers to keep them low. In dry seasons "almost any spark could touch off a conflagration that might rage far and wide for miles."[101] In the lands between the Battle and the North Saskatchewan, ranchers did not appear in advance of sod-busters with sufficient power to completely restock these vacated grasslands with an alternative to the bison, as had happened in southern Alberta.

The fires of the 1890s and their association with agricultural settlement, moved federal government agent, E.F. Stephenson, to set aside several sections of land as a timber reserve in 1892.[102] The Cooking Lake Forest Reserve was given formal legal status in 1899 and in its new definition it covered about 170 square miles. Systematic fire prevention dates from this period when two fire rangers were appointed, William Stephens, a former scout at Fort Edmonton, and the Lakota-Sioux Indian, "Black Jack" Sanderson, previously mentioned, who had been a guide for Middleton's troops during the 1885 Riel troubles. Their surveillance facilities and cabin defined the first forest ranger station on the public lands of Alberta.[103] Sifton's policy of establishing public conservation lands in the Beaver Hills continued under his successor at the Department of the Interior from 1905, Frank Oliver.

Intimations of the recreational future of the hills may be noticed as early as the year 1894. Dr. A.H. Goodwin of Edmonton purchased Pine Island in the western corner of Cooking Lake and renamed it "Koney Island." The name involved a play on words, originally referencing the abundance of spruce cones found in the area.[104] With a private resort establishment in mind, this enterprise became known as the Koney Island Sporting Company.[105] The mode of access was the old trail from Edmonton which led through the hills and then carried on towards Battleford. The resort remained a fairly exclusive affair until the survey of the Grand Trunk Pacific Railway along the north shore in 1907 put it within reach of the general population of Edmonton. The opportunity to promote summer camp sites was then seized, and 188 lots were soon surveyed on Koney Island and 344 lots at Oban Beach town site.[106] Pleasure boats and picnics thereafter became popular pastimes on this the dominant regional lake, hinting at the important future role of the Beaver Hills as a recreational landscape.[107]

CHAPTER FIVE

Conservation, Communities, and Egalitarianism, 1905–1930

After granting provincial status to Alberta and Saskatchewan in 1905, the Canadian Government had still to give close attention to its selection for the Cabinet position of Minister of the Interior, a position of the greatest interest to western Canadians. Under the new political arrangements, administration of natural resources on the prairies remained in Ottawa's hands. The year 1905 was also a federal election year. Wilfrid Laurier, when returned to office for a second term as Prime Minister, appointed Frank Oliver, the veteran Edmonton journalist and Territorial Member of Parliament, to the portfolio of the Department of the Interior, which included administration of Indian Affairs.

This was an opportune appointment, for during the federal debates conducted over the last year on proposed provincial autonomy for Alberta, Oliver's editorials had been lukewarm owing to the lack of an adequate federal subsidy being proposed. At the time of the Bill's passage Oliver chose not to become the first Premier of the new province.[1]

Frank Oliver (1853–1933)   He arrived at Edmonton from Ontario in 1874 and in 1880 founded the *Edmonton Bulletin*. A tough-minded promoter of western settler interests, he had a long and influential political career, first in the North West Territorial Council and then in the federal cabinet of Wilfrid Laurier. He served as Minister for the Department of Interior from 1904 to 1911, and also had responsibility for Indian Affairs.

A strong booster of the West, Oliver chose to work for Alberta from his federal office. As a promoter of agricultural development, his appointment to the cabinet reflected the shifting tide of opinion towards farmers as opposed to ranchers.[2] In replacing the effective Clifford Sifton, Oliver continued to promote immigration, but in a different manner. He had been a strong critic of the wide net Sifton had cast in his recruitment zeal. There were limits to Oliver's liberalism. Although the slogan of the *Edmonton Bulletin* was "Read the Bible and the Bulletin" his attitude towards central Europeans was not always charitable.[3] One of his first acts was to cancel Sifton's arrangements with the North Atlantic Trading Company, which actively sought settlers from central and eastern Europe. He reoriented efforts towards western Europe and the United States by means of the amended Immigration Act of 1906.[4] Not only people from these areas were interested in the new West. There were also many from eastern Canada, including small and large investors.

If Oliver's was a rather WASPish view of the world, he adopted a fairly broad approach to community requirements which allowed him to respond openly to the practical requests of settlers and of wildlife conservationists. He revised the pre-emption provisions in the Land Act, making it easier for established settlers to obtain additional acreage contiguous to their property.[5] His assistance in the establishment of the so-called "Elk Park" in the Beaver Hills revealed his changing attitudes towards wildlife. The circumstances which allowed for the declaration of a special game sanctuary in the Beaver Hills can be traced to withdrawal from settlement, in 1892, of six townships and their later definition as the Cooking Lake Forest Reserve. The 1892 action came about in the aftermath of six years of sustained fires in which timber cover and soil quality were severely diminished in the hills. The effect, contended Edo Nyland, "was utter desolation." The land which later became Elk Island National Park "was burned so severely that only a few scattered trees in places sheltered by water, muskeg, or on north slopes of hills escaped."[6] The lands around Cooking Lake, segregated from settlement, provided the potential answer for a group of individuals who had recognized that the last pools of local game were under serious threat. W.H. Cooper, the Territorial Game Officer in Edmonton, brought Frank Oliver into the discussion, making him aware of the danger currently posed to a herd of elk frequenting the lands directly north of the forest reserve. His message stated:[7]

> I take the liberty of drawing to your attention that in the Beaver Hills near Island Lake, there is a large herd of Elk about 75 head roaming through a rough uncultivable country. It would be a commendable action on the part of the government to preserve these noble animals and allow a parcel of land for a reservation for their special use.

The following winter at least twenty of these animals were shot by hunters. Clifford Sifton, upon receipt of a petition signed by over seventy local residents, moved to set aside portions of the reserve and establish a special fenced zone for the protection of the Elk. The response from the government was positive and a bond was signed with some of the original petitioners to complete the fencing around six sections carved out of the Cooking Lake Forest Reserve in 1906 as a game reserve.[8] One of the Parry Sounders, Ellsworth Simmons, went on to become the first superintendent of the new Elk Park. The ingenious conservation plan involved fencing the east, north and west sides of this property, and then driving animals north out of the forest reserve into what was in fact a grand variation on the ancient Native game pound. Once the animals were trapped, the contractors moved quickly to fence in the southern limit. Much of the fencing was done by local volunteer labour.[9] By 1908 the Commissioner of Parks, Howard Douglas, was able to report that about twenty-four elk and thirty-five mule deer had been enclosed.[10] Astotin Lake became the centre of this new reserve and

Ellsworth Simmons   Among the settlers who came to the Beaver Hills from Parry Sound, Ontario, in the 1890s, Simmons served as the first Superintendent of the new "Elk Park" established in 1906.

The second Superintendent at Elk Island, Archie Coxford and family in front of
what is now the oldest Superintendent's Residence in the National Park system
at Astotin Lake.

it was here that park officials authorized construction of a superintendent's residence in 1907. This structure is still in use today
and is the oldest residence in the Canadian National Park system.[11]

Some already on these lands were forced to relocate, including
the Reids, who were Parry Sound pioneers. In 1902 they had settled
within the boundary of the Cooking Lake Forest Reserve in the
vicinity of Good Hope, just west of the present boundary of Elk
Island National Park. Many years later Ida Reid recalled that "No
hunting or trapping was allowed on the reserve and after 16 square
miles had been fenced and named Elk Island Park, homesteaders on
the reserve were bought out and moved away."[12] Only the Osters
on the western edge seem to have held out against the pressures
to sell. Ross Chapman observed that their "small homestead was
meticulously cleared and burned for planting and grazing." Charles
Oster did eventually sell. His family name, along with those of
other early settlers, such as Hayburger and Moss, are still found
as place names in the park.[13]

The main conservation objective at Elk Island, that of elk conservation, had seemingly been realized by 1906. The situation was to
change rapidly owing to the sudden interest shown by federal
authorities in an opportunity to obtain for Canada one of the last
great herds of plains bison. In the later nineteenth century the
western portions of North America were rapidly enclosed by the steady
advance of railway enterprise, mining rushes and overland trails.
These post-1860 invasions facilitated the second onslaught on the
great animal which, for so many centuries, had been vital to many
Aboriginal peoples on plains and parkland. The first wave of
destruction had come about in the 1830s with the rise of the buffalo
robe trade on the Missouri, the preferred activity among veteran
fur traders. That wave had taken its toll on the bison but the second,
aided by rail access, rendered the remaining herds particularly
vulnerable to hunting practices conducted on a scale unknown in
all previous centuries. Not for nothing was the young railway town
of Regina known first as "Pile o' Bones." The story of the bison's final
eclipse by the mid-1880s has been told on many occasions.[14]

Between 1870 and 1880 the last remnants of these herds on
the northern plains huddled in the Cypress Hills, near the American
border, along with various desperate Native and Métis peoples still
seeking to make a living in the traditional way. In a few short years
the forces of change and settlement removed most traces of the old
bison and fire-marked landscapes which had for so long provided
the context for human survival.[15]

By the mid-1880s the bison had all but disappeared. There
remained but a few small protected pockets surviving mainly on
various private ranches. In 1906, a herd owned by Michel Pablo
of the Flathead Reservation of Montana came to the notice of Canadian
officials. The main players were the Commissioner of Dominion
Parks at Banff, Howard Douglas; Mr. Alexander Ayotte of the
Canadian Immigration Department, based at Great Falls, Montana;
and Frank Oliver, Canadian Minister of the Interior. Arrangements
were quickly made to pay Pablo for his herd and to offer him
a contract to round up and then deliver the animals to Canada.

The potential of the Canadian application grew out of Pablo's frustration with the American government, which intended to open the Flathead Reservation to settlers without purchasing the free-ranging herd as a national asset. To be sure, President Theodore Roosevelt showed interest, but even this enthusiastic sportsman could not succeed in putting sufficient pressure on Congress to advance a satisfactory offer. Only after the Canadian government had made a firm arrangement with Pablo did American interests suddenly rise to the alert. Pablo was sufficiently insulted that even when U.S. authorities upped their offer, he maintained his understanding with the Canadians.[16]

Howard Douglas, keenly aware that time was of the essence, spent much time lobbying his own officials in Ottawa and traveling to Montana to reassure Pablo. The cowboy's work was not easy. He began the round-up in May, 1907, obtaining much needed labour relief late in the summer when the devil-may-care Charles Allard Jr. (the son of Pablo's deceased partner) arrived on the scene and

Michel Pablo, the Mexican cowboy who was in partnership with Charles Allard, Sr. He entered into contract with the Canadian Government to sell and deliver his Montana bison herd to Elk Island.

Left to Right: Alexander Ayotte, Charles Allard Jr. and Howard Douglas on the Flathead Reservation during the final round-up of the bison for shipment to the Beaver Hills. Ayotte, Canadian Immigration Agent at Great Falls, Montana, and Douglas, Commissioner of the Canadian National Parks, based at Banff, were instrumental in negotiating the purchase of the herd. Allard's late father had been the main force in conserving the animals.

offered to buy into the project. The two men soon came to an under-standing and young Allard "launched 20 hand-picked cowboys and 125 horses into the campaign against the elusive buffalo."[17] The bison were sufficiently wild that it took four years to complete the project. Norman Luxton and Howard Douglas of Banff were on hand to witness the round-up and loading of the animals onto trains for shipment north to the town of Lamont, just north of Elk

Island National Park. Luxton left a memorable account of the difficulties of the round-up at the Montana end.[18] Sheilagh Ogilvie tells us that "even amateurs" took part in Pablo's round-up: "one lady of sixty years had a legendary 100 mile ride to her credit and single-handedly prevented a stampede."[19]

It was not certain in 1906 just how many head were loose on the Flathead Reservation. Pablo had at first estimated around 400 and had contracted on that basis. By the middle of the summer in 1907, he had sent 199 animals north, but had also come to realize that he might have as many as 600 head in his herd. Adjustments were then made to the contract, allowing for a per-head shipping allowance. Pablo sent a second shipment of 211 bison from Ravalli Station that year, the animals arriving at Lamont in mid-October via the newly completed Canadian Northern Railway line. Difficulties with the round-up plagued Pablo in 1908, resulting in a delay of shipments. At the same time, progress was being made on the establishment of a new "Buffalo Park" at Wainwright, Alberta, the intended home for the remaining Montana bison and those

Ellsworth Simmons is shown here with bison prior to their shipment to the new "Buffalo Park" at Wainwright, Alberta, 1908.

Coyote Hunters in the Beaver Hills   Hunting was an important subsistence activity among the early settlers. Bounty policies made the group hunting of coyotes a rewarding pastime until after World War II.

already at Elk Island. By the spring of 1909 the new Buffalo Park was in a sufficient state to take shipment of bison from Elk Island. When Pablo completed his work in 1912, over 700 bison had been shipped to Canada.[20]

It was the original intention of Canadian park authorities to relocate all of the bison from Elk Island to Wainwright but some proved difficult to capture and the final round-up estimates indicated that about forty-eight head remained at Elk Island. The standard response was that they were considered "too wild to catch" but one park employee, M.H. Butler, felt that some of the Park staff were anxious to retain some of the bison for Elk Island and did not work too hard at capturing the "outlaws."[21] The stragglers provided the nucleus for a herd which eventually rose as high as 2,000 in the 1930s. Intimations of a future population explosion were contained in a letter to the *Fort Saskatchewan Reporter* in 1906, which expressed the conventional wisdom of the day that species were not to be seen in any special ecological relationship except negative ones:[22]

> The Government in securing this grand herd should at the same time bear in mind that the timber wolves are the natural enemies of the buffalo, and provide by bounty for their extermination, and also take notice of the large number of coyotes and provide for a like bounty.

Moving a hunting lodge in the Ryley district. c. 1920

The conservation actions taken between 1903 and 1912 were, nevertheless, timely, for the progress of settlement and improved transportation were steadily closing in around the hills and large large-scale land assembly for conservation purposes would become more difficult in the future. In 1913, Elk Island was declared a National Park, in line with new federal legislation.[23]

There were other special lands set aside in the Beaver Hills besides the Elk Park. While Cooking and Hastings lakes occupied the very centre of the hills, a second chain, composed of Ministik, Miquelon and the Hay Lakes, ran to the south. Miquelon attracted the attention of biologist R.M. Anderson, whose survey in 1917 found the lake was being degraded by local agricultural land use. An important pelican colony, for example, located on what is still known as Pelican Island, had been destroyed by pig-grazing practices. In 1920, local citizens were successful in having Ministik Lake set aside as the first official bird sanctuary in the province.[24]

In this same region, land manipulations of another order had arisen by 1910, centred around Little Hay Lake. Numerous unpredictable wetlands associated with the seasonal waxing and waning of this body of water had led individual farmers to begin drainage practices, beneficial to their own unit of land, but without considering their effects on lands held by others. An Inspector of Irrigation from Calgary arrived in the area in 1914 to inform certain parties that their actions were illegal. Community action and petitions eventually led to the establishment of the Hay Lakes Drainage District in the early 1920s. A system of large ditches was gradually put in place, but to curtail the natural tendencies of such a contorted landscape required eternal vigilance. "Growth of tall grass, brush, beaver dams and the general build up of silt and dirt always tend to block the free flow of water through the network of ditches" which now led the water into Stoney Creek and thence towards the Battle River drainage. For good reason the Cree had called the Hay Lakes area *Apichikoochewas*, the land of "grassy swamps."[25]

Other adjustments to public reserves were made in this period. In 1895, William Stephens was appointed as a Forest Ranger in the townships which would soon be formally established as the Cooking Lake Forest Reserve. His cabin was located close to the Beaver Lake Trail on the south-western boundary of today's Elk Island National Park. North Cooking Lake became the setting

Field near Beaverhills Lake   This photo gives a clear indication of the labour involved to reclaim workable land from the bush in the hills.

for Alberta's first nursery in 1910, under the direction of C.F. Brandt, a German forester who had been promoting prairie shelter-belt planting since 1906. The initial site of the nursery failed owing to inadequate soil conditions for coniferous plantings, but was relocated in 1912 to an area near the Dominion Forest Administration Building at Cooking Lake. From this location, under the guidance of Freeman Kelley, the first large scale plantations in Alberta were planned. Nyland observed that "nearly 1,000 acres of white spruce, Norway spruce, jackpine, lodgepole pine, Ponderosa Pine pine and green ash were seeded and planted between 1919 and 1930."[26] Fire continued to plague such systematic efforts however, and when the Province took control of these public lands in 1930, the replanting programmes ceased.

Another experiment in public land use took place south of Elk Island National Park on a complex of lands known as the Blackfoot Grazing Reserve, an initiative in community pasture development. This was Alberta's first experiment in such a communal concept,

William H. Stephens The first Forest Ranger for Alberta, he served between 1895 and 1912 in the Cooking Lake Forest Reserve.

The Provincial Forestry Headquarters at Cooking Lake, built in 1912

Ranger Freeman Kelley and his wife Elizabeth at work in the Cooking Lake Forest Reserve in the 1920s. Kelley did much work preparing seedlings and replanting trees in the reserve.

Freeman Kelley setting out seedlings at Cooking Lake Nursery. For some years this operation was a source of shelterbelt planting stock.

started in 1920 by the Blackfoot Stock Association. As with the Elk Park before it, it was carved out of the Forest Reserve and then leased back to the association which, in 1920, consisted of some 150 local farmers and ranchers. Having leased about 40,000 acres from the Province for one dollar a year, the associates then arranged to finance improvements in the form of fencing and to set the rules for the use of the pasture. In the relatively dry years of the 1920s, demand was brisk enough, horses being brought in from as far south as Stettler and Big Valley. When financial difficulties beset the organization, the lands reverted to the Province. A second effort was later begun, the Blackfoot Grazing Association, constituted as a non-profit body working in cooperation with the Province.[27]

Game populations expanded at Elk Island in the early 1920s, evidence of the conservation efforts. In 1922, the Department of the Interior "took over 34 sections of the Cooking Lake Forest Reserve to be fenced and added to Elk Island Park." It was contended that the action would "extend the total area of the park to 32,000 acres" and will much relieve "the present overcrowding of animals" making room for "the addition of a goodly number of elk, moose and deer within the new enclosure."[28]

These experiments in land use and conservation commenced with a minimum of political friction during the early years of Provincial autonomy when Ottawa still exercised control over natural resources and settlement. These conservation measures had not taken place in a social vacuum however, and it is to the consolidation of pioneer settlements and landscapes that we now turn.

Scenes along Beaverhills Trails

> How we loved to see people come and feel at home with us. There were the traveling clergy and laymen of every denomination who stopped at our doors, and shared our meals and family gatherings. One that I remember asked to lead in prayer before breakfast. He said he was a Roman Presbyterian, at least that was what I understood him to say. However I have wondered since if it wasn't Roamin' he meant.
>
> – Ida May Reid
> *Good Hope Days*

By 1905 the hills were dotted with fledgling communities, each with local industries responding to similar calls of necessity: Clover Bar on the west; Josephburg, Bruderheim and Bruderfeld to the northwest; Ukrainian and Polish settlements were filling in to the north-east. On the southern flank, a large protestant element had been added by means of a strong contingent of German, Swedish and Norwegian Lutherans settled between the Hay Lakes and Kingman.[29] In the rougher interior and in the Tofield districts was a mixture of eastern Canadian, American, and European immigrants.

Local historians at Tofield have noted that Cooking Lake, as a stopping place, may be traced back to the days of the old Carlton Trail, the main overland route from Winnipeg to Edmonton in the 1880s. The setting would naturally have been ancient with Native peoples. The Cooking Lake Trail was so named by local Cree, designating the "place where we cook."[30] The trail was used regularly after 1900 by homesteaders entering from the west. Before long the trails would be replaced by both road and rail, but during the first two decades of the twentieth century they continued to serve as the sinews of life in the hills. The main routes were the Cooking, the Battle, the Baseline, and the Victoria, although there were many others variously named such as the Beaver Lake Trail and the Duhamel.[31]

During the early years of the century, nothing was quite as important as proximity to these trails. The problems associated with moving through the hills were formidable owing to the unstable quality of the soil and water movements. Anna Busenius of Glen Garden recalled that "down at our place we had a lake about a mile long. A little bit north there was a slough. With all these sloughs to go around we'd be going miles and miles before you got anywhere."[32] The main object, when going through the hills, was to head for high ground and ridges of moraine. Keeping such natural lines of transit open did not always conform to the primary efforts of new settlers who, when filing on land, were inclined to take out homesteads identified by land appraisals that sought to maximize purely local convenience. Such practices often led to conflicts with old established trail patterns. The *Edmonton Bulletin* reported in 1894 that "Grievous complaints keep coming, in which old travelled trails to Beaver Lake are being fenced in to the detriment of all travelers." The preference was to go around the hills rather than through them and a number of new or historic trails, supplemented by log "corduroy" features in low wet spots facilitated travel. Yet, the vagaries of weather could render even short-distance travel almost impossible.[33]

The ability to assess land was therefore an important factor determinant of success for those who chose to settle within the hills. The experience of a group of Irish and American settlers who arrived at what became Deville in 1906 illustrates the general situation. John Morrow related the story of how his party "wended their way east from Edmonton by the old base-line trail for eighteen miles" and "as best they could for another fifteen miles through brush, swamp and muskeg." The men then "pooled their resources to buy a team of horses, a wagon, and supplies for the coming winter." After reaching the north-east shore of Cooking Lake, they scouted out a quarter section of land on which they could "squat and establish a home." This land was actually part of the Cooking Lake Forest Reserve, and although "it was all burnt over and not yet surveyed or open for homesteading," the virtue of the land consisted in the presence of good rich sandy loam. "It lay in a sloping valley between Wannison Lake and Hastings Lake, with Cooking Lake on the west and Islet Lake on the east."[34] Part of the thinking of the Deville settlers was that they should locate close to the location of the anticipated Grand Trunk Pacific Railway. In this they were rewarded, for the line did eventually run just north of Cooking Lake. Many of the settlers in the forest reserve were able to gain work during the construction phase of the railroad. "This was slow hard work, but it paid $2.00 a day, and I honestly believe few of the settlers could have stuck it but for this ready cash."[35]

The attempt to control fire was closely linked with trail and road preparation. These requirements can be traced to the earliest forms of municipal organization in the Beaver Hills. Ezekiel Keith, born at Clover Bar in 1883, saw the early approaches to local improvements as related to the establishment of a Labour and Fire District in 1890. The "chief duty was to fight the prairie and brush fires which often broke out in the pioneer settlements." This body in turn, proved to be the template for the Local Improvement District, which then graduated to become Strathcona County in 1943.[36]

Cutting fireguards out of the bush was an important priority for Archibald Coxford, the second Superintendent at Elk Island National Park. Coxford was on one occasion questioned by a visiting public servant: "How did you get the money for this nice road?" to which he replied: "That's not a road, it's a fireguard." This brought a second question: "Who did your surveying for you?" to which came the reply: "No one. I just followed the buffalo trails. I knew they would pick the high and dry spots." The visitor was sufficiently impressed to finish by saying: "You'll have to come to our Park and teach our engineers how to build roads."[37] Thus, as in many parts of the hills, defining straight lines of communication was seldom essential.

A more predictable route stretched from Fort Edmonton around the north side of the Hills. The old Victoria Trail took the traveller to the mission site of the Methodists, established in 1863, some forty miles east on the Saskatchewan River. The southern branch of the Victoria Trail followed a course from Fort Edmonton slightly to the east of Clover Bar and then ran northeast towards Partridge

Grand Trunk Pacific Railway construction in the Tofield area. c. 1906 Construction work provided supplementary employment for many attempting to settle in the inner reaches of the Beaver Hills.

Hill, Josephburg and Bruderheim, before turning east and running a course between Edna and Star. Before passing Edna, another trail branched to the south, taking one along the outer rim of the hills towards Ross Creek and Beaverhills Lake where it then ran along its western edge through Logan and down to Tofield. On the south-west side of the hills an old trail ran from Fort Edmonton towards the Battle River, crossing the Papaschase Reserve, past Breton and then through the lake country south of the old Cooking Lake Forest Reserve towards New Sarepta. After 1892, the central interior of the hills was accessed by the Baseline Trail running east from the Clover Bar area, making possible establishment of communities such as Bremner, Uncas and Good Hope via a north-running extension. Many of the settlers from Parry Sound helped open up these interior townships.[38]

The complexities of travel in the years before railway construction helped foster a strong sense of local self-sufficiency in the hills. McCauley's sawmill had been built in 1893 at Hastings Lake, shortly after declaration of the forest reserve. A form of barter economy was popular amongst the settlers in the years of restrictive travel. "Exchange of work for commodities was the order of the day." Small scale basic industries made an appearance in the form of a creamery, cheese factory and flour mill.[39]

Settlers making the trip in to Edmonton had gained some relief by 1910, for the hills were now flanked by two railways. On the north side, the Canadian Northern Railway had reached Mundare by 1905 and was then built through to Lamont, Fort Saskatchewan and Edmonton. In the central portions, the Grand Trunk Pacific was constructed through Ryley, Holden and Tofield by 1909. A third line, built by the CPR in 1912, ran from Edmonton through Wetaskiwin and Camrose, and on to Saskatchewan, giving access to the southern prairies. With the completion of these railways, rural industries started to appear, such as the short-lived Tofield Foundry. Enterprises of this kind gave way fairly rapidly to the locational transportation advantages and economies of scale enjoyed by the main railway cities.[40]

More lasting were the local coal mines in the Bardo and Tofield district. Three were active by 1913: the Dobell, the Tofield Coal Company, and the Pioneer. The first two were strip mines which exploiting open seams, while the third was an underground operation. J.W. Robinson stated that since "the Pioneer had no railway facilities, wagons came in groups so that the combined efforts of the teams could be utilized to haul the loaded wagons up the hills. Wagons came from as far as fifty miles away for coal."[41] Engineering innovation was also in the air at that time. The Tofield mine had, in fact, first been an underground mine. "When I came in 1913," said Robinson, "it was a strip mine" but in 1912 "the management imported a dirt-moving machine called the Lubrecher." This device was "self-propelled" with "a number of buckets similar to the ones used in a grain elevator which loaded the dirt on a conveyor belt and dumped it where the coal had been taken out in the previous year." Also in use was a "steam dragline called the Ledgerwood which followed behind the Lubrecher."[42] The local coal industry went through a

Local spinning in the Bardo area, c. 1910

number of stages with the Tofield Coal Company eventually emerging as the main producer. With the important discovery of oil at Leduc in 1947, the local coal industry went into decline and was closed down in 1957, ending a phase in which the mines had been important sources of employment, supplying regional industries and domestic consumers.[43]

The 1920s were years of relative prosperity in the hills, a time when small-scale commercial town life took hold and second-generation properties were improved. Educational institutions advanced with a corresponding injection of enthusiasm from the younger generation who sensed that style was as important as learning. The climate and environment were more predictable than in the southern reaches of the province, where many areas began to experience the droughts and dislocations which became so famous in the 1930s.[44] In these relatively good years, the reputation of the hills as place of recreational appeal increased as Cooking Lake and

Small scale coal mining at Tofield, c. 1910

Astotin Lake gained improvements, providing the citizens of Edmonton and other communities with good swimming and fishing.

Landscape and the Human Imprint

"God is under the poplar trees...You can speak to Him there!"

—Memoirs of a Ukrainian Immigrant

Landscapes are cultural as well as natural and industrial. They bear upon them not just the outward signs of ecological adjustment and geological accumulations, but also historical achievement and symbolic memories of times past. The manner of building a home, the design of a field, fence or hedgerow, the architecture of church and store, town plans and housing arrangements, all of these things may have suspended in them skills and dispositions fostered centuries ago. The centre of a compass positioned at Elk Island National Park, defining a radius from Edmonton in the west, to Victoria in the north, Vegreville on the east and Camrose to the south, would bring into view one of the most diverse patchworks of group settlements in Canada. The fashioning of such an imprint within a space of some thirty years allows for a certain retrospective reading of the landscape. The signs of pioneer cultural diversity may be recognized in the varied institutional and domestic architecture. Indeed, Lamont County has been described as the "Church Capital of North America."[45]

This cultural mosaic raises questions concerning local politics and institutions, for the ability of so many diverse groups to rapidly accommodate themselves to an unknown frontier suggests a certain spirit of egalitarianism, not unknown in the history of other parts of western North America. Many of the central and east European settlers had emigrated in order to free themselves from various types of economic squeeze and from the lingering claims of feudal, class or aristocratic privilege. If the prejudices and practices of the established folk from the British Isles often set much of the social and political agenda in the "New West," the huddling together of these groups was less fractious than might have been expected. "The poverty on the frontier is shared by all" said W.C. Pollard.[46] The daily requirements for communal self-help or neighbourly assistance suggest that egalitarianism united more easily than it divided. While the driving ambition for most settlers was to "prove

Teacher. James R. Levy. Deep Creek School. c. 1912

Teacher Mary Rowe. Clover Bar District, 1920s

up" and gain possession of a private landholding, the importance of communal effort in such undertakings was also recognized. Few in Canada at that time, with the exception of pockets of old Quebecers, were very far removed from memories of the old world. Established settlers in western Canada had arrived only slightly more recently than the waves of post-1890 immigrants, and they had, by and large, come for similar reasons.[47]

If hereditary privilege had been formally abandoned in Canadian law, there nevertheless came to be in the Canadian West, as in the United States, a distinct new "landed class" other than that composed of the ambitious "everyman" of the American frontier.[48] To Frank Oliver, and many others, this new landed class combined the forces of "big business" and "government." The power of new federal agencies and the special landholding privileges of the CPR, the Hudson's Bay Company and chartered colonization companies, all became regular targets of Oliver and his *Edmonton Bulletin* after 1880. As an arch defender of the freehold system, Oliver's negative view of the location of the Papaschase Reserve, so close to Edmonton, was as much a product of his opposition to the power of these large corporate bodies, as it was to Native rights as such.[49] There remained, nevertheless, a large disenfranchised class. Born of land-surrender "treaties," this class was composed of the original inhabitants, along with many of mixed inheritance, increasingly restricted to reserves of varying quality.[50] This policy was pursued in the interest of the greater "getting on" and of reconfiguring the post-bison landscape into units appropriate to the advancing ranching and agricultural economy.[51]

Treaty No. 6 (1876) led to the setting aside of several reserve enclaves in the vicinity of the Beaver Hills. Besides Papaschase, these were at Enoch, Alexander, Paul, and Saddle Lake north of the Saskatchewan River. The visible signs of ancient traditional hunting grounds, however, were to become subject to rapid transformation in much of the province.[52] South of the boreal forest, what survives of much of the old aboriginal landscape today lies beneath the ground. With much of the Beaver Hills remaining as unsettled public reserves throughout the twentieth century, there has been a chance to recover elements of the ancient past. At Elk Island, evidence of prehistoric life survives in "circular stone rings, scattered bone fragments from butchered game, hearth remains from cooking activity" and "broken or discarded tools and chipped waste flakes from tool manufacturing."[53]

The tangible remains of Native cultures have long fascinated settlers but less so their customs. Whereas the institutional and cultural "baggage" brought by new immigrants was widely tolerated in public policy, and even encouraged in some cases, the Native peoples in the later nineteenth century were generally expected to become the beneficiaries of European religion and new educational institutions. The guiding policies, which commenced in earnest under the newly consolidated Indian Act of 1876, were designed to get Native peoples through a difficult time, after which, according to the conventional wisdom, their ways of life would presumably disappear altogether in favour of collective adjustments to the new Canadian order. The fruits of this policy have accumulated over the years with differing and often remarkably negative results, particularly with respect to education and community living conditions.[54] In any review of the debates in the House of Commons for the mid-1870s, when the consolidated Indian Act of 1876 was being prepared and administrative policies devised, what is remarkable is not the presence of illiberal arguments made by Honourable Members concerning the future of the Indian as much as the lack of any arguments whatsoever.

In the wake of the complications of the Manitoba Schools question of the 1890s, several standards came to prevail in prairie public life with respect to language, religion and cultural survivals and their perceived value. Immigrants from areas outside of the Anglo-Saxon stream were allowed, even encouraged on occasion, to conserve certain aspects of their collective heritages, but not by drawing upon the public system of finance.[55] This was seldom a policy extended to Native peoples, where suppression of the traditional was actually implemented by means of public finance, with the occasional exceptions for exotic, tourism-related performances. Thus, the banning of the Battle River Sun Dance in 1893 anticipated new regulations in the Indian Act of 1895 which outlawed many aspects of Native ceremonialism on the plains and across Canada. The revival of the "Sun" or "Thirst" dance by Chiefs Samson and Ermineskin at Hobbema in the early 1920s was only reluctantly tolerated and was firmly attacked by many churchmen. There were, to be sure, individuals who took a more enlightened view, such as Indian Agent Robert Wilson. He possessed a genuine interest in the details of indigenous ceremonies and wrote intelligently about them; but post-Confederation community leaders were generally on a different course and had little time for cultural revivals other than of their own preference. The continuation of such ceremonies was seen to be unrealistic, arcane, and probably degenerate.[56]

The long-lived guide and interpreter, Peter Erasmus, was uneasy about the new dispensation. He had grown up in the old fur trade economy but, by his middle years, the demographic and economic conditions supporting that relationship had, by and large, disappeared. Erasmus had a foot in both worlds, but the one in the Native community at Whitefish Lake was more firmly planted. Having been an interpreter in treaty days, he continued to do his best as an intermediary between the old peoples and the new.[57]

Settlers arriving in the Beaver Hills had their own pasts to deal with and most could not appreciate the depth of the historical drama to which Erasmus had been a witness. Within the new communities there was an attendant bonding which tended to encourage clannishness in some respects but rural life was also subject to the pressures of local politics. Settlers became accustomed to a day-to-day rubbing of shoulders with people who, because they had shared the trauma of up-rootedness, were only partially strangers. Religion was the main vehicle of culture and the glue of social cohesion for these pioneer groups. The vitality animating these local versions of Christian organization was not easily supplanted by resident French Canadian or Anglo-Saxon missionaries.

A certain nativist reaction set in after 1900, undoubtedly related to Canadian participation in the Boer War and the successes of the second British Empire. The impulses which caused Frank Oliver, the new federal Interior Minister, to redirect Clifford Sifton's immigration policy away from Central and Eastern Europe and towards Americans, also informed the outlook of certain energetic churchmen.[58] As they had with Native peoples in the 1870s, politicians and community leaders now perceived a parallel need to socially engineer members of the new pioneer classes who, for cultural reasons, were understood to be incapable of appreciating the terms and conditions of English liberty and institutions. For J.S. Woodsworth, that muscular, if doubting, Christian soldier of the Methodist-sponsored All Souls Mission in Winnipeg, severe doses of education and reform were required. In 1908, Woodsworth set out the rules of engagement for this new campaign in stark Anglo-Saxon terms.[59]

> The great majority of the people from Austria and Russia are Roman or Greek Catholics. They are peasants; the majority illiterate and superstitious. Some of them bigoted fanatics, some of them poor, dumb, driven cattle, some intensely patriotic... The Slav is essentially religious, but his religious instincts have never found true expression..."Light and liberty" these are what are needed.

This was certainly a bold reaffirmation of the view of history advocated by British historian Thomas Macaulay. Woodsworth's version reinforced the preferred nineteenth-century English tale of progress, much favoured in Edwardian Canada, implicitly wrapped up in the rhetoric of Kipling's "White Man's Burden." Woodsworth's writings echoed the views of his colleague, John McDougall. Convinced that he had correctly characterized the shortcomings of the immigrant outlook, he set out a complete strategy by which the main body "could be weaned away from their ancient errors and dispositions" and brought into the necessary "light" of British democratic traditions. "It would seem as if the Methodist Church might work amongst the Poles in some such way as the Presbyterian Church has been working amongst the Ruthenians." This would lead, in the long run, to the proper group frame of mind, for "Independence affords the opportunity for Reformation." More recent commentators have noted that reformers seeking to assimilate these "strangers within our gates" tended not to see that, as groups, the immigrants suffered from poverty and not from an inherent cultural deprivation.[60]

The promotion of technical education, with a view towards the eventual assimilation of new immigrants, was not limited to Protestant initiatives. Before 1905, the Roman Catholic hierarchy in St. Boniface, Manitoba, had also made efforts to bolster its presence in the West by ministering to the new arrivals in the national language of their choice. This had come about largely upon the initiative of Archbishop Langevin, who had travelled from St. Boniface to Rome in 1896 to discuss the needs of East European pioneers. Other visits by his bishops to Western Ukraine were sponsored in 1898. In 1900 he sent Father Albert Lacombe to Rome, Lviv and Vienna to press the issue of Ukrainian missionaries. These actions bore fruit by 1902 when four Basilian missionaries arrived in Edmonton, accompanied by four teaching sisters of the Oblates of Mary Immaculate order. Their arrival was timely, for in 1904 Langevin estimated that there were over 60,000 Ukrainian settlers in the west, most of whom followed the eastern Catholic rite.[61]

The progressive policy of Langevin appears to have been the cause of some division in the ranks of the church, particularly between Irish and French Catholic priests. Policies of social and educational reform were not priorities for all members of the clergy. One figure who illustrated this position was the young Franciscan, Father Boniface (1880–1960), who had arrived at Fort Saskatchewan in 1908 from Quebec. He was content with the more modest ambitions of his order, which he understood to primarily concern the cure of souls. Assistance from the venerable Franciscan order had been requested by Bishop Grandin as early as 1898, to bolster the long-standing efforts of the thinly-stretched Oblates. The sheer number of Catholic immigrants into the West had put strains on the church's capacity. This was now complicated by the heavy intrusion of "Uniate" (Ukrainian) Catholics into a setting where the Western Roman Catholic rite prevailed.[62]

Father Boniface took up his duties at the Franciscan Monastery at Lamoureux, just across the river from Fort Saskatchewan.[63] Late in life, Father Boniface recalled that "Fort Saskatchewan was to us in Quebec in 1908, what Quebec was to the first missionaries of Canada, the Recollects of 1615 – the land of Promise!" While en route back to Alberta from Wisconsin in 1909, Father Boniface chanced upon a copy of Woodsworth's *Strangers within Our Gates*. The book made a strong impression on him, but not the one Woodsworth sought to impart. To Father Boniface the book openly disclosed "the tactics of those Protestant organizations that stopped at nothing in tearing the Catholics away from the Church in

The School at Beaver Lake, c. 1914

Teaching Sisters. Servants of Mary Immaculate, c. 1914

Northern Alberta."[64] The old competition between Protestant and Catholic clerics for the salvation of the Native peoples had taken on a new aspect. It was the start of what Vera Lysenko called "the tug-of-war for Ukrainian souls."[65]

Father Boniface was part of a shifting set of church relationships. In 1902, his superior, Father Legal of the French Canadian Parish in Edmonton, travelled to Beaver Lake, escorting the recently arrived Basilian missionary, Father Filias. Along the way, they stopped at a Polish Roman Catholic parish, thereby revealing the cosmopolitan nature of the task facing any mission worker of those times. Bridging the gap between the Byzantine (or Greek) and Roman rites would be one of Father Boniface's first tasks, and shortly after taking up his duties, he too was in touch with the Ukrainian Catholics at Beaver Lake. Here, the small homestead and house of Father Filias was soon supplemented by a small Basilian Monastery and a chapel that had quickly come to serve as a school for Ukrainian children.[66]

The Ukrainian Catholic Church had its origins as a compromise form of worship combining elements of the Roman and Greek rite, established in 1596 at the Council of Brest-Litovsk. It was the outcome of complex historical and political relations among the Jesuit-advised rulers of Poland-Lithuania, elements of the Ukrainian gentry, and the Papacy.[67] By the agreement, those in the Ukrainian Catholic Church would retain the form of rite customary in Eastern Orthodoxy, but would acknowledge the authority of the Pope as head of the one universal church. At the time, many old believers wanted nothing to do with this, and so both traditions continued to function, side by side. Adherents of each group were subject to intense political manipulation up until the late nineteenth century.[68]

We have seen that many of the first Ukrainian immigrants to Canada were Ukrainian Catholics from western Ukraine, lands long under the control of the Catholic Austrian Hapsburgs. Still, there were also many adherents of the Ukrainian Orthodox or Russo-Orthodox rite, and thus, a variety of religious outlooks were represented in the bloc settlements of central Alberta.[69] Unlike conditions in their homelands, where religious conformity had, since the mid-eighteenth century, been a reason of state, in Canada believers were given the chance to make up their own minds on such matters. The consequences of such unfamiliar freedom led in a number of directions in the future social relations of Canadians of Ukrainian origin.[70]

The potential for sectarian friction in this situation was real and a "clash of religious sentiments and affiliations ominously surfaced in the first Ukrainian settlement in Canada at Star."[71] The situation involved a legal dispute with the nearby Wostok settlers concerning proprietary rights to the local church, which had been built by sweated labour. But who controlled the church? Was title to reside with the local trustees of the church or with the Roman Catholic Church hierarchy in far-away St. Boniface? And which rite was to be recognized: that of the Ukrainian Catholic, the Ukrainian Orthodox, or the Russo-Orthodox? The legal case was initiated in 1898 and it took years to crawl through the courts, finally ending up before the Lords of the Privy Council in England for final resolution in 1907. The decision finally rendered favoured the breakaway Russo-Orthodox. The decision provided, however, that those who wished to remain Ukrainian Catholics would receive proportionate compensation for the value of the land upon which the church stood.[72]

There were political consequences of these old divisions. The first wave of Ukrainian immigration to Canada had coincided with a late nineteenth-century flowering of Ukrainian nationalism, and it is perhaps not surprising that long-frustrated ideas about democracy or about national control of fundamental institutions quickly took root among many of the pioneers. Under the conditions of frontier life there was little to curb and much to encourage them. The ability of immigrants in the Ukrainian bloc settlements to exercise political choices came quickly to the surface. They were exercised, haltingly at first, but then with increased confidence. Myrna Kostash made the graphic observation that in Canada there was no longer any need to "accept everything that was dished out by authorities in the manner of a Galician peasant accepting the kick-in-the-pants from a Polish landlord."[73]

The secular and political aspirations of many Ukrainian immigrants added another element of confusion to the activities of churchmen, and others, working for the improvement of the new arrivals. In his memoir of the Chipman area, Father Boniface attempted to put as good a face as possible on the situations he faced with the more radical elements of the community. It is clear from his words that many labour advocates were quite hostile to church authorities of any kind. While Father Boniface and other church workers outside the Ukrainian tradition had their own agendas, it was nevertheless difficult for even objective outsiders to pick up on the many local nuances. Divided opinions in the Ukrainian community, scarcely visible to non-Slavic fellow settlers or to their political representatives, progressively manifested themselves passionately in local church politics and in the local community halls and reading rooms.[74]

Wedding at Mundare, c. 1912

The appearance of the Basilian Order at Beaver Lake in 1902 was clearly a welcome event for many Ukrainian Catholics, both in terms of religion and education. By 1910, it was obvious to Father Kryzanowsky that the small school run by teaching sisters was now inadequate, so he sponsored construction of a more spacious facility, completed in 1913.[75] It reflected the general growth of the area. The landmark Sts. Peter and Paul Church was still under construction in 1910 when a thousand people received communion. Mundare continued to grow and became a lasting centre of influence for Ukrainian Catholics in the region.

Events around the town of Chipman on the northeast side of the Beaver Hills, provides an illustration of the increased pace of building in the settlements, but also the relevance of the earlier court case at Star. A main founder of the local parish in 1901 was Vasyl Eleniak, one of the first Ukrainian settlers in Canada. In 1908, the first St. Mary Ukrainian Catholic Church was built about two miles east of Chipman. In 1915 the congregation split "with several members expressing a wish to convert to the Russo-Orthodox faith." The outcome was based on the legal precedent set in 1907.

Building Our Lady of Lourdes Grotto by Polish Roman Catholics at Skaro, c. 1912

The converts "were allowed to continue holding their services in the original church." The Ukrainian Catholic contingent decided, in response, to relocate to Chipman proper, where the present St. Mary's Ukrainian Catholic Church was built in 1916.[76]

The appearance of the Basilians at Mundare, then, was less of a blessing to some of the Orthodox believers. Neil Savaryn has identified the priests of this order as potential sources of social friction. "In the spectrum of Ukrainian Catholic Church politics in Western Ukraine" the Basilian Order was "in the forefront of a reformist trend," one which sought to strengthen the church by "bringing it more closely in line" with the predominantly Polish Roman Catholic Church.[77]

For local Polish immigrants, of which there were a good number after 1896, the presence of the Basilians was seen in a more positive light. The loyalties of Polish immigrants settling at centres such as St. Michael, Chipman, Round Hill and Kopernik were to the Roman Catholic Church.[78] When the Franciscan order was asked to assist in ministering to Polish communicants in the vicinity of

Store front, Mundare, c. 1912

St. Mary's Ukrainian Catholic Church, Chipman

Krakow, Wostok and Skaro, Father Aloysius encountered what he took to be similar secular trends as among the Ukrainian community. Father Boniface, in his old age, spoke of Aloysius and his "heroic" efforts and of the "many difficulties" presented in those areas "on account of the Bolshevistic and Communistic undercurrent and of the religious ignorance of the people."[79]

Egalitarianism was severely strained after the outbreak of war in 1914 when things took a nasty turn for landed immigrants from central and eastern Europe, not just on the prairies but across Canada. Many were suddenly classified as "enemy aliens" and consigned to internment camps. This crackdown, admittedly, had less effect in remote pioneer agricultural communities and more on urban workers and transients seeking work. The psychological effects were, however, serious, long lasting and not forgotten.[80]

Community life in the new settlements continued to strengthen, nevertheless, drawing on strong residues of traditional belief and practice, sufficient to inspire volunteers to complete or initiate many churches, institutions and community projects in the postwar years. In 1919, for instance, the grotto at Skaro dedicated to Our Lady of Lourdes was completed, a site which attracted thousands of the faithful. It was finished under the direction of Father Anthony Sylla, in association with an Oblate priest, Philip Ruh, the Belgian-born church architect of "prairie cathedrals."[81] The proliferation of new churches in the hills provided an outlet for craft and artistic talent associated with the elaborate interiors. St. Mary's at Chipman for example, was finished with the assistance of Jarema Janishewski, a well-known local craftsman.[82] Many a landscape in and around the hills was graced with a church of landmark beauty in the 1920s, and many still survive.

On the cultural and political side, national halls started to appear, providing the context for a rich range of views and discussion on cultural and political matters. Music and stage productions were important forms, although it has been noticed that original local dramas "had a frankly didactic function." In 1910, the *Vegreville Observer* reviewed a production called "The Old and the New Country"

Theatrical Event in Ukrainian Hall, Mundare, 1940s

put on by the Young Ruthenian Club. An English synopsis was provided for the consideration of any Anglophones in the audience.[83]

The local halls and reading rooms provided settings for widely divergent views on political and theological matters and much wry humour emerged from incidents and disputes. Peter Shevchook, who taught school at Hairy Hill, recalled his conflict with local communists. They "had a strong organization there" and "had the hall and they were writing letters against me." At one point "a Communist from Two Hills became secretary of the church." Upon enquiry made to the local Metropolitan about the suitability of burying church members in the Two Hills cemetery, where communists were also buried, the reply came that "a Christian should not be afraid to see the Devil himself."[84]

CHAPTER SIX

Hard Times and Good Times, 1930–1950

I eat my own lamb
My chickens and ham
I shear my own fleece and I wear it,
I have lawns, I have Bow'rs
I have fruit, I have Flow'rs
The lark is my morning alarmer.

From: *Anyfoolcanbeafarmer*
Henry Brewis, Hay Lakes

The year 1930 was a significant one for western Canadians, marking the end of the lengthy "autonomy" negotiations between Ottawa and the prairie provinces on the transfer of authority over natural resources from Ottawa to the provincial capitals. This transfer was expected to provide an important stimulus to regional development, but the stock market crash of 1929 put a severe damper on economic life in western Canada, as elsewhere, and a year later nobody knew just how severe the Depression would become. The Parliamentary Speech from the Throne in February referred to the "temporary slackness" in the economy. In April, the soon-to-be-defeated Prime Minister, Mackenzie King, still felt confident that unemployment insurance was not a measure required in the current circumstances.[1]

The effects of the stock market crash did not begin to register in full force on western farmers until 1931. Long after the Depression, residents of the Beaver Hills such as John L. Blackburn offered their views on the consequences of the severe years of the early 1930s. Blackburn's father was originally from Lancaster County in Pennsylvania. Having followed his brothers to Alberta, he settled with his family near Tofield in 1911. He successfully tamed some 255 acres, following which his son took up land at Lavoy, near Vegreville. Two years into the Depression, the younger Blackburn recalled that "the price of grain dropped lower than it had been since the Alberta Wheat Pool started operations in 1923."[2] Capital had dried up across the country with the result that between 1929 and 1932 the Gross National Product fell by about 42 per cent.[3] Many lost their farms altogether in the rural areas. "One of the great hardships," said Blackburn, "was the humiliation of not being able to make payments due to the banks, mortgage companies and farm machinery companies."[4] One of his fellow farmers in the Beaver Hills, Henry Schroeder, recalled the Dirty Thirties on the Trent Ranch: "One poor crop after another and no other income – nothing with which to make payments on the land...gradually the people gave up. Some went to the Debt Adjustment Board to get straightened away; one by one, they left the ranch. My father alone chose to stay rather than to move again."[5] For those who could hang on to the land, there was at least the advantage of being able to eke out a subsistence living. John Blackburn again:[6]

> It was possible only because we lived on a farm. We grew our own beef, pork and chicken. We also produced eggs, butter, cream and vegetables. Once a year we took wheat to the mill at Vegreville and came home with ten one-hundred pound sacks of flour. Our fruit consisted of raspberries and rhubarb grown in the garden, and wild saskatoons and chokecherries, which we picked each summer.

Such capacity to live off the land was captured in *Anyfoolcanbeafarmer,* a witty piece of doggerel by Henry Brewis, a Scottish-Canadian farmer from Hay Lakes. Robert Shroeder remembered his father "sending a cow to market just before Christmas one year and getting a cheque for sixty-six cents after trucking and expenses. Can you wonder at Santa Claus sort of sneaking by that year?"[7] Even transportation was not as reliable. These were the years of the "Bennett Buggy." The new horseless carriages, for reasons of expense, were now being ingeniously readapted to a horse-drawn state.

Accounts such as these reveal the adaptability of prairie people in hard times, but they also demonstrate that the specifics of locality were also important in allowing some to get by on agriculture subsistence. Moisture was not totally lacking in the hills region as it was in many other pockets of the prairies to the east and south. In his analysis of the weather that made the thirties "dirty," James Gray wrote: "It was never wholly bad everywhere at once. However, within the Palliser Triangle – from Lethbridge to Battleford to Melita – it was bad all the time." Alberta came off best. Except for "the disaster years of 1933 and 1936" its central and northern areas tended to escape much of the drought.[8]

The political response of Albertans to the Great Depression is well known. The call for radical reform was taken up by a Calgary school teacher and preacher, William Aberhart, who guided his new Social Credit party to power in 1935. The Social Credit movement of that time bore a closer resemblance to the programmes of the socialist CCF in Saskatchewan than did its later manifestations. The early emphasis of "Bible Bill" Aberhart's movement was on collective economic security through the stimulation of individual buying power. While he drew his strength from the older areas of southern Alberta, peopled heavily by British and American settlers, his appeal was also relatively strong in the newer districts of more recent European immigration, even if his religious message was unfamiliar. Elements of the argument of Social Credit, although served up in an unusual format, might still appeal to a Ukrainian or Finnish worker of socialist or even communist persuasion. The secret and significance of his political appeal have been subjects for debate ever since.[9]

John Blackburn had his own explanation for Aberhart's success. The result of the election of 1935 "came as quite a surprise to almost everyone" because few had "openly acknowledged that they intended to vote for Social Credit." This applied to Blackburn's mother-in-law, a Mrs. Olson, a woman of solid Norwegian pioneer background. Blackburn thought it "incredible that after practising such rugged independence throughout her life" she could then 'support a party that promised a handout of twenty-five dollars a month."[10] Mrs. Olson pondered her reply to this suggestion and then said: "I listened to our premier Mr. Reid, over the radio, and he said there was nothing the government could do about the Depression. Mr. Shaw, the leader of the Liberal Party, said there was no solution; that we would have to wait and stick it out until times got better. When I listened to Mr. Aberhart, he said he would try something to bring better times."[11] This was the short answer from many of the working people on the farms and in the towns of the Beaver Hills: Aberhart was offering hope.

Aberhart's was not the only answer being suggested, particularly in the National Halls of many of the Ukrainian communities where left-wing proponents had made strong headway. Among the heavy Ukrainian population around Two Hills, the affiliations were reported as follows in 1937: 50 per cent Ukrainian Greek Catholic; 15 per cent Greek Orthodox; 10 per cent Seventh Day Adventists; and 25 per cent members of the Ukrainian Labour and Farm Temple, an affiliate of the Communist Party of Canada.[12] A penchant for radicalism, often attributed by many to the Ukrainian community as a whole, was of course only very partial. The actual suggestion however, induced its own reaction in the form of such conservative and main-stream organizations as the United Loyalists of Canada which took form in the Vegreville-Mundare area in 1931. There was, in fact, a strong push from the political left in many of the settlements, mounted against conditions which were seen to be a product of both bad capitalist management and overt discrimination. The trial of the "Mundare Ten" in 1934, in connection with local efforts to boycott grain shipments from the local elevators, was just one of many violent incidents which do not show up in many of the local histories.[13]

It was a measure of the desperation of the times that the federal Conservative Government had attempted to experiment with social programmes bearing a similarity to the "New Deal" legislation sponsored in the United States under the Roosevelt administration after 1932. This happened, with increasing momentum, under the leadership of the wealthy lawyer and businessman from Calgary, Robert B. Bennett. At the provincial level, Aberhart got into trouble for advocating the printing of certificates (so-called "funny money") as a way of putting more spending power into the hands of Alberta consumers. In the view of many progressives, the more acceptable approach was to turn to the ideas of the British economist, John Maynard Keynes, who advocated that, in certain circumstances, those in power should attempt to spend society out of debt through formal government initiatives and adjusted monetary policies. Bennett was not entirely hostile to this approach, but the reform pictures he painted were not executed with bold enough strokes. They remained tentative, tending more towards relief than reform. Bennett was turned out of office before much in the way of results could be noticed from the efforts of his administration.[14]

Elk Island National Park became one of many public land units designated as settings for relief projects for the unemployed. Work camps were set up there as early as the fall of 1931. In late 1932 the *Lamont Tribune* reported that forty men had been "transported from Edmonton...the nucleus of 200 men to be so engaged this winter." They "will receive $5.50 per month, 50 cents of which

Road Construction, Elk Island National Park, 1930s

will go towards hospital dues." At Elk Island, the tasks included much underbrush clearing to open up grazing habitat for bison, elk and moose, as well as work on a new road right of way to the south end of the park.[15] Sharing the cold winter with so many large beasts did not sit well with many of the men. A reporter in Lamont wrote that there was trouble on one occasion, for "about six agitators" were "stirring up unnecessary strife." Superintendent Coxford ordered them to return to Edmonton, where they were soon joined by fourteen others.[16] Still, the camps did carry on for some years and the workers completed a considerable range of park improvements.

Relief projects made other improvements in the hills. At Cooking Lake, an air base was developed in 1935 through a special programme coordinated by the Corps of Royal Canadian Engineers and the Directorate of Civil Aviation. The object was to improve the national distribution of airports and related facilities.[17]

The persisting general economic strife of the times led community leaders to think more systematically about local development and public works of a more commercial and recreational kind. In 1933, J.B. Harkin, Commissioner of National Parks, attended a round

Air Base, Cooking Lake, 1938

table meeting at Elk Island with representatives of various local organizations, including the Edmonton Chamber of Commerce and the Elk Island Park Association. Discussion centered on projects for Elk Island and other sites of interest to regional tourism promoters. Harkin and his Chief Engineer, James Wardle, were supportive of many of the proposals, but they informed the assembly that the financial restraints of the times would cause delay and that all projects would have to be reviewed within the context of general government policies.[18] New cottage and recreational facilities were built in the later 1930s, particularly around Sandy Bay on Astotin Lake. Locals who since the 1920s had been advocating for addition of a golf course to Elk Island were pleased to see such a project brought to completion in 1935.[19] The Agape church camp was added to the south side of Astotin Lake in the same year.[20] These were some of the more visible achievements of the relief camp work programme.

A limited opening up of the park to free enterprise was encouraged as a result of discussions, but of the few efforts made in this direction, not many turned out favourably, even after the war. There were leased sites for two bungalow camps, a restaurant,

The beach and recreation area, Astotin Lake, 1940s

service station and a dance hall at Sandy Bay, but none proved profitable owing to the limitations of local demand, which was mostly restricted to weekends. The main recreational successes enjoyed by the park over these two decades remained associated with its setting as a place for special events such as group picnics, church events and youth camp activities.[21]

In those quieter times, when transportation and outings required more of an effort, the park clearly played a strong role in the social life of the surrounding communities, reflected in the founding of a citizen's cooperative organization, the Elk Island National Park Association, in 1934.[22] Interested local citizens and their political representatives gradually introduced new initiatives. In 1949 a gathering was held "for the purpose of organizing a committee which would help plan certain improvements within the Elk Island National Park."[23] Dr. A.E. Archer of Lamont was the main voices in this committee and an early group achievement was the completion of a replica of a typical Ukrainian homestead near Astotin Lake.[24] The effort anticipated the later establishment of the Ukrainian Heritage Cultural Village east of Elk Island.

Science and Nature in the Beaver Hills

Since 1906, the Beaver Hills had gradually gained a reputation as a refuge for birds and wildlife, but the management of the lands associated with these resources progressed unevenly, often along intuitive as well as experimental and scientific lines. The popular imagination is easily drawn to the life histories and drama of big game animals, but there were many other life forms in the hills of interest to naturalists. Beaverhills Lake, in particular, became one of the main theatres of enquiry for an important natural scientist of mid-twentieth century Canada, William Rowan. He was born at Basel, Switzerland in 1891, and took advanced degrees at the University of London. Rowan visited a ranch in southern Alberta in 1908 and this may have influenced his decision to come to the University of Manitoba in 1919. A year later he accepted a position at the University of Alberta, where he established the Zoology Department, which he chaired until his retirement in 1956.[25]

Rowan was greatly interested in avian studies. Much of his research on the ecology of bird behaviour was conducted at Francis Point on the southern shore of Beaverhills Lake. Early in his university career he argued for a field station at that location but to no avail. He did manage to negotiate collecting and hunting rights with the owner, Daniel Francis. After extolling the virtues of Beaverhills Lake to colleagues in England, he was commissioned to prepare a series of illustrated articles on Alberta waders.[26] In one of these articles, Rowan praised the qualities of Francis Point as a place for research, one that has "proved so extraordinarily fruitful that I have worked but little elsewhere."[27] Those who collaborated with Rowan acknowledged the way in which he balanced artistic and scientific impulses. The close student of bird life in the Beaver Hills, Robert Lister, noted that Rowan "illustrated much of his scientific and popular writings with delightful pencil and pen-and-ink sketches" and that "his notebooks are full of life-like-drawings of birds and mammals made in the field."[28]

Rowan continued to make his mark over the years, despite having to continually justify his "field work" to Henry Marshall Tory, the President of the University. Tory, a man of scientific achievement himself, was of the opinion that field work was not a prerequisite of science.[29] To Rowan and his international colleagues, then attempting to develop the young study of ecology, Tory's view on field work was anathema. Rowan opened up communication with some of the best minds of the day: George Bird Grinnell, Sir Julian Huxley and Charles Elton. These colleagues all admired his work and attempted to further his career, despite the stubbornness of Tory.[30] Rowan's main contributions were in bird anatomy, migration theory and the nature of population cycles. His elaborate studies of crows, partially undertaken in the Beaver Hills, issued in several papers and provided the basis for his important book *The Riddle of Migration* (1931).

William Rowan and raven

    Rowan's interests in the natural world extended beyond birds. He got involved in what came to be called the bison-transfer issue of the 1920s. This came about following the discovery of an isolated population of Wood Bison in the Alberta-Northwest Territories border region. The point for debate was the appropriateness of shipping some of the excess Plains Bison north from the Buffalo Park at Wainwright, Alberta, into terrain where they might mix with and infect the isolated northern Wood Bison, a slightly different form of the species.[31]

The activities of Rowan and his associates provided a stimulus for others, and reflected a growing desire for various forms of concerted conservation and education action. More Canadians were becoming concerned with wildlife. They started to give attention to organizational matters, to the development of a domestic body of theory concerning conservation management, and to the tapping of local pools of expertise for educational purposes.[32] By the onset of the Great Depression, Alberta citizens had formed organizations oriented towards outdoor field studies such as the Alberta Fish and Game Association, founded in 1929. President C.A. Hayden stated: "I firmly believe that your association has justified its existence" and that it will "be responsible for the creation of one of the finest fish and game countries in the world."[33] There was reason for optimism. The 1920s had been years of high water in central Alberta and the records kept of fish taken around Beaverhills Lake provided a rationale for the confidence of the new fish and game president. Throughout the 1930s, Rowan continued to take an interest in the requirements of sound conservation policy, as did many of his fellow naturalists and ecologists.[34] An active hunter himself, he devoted considerable attention to the education of hunters and public policy makers who too often, he felt, had little understanding of the interrelations of wildlife species. They thus fell into erroneous thinking about the role of predators. His arguments grew out of his extensive studies on wildlife population cycles.[35]

There were others besides Rowan who took a passionate interest in the flora and fauna of the Beaver Hills, men such as C.G. Harold, Frank Farley and H.B. Conover of Chicago's Field Museum.[36] Local journalist and creative naturalist Robert Lister was a steady force in the cause of promoting field work. He helped found the Edmonton Bird Club and recorded local natural history achievements.[37] Having arrived in Tofield in 1920 from his native Norfolk, he later recalled the first impression made on him by Beaverhills Lake:[38]

> The lake lay flat as glass under the heat of the afternoon sun. The haze shimmering above the water veiled the far shore so that one looked out over what appeared to be a strangely quiet sea. Only where the wavelets lapped listlessly on the mud and sand was there any motion and from where they rippled in the wrack came a strong stench of rotten weeds. This was my first look at Beaverhills Lake and I was not impressed.

It would take some time for the lake to begin to exercise its magic upon Lister, who became one of its great observers and defenders.

In the offices of the Canadian civil service, intimations of the new ecological thought developed roughly in parallel with U.S. experience. Hoyes Lloyd had been hired by the National Parks Branch in 1918 to administer the Migratory Birds Convention Act.[39] Under the direction of Harkin, park officers started to question the traditional view taken of predators. For example, in 1920 the official predator list still identified the following species: "Puma, wolf, coyote, lynx, bear (if nuisances), gopher, porcupine, eagle, hawk, woodpecker and blue heron (for eating geese eggs)." This list was greatly reduced in 1924, particularly with respect to birds. In 1925, Harkin released a statement which set out a comprehensive philosophy for the conservation of species in the National Parks, confirmed later in that year by the Department of the Interior.[40]

By 1930 the developing science of ecology had helped produce a much more focused body of wildlife management practices. In this body of practice, the name of the American, Aldo Leopold, came to the fore. His book, *Game Management* (1933) became a landmark of the literature, for it revealed a shift in attention from pure field recording towards theory. He argued that earlier attempts "to apply biology to the management of game as a wild crop" soon disclosed the fact that "science had accumulated more knowledge of how to distinguish one species from another than of the habits, requirements, and interrelationships of living populations." Until recently, he said, science could tell us "more about the length of a duck's bill than about its food, of the status of the waterfowl resource, or the factors determining its productivity." It had now become more realistic. "Scientists see that before the factors of productivity can be economically manipulated, they must first be discovered and understood."[41]

These were just some of the critical ideas starting to circulate among park and wildlife managers in the early 1930s. An ecological viewpoint was strongly evidenced in William Rowan's growing preoccupation with conservation and the wildlife cycle. A host of professional organizations and journals started to appear seeking to criticize and revise past practices with the precision of science.[42]

In addition to completion of the Federal-Provincial "autonomy" agreements for transfer of natural resource lands, the year 1930 was also significant for passage of a new National Parks Act. Elk Island National Park was given increased protection as a result, but it was also the start of a new *modus operandi* in which managers found it necessary to deal with provincial agencies and authorities with respect to the planning and coordination of adjacent public lands. Negotiating land additions to the western parks would henceforth

Birds in flight over Beaverhills Lake

be more complex, involving the give and take characteristic of Federal-Provincial relations.[43]

These new political relationships, combined with developments in ecological thought, began to impact the administration of Elk Island. Archibald Coxford's long tenure as park superintendent came to an end in 1935. His successor was appointed in the fall of 1936 in the person of Dr. B.I. Love, a veterinarian by profession. The early years at Elk Island had required the rough and ready skills of practical men of the field. It now seemed fitting to turn the park over to a manager trained in the sciences. The next quarter century saw considerable experimentation in wildlife management procedures, accompanied by attempts to rationalize earlier policies. It was a period when theories of wildlife carrying capacity were invented, debated and contested. Early in Love's tenure, a southward expansion of the land base of Elk Island National Park was negotiated with the Province of Alberta.[44]

Harkin's adjustments to conservation policy between 1925 and 1935 were appropriate beginnings for the redress of some of the specific conflicts developing in the National Parks. These conflicts were frequently of a kind in which conservation aims ran afoul of recreational demands. At Elk Island, wildlife conservation had to be achieved on a fairly small and confined land unit without the normal cross-country flow of wildlife. This particular condition was aggravated by the growing isolation of Elk Island from the agricultural lands surrounding it. Given the borderless manner in which ecosystems operate, this isolation was only partial; but it also reinforced what managers had sought to achieve, ever since the first years of the Elk Park, for close attention had always to be given to the agricultural interests and actions of landed neighbours. With the addition of a bison conservation programme, the question of just what constituted a valid carrying capacity for the park was regularly posed. In 1936, John Buie, an inspector with the Department of Agriculture, recommended a reduction of the ungulates by a half.[45] The question was complicated by the restricted and

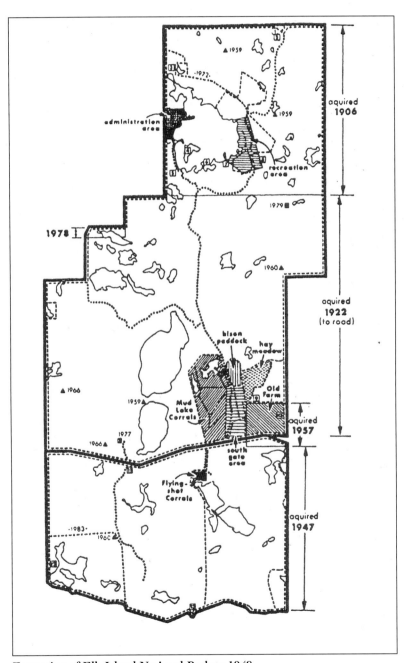

Expansion of Elk Island National Park to 1948

fenced range of the park in which cross-boundary movement of large ungulates was generally restricted to deer.[46]

A second source of conflict, closely related to the conditions imposed by the first, came about as a natural side effect of the rapid growth in scientific thinking about animal ecology and disease control that commenced in the 1880s. Relations with neighbours were especially important on the question of communicable animal diseases. Understanding prevention methods for hoof-and-mouth disease, rabies and tuberculosis were major preoccupations of park managers. In time, it became clear that certain animals diseases were particularly hard to monitor and eliminate, and that the degree to which it was possible to do so had much to do with the promotion of proper range conditions and animal proximity.[47] The shrinking range conditions in the vicinity of Elk Island were directly contrary to what was required, according to developing post-1930 theories of wildlife ecology and carrying capacity. Free of natural predator control, the continually growing ungulate populations at Elk Island had to be contained by one means or another. One obvious solution was to add to the amount of available range. Thus, in 1947 the park underwent its second major expansion with the addition of some twenty-four sections of the Cooking Lake Forest Reserve along the southern boundary.[48] The expansion was based on a

Blackfoot Grazing Association, 1948

Cattle grazing in the Cooking Lake-Blackfoot Recreation Area, which shows the mix of terrain conditions characteristic of the Beaver Hills region.

complex set of land transfers between Canada and Alberta, ending negotiations that Dr. Love had initiated ten years earlier.[49]

Another approach to controlling wildlife numbers involved the direct marketing of meat from slaughtered animals, through contracts to major meat-packing houses.[50] From the mid-1920s through the 1960s, Elk Island National Park was committed to a form of ranching, as a necessity, and staff had gradually put in place all the necessary support facilities, including in-park agriculture. Similarly, the early experiment in cattle grazing known as the Blackfoot Stock Association continued in various forms on what were now Provincial lands.[51]

World War II interrupted the national conservation momentum, but in 1947 the Canadian Wildlife Service was formed to bring greater focus and more systematic attention to wildlife issues.[52] For the previous thirty years, officials of the National Parks Branch had administered the statutes relevant to wildlife protection. The new unit was given broader powers and responsibilities, and the establishment of this branch indicated that wildlife was starting to be seen in landscape contexts other than those of just parks and wildlife sanctuaries.[53] Its establishment was in part a recognition of the excellent advisory work accomplished by such eminent field biologists as A.W.F. Banfield, Ian McTaggart Cowan and J.D. Soper. The Canadian Wildlife Service would play an important role in the postwar Elk Island National Park.

CHAPTER SEVEN

Postwar Urbanism

The First World War drew many soldiers away from the Edmonton area but did not precipitate any substantial economic growth in the city. This was not the case during the Second World War. The city's population grew from some 90,000 in 1939 to over 113,000 in 1945. Much of this growth was driven by war industries, particularly in aviation and air training. Aviation was built on the base of regional industries that had taken root in Winnipeg and Edmonton before 1930, oriented towards serving the north. Another factor was the push for construction of a wartime transportation corridor from Edmonton to Alaska to counter a potential threat from Japan. A substantial military and engineering presence in Edmonton induced a boom in home construction.[1]

As in the rest of Canada, the immediate postwar years were a time of economic restraint in Alberta. Non-essential government expenditures were held in check, including those associated with recreational roads and tourism. The countryside still remained distinct from the city, although Edmonton was on the eve of a great transformation. In 1947, oil was discovered at Leduc, a few miles south of the city. This event transformed the province, changing the economic base of many communities into a mix of agriculture and industrial resource extraction. It marked the beginning of Edmonton's rise to prominence in the oil industry. In addition, the Redwater field north-east of Edmonton soon came into play, a development that transformed the small community of Fort Saskatchewan and which would eventually outdistance the Leduc field in terms of production. On the western edge of the hills, the quiet rural hamlet of Clover Bar was suddenly graced with a refinery while, by 1951, the Hay Lakes area found itself at the centre of the Joarcam oil field. There were at least twenty-one oil fields in production in the Edmonton region by 1953. These postwar finds merely confirmed what had been known for some time about the general possibilities for petroleum in central Alberta. As early as 1912, Tofield experienced a short-lived gas boom. The Viking gas field east of the hills had seen minor development as early as 1923.[2] Petroleum was on the way to becoming the substance of Alberta's future. Its accessibility, combined with the rising popularity of the automobile, assured that the relative isolation of the Beaver Hills would soon end.

Agriculture was also poised for a revival after the Second World War. Mixed farming, grazing and the maintenance of wood lots continued to be seen as the best way to balance the effects of unpredictable soils and weather patterns. Unlike practices on the open prairies, where large land units had long been in favour, subdivision into smaller holdings was the trend in the hills after 1945.[3] In order to foster employment for returning servicemen, the Federal Government had passed the Veteran Lands Act as an inducement to soldiers to take up land. This well-intentioned legislation had mixed results, for much of the land made available was either in the north, or was otherwise marginal, such as the Beaver Hills. Also, the legislation was offensive to many in suggesting that established Indian reserves should, as in 1919, be thrown open to soldier settlers.[4] From an economic perspective, the northern and rural areas could not compete with the growing cities in their ability to offer the support facilities needed by many veterans or by the young and unemployed. The fledgling oil industry was a stronger lure than farming for the ambitious job-seeker. Nevertheless, the traditional advantages provided by relatively low-investment grazing remained strong in the hills. At the C.J. Kallal Ranch, on the southeast side of Beaverhills Lake, the nucleus for a highly successful commercial herd was developed in the 1940s, based on registered Herefords.[5]

Postwar economic circumstances led to revival of the Blackfoot Grazing Reserve, even though the quality of the fenced-in grazing land had declined with the growth of trees. In 1947, Jack Gray and his associates, having taken over the old Dominion Forest Administration Buildings as headquarters, coordinated many improvements over the next 20 years. The Blackfoot Grazing Association became the vector by which local grazing herds made adjustments to the landscape, and in which communal and leased landholdings played a role.[6]

Jack Gray at work, c. 1967

Increased demand for recreational use of the hills in the later 1970s led to discussions between the association and provincial land officials on defining a new multiple-use resource area. Under subsequent arrangements "a part of the area was cleared, broken and seeded with a mixture of forage plants" and the remainder "left forested." Thus, the revamped Cooking Lake-Blackfoot Grazing, Wildlife and Provincial Recreation Area officially opened in 1988. A system of fences now surrounded the area to enclose both game animals and cattle grazing areas. A network of recreational trails was added, some of which link up with Elk Island National Park directly to the north. The process by which a working landscape was reconfigured into one with connections to the growing city of Edmonton dovetailed well with other ongoing assessments of land use in the hills.[7]

Science and History in the Beaver Hills

It has already been noticed how conflicts growing out of the initial designation of the "Elk Park" as a game preserve led to its incorporation within the growing system of National Parks in 1913. This inclusion meant that Elk Island came to be administered with a view to fulfilling the various mandates outlined in Dominion Park legislation. In response to public expectations that the Dominion Parks represented "pleasure grounds," recreational improvements were authorized, both after the First World War and during the Depression. The tandem pursuit of conservation and recreation objectives was not viewed as particularly anomalous. Consider the words of National Park historian, W.F. Lothian, in a popular article from 1940:[8]

> As one of the older units in the great system of public reservations... of Canada... Elk Island National Park, for more than a quarter of a century has been fulfilling a dual purpose. As a sanctuary for wild-life it has not only helped to save for posterity the buffalo...but it is preserving in their natural surroundings

other interesting big-game species and wild birds. As a public resort it is also providing opportunities for outdoor life and recreation amid the unspoiled beauties of a beneficent Nature, and as time goes on it will continue to render an increasingly useful service as one of Canada's National Playgrounds.

The quieter and less-congested world described here has long since vanished. In the hills, encroachment came about incrementally, but steadily, as happened on the peripheries of so many other urban centres of North America. In the immediate postwar years, National Parks officials adopted a policy of caution with respect to new in-park developments, just as they had during the late 1920s and 1930s.[9] Despite previous unprofitable ventures in the commercial concession sector, managers did respond to demand for accommodation facilities, but by 1968 these efforts also succumbed to the economics of seasonal demand. Other ventures considered appropriate were approved, including church recreation camps, tent rental operations, a facility built by the Canadian Youth Hostel Association, refreshment booths, the Wapiti Inn, and boating concessions. Many of these agreements were cancelled between 1960 and 1970 owing to lack of sufficient use, changing public tastes or as responses by administrators to changing policy directions.[10]

New conceptions of park management and of the conservation and heritage mandate came up for debate in the 1960s, along with formal revisions to public policy. One student of Elk Island history commented that previous arrangements for the park were "tolerable until after the Second World War when a more sophisticated and professional view of the role of national parks as islands of relatively intact ecosystems" started to surface. These new environmentalist points of view had to mesh with the reality of more "intensified recreational use of these same areas." The need to cater to these diverse demands came to complicate administrative, professional and lay perceptions of desirable land use. Seeking the right balance between "conservation and use" was one of the main tasks facing park managers across North America after 1970.[11]

Increased demand for access from an expanding regional population caused managers at Elk Island to re-evaluate the role of the park. At one level, the conflicts between conservation and human use were seen to be rather minimal. The areas of most intense use were well known, localized, controllable, and seasonal. Of more interest to park managers after 1970 was the definition of the park's ideal character and its proper conservation role. Debates about the nature of Elk Island's ecology had commenced shortly after the retirement of longtime superintendent, Dr. B.I. Love, in 1959. In the first half-century of park administration only three men had held sway, but the next eighteen years saw no less than six superintendents come and go, each attempting to alter policy and prepare a suitable park management plan.[12] In doing so, they had to pay much more attention than their predecessors to the claims of science and their application.

Bison processing facility, Elk Island National Park in 1992   These corrals were built in the 1930s to assist in rounding up bison for slaughter, for disease inspections, and for transporting to other centres.

Love's successor, H.R. Webster, quickly demonstrated a keen interest in gaining accurate estimates of the big-game population and utilizing academic research in the interests of policy. The ethos concerning animal reduction methods inherited by Webster is interesting to note in retrospect and may be taken as a measure of how frequently public attitudes have altered since 1907. Initially, the park was a kind of holding tank for threatened species, in which numbers were encouraged. The policy was all too successful. A shift in attitude came in the mid-1930s. Dr. Love saw the need to reduce animal numbers to a much lower figure than those common in the 1920s. Elaborate control facilities were built to assist in the monitoring of the health of bison. The notion that the park was, in some respects, a ranch, persisted during his time, making acceptable methods of animal reduction quite straightforward.

The purpose of a ranch is to raise and then sell meat on the hoof. So it was at Elk Island during the 1950s and early 1960s. Large contracts were let by tender to major meat-packing houses, calling on them to look after the animal reduction problem in ways which would generate revenue.[13] Often the slaughter would be conducted at the park, but the companies clearly would have preferred to carry out such activities at their own well-equipped facilities. In 1961 Webster noted that Canada Packers "have again raised the question of the possibility of shipping the buffalo to their city plant where they could handle the complete kill of about 200 animals in one morning. That suggestion has been turned down by the Health of Animals Division in the past."[14] The next year the Department of Indian Affairs and Northern Development took a very business-like attitude to the entire situation. One of its news releases declared that "Sweetgrass buffalo steaks will soon be adding northern sizzle to Canadian menus" for "250,000 pounds of top quality meat" from Wood Buffalo National Park were "to go on sale from coast to coast on January 17." Not only would the supply come from the northern herds, but "Buffalo meat from Elk Island National Park" would be "on sale this year with the sweetgrass variety." There would be everything "from streamlined hind quarters to packaged buffalo burgers" all prepared "to give jaded after Christmas appetites a lift." The number of beasts culled for these purposes was by no means negligible and indicates how quickly the populations could burgeon under conditions of protection and winter feeding. Webster reported that 337 animals were slaughtered in 1964, mainly for meat.[15]

The identity of Elk Island National Park had become a curious amalgam of game ranch, zoo, recreation centre, and nature area. Such were the operational necessities of the day and such was the flexibility of the National Parks Act. For the future, however, Webster was anxious to identify more lasting forms of control through applied ecology and a consideration of carrying capacity. He facilitated research and aerial surveys of animal populations in 1959. The contemporary reports of W.N. Holdsworth became the subject of some confusion between Webster and the Canadian Wildlife Service. Chief Mammalogist W.E. Stevens took the view that Holdsworth's work indicated that ungulates (elk, bison, moose, deer) were tending to reduce the plant variety of the park landscape. In the long term, these grazers might prevent new deciduous growth, perhaps reducing northern areas of the park to a meadow-like condition in due course. Webster himself interpreted the scientific reports as questioning the very idea that Elk Island was a suitable place for a bison sanctuary. In his opinion, the park, as with much of the Beaver Hills of old, constituted a spruce forest, one which had been home only to moose and elk. Any bison in the area were likely only passing through on the more open fringes of the hills. The present vegetation, according to Webster, resulted mainly from fires during the homestead period, while subsequent animal use had prevented regeneration of the natural spruce forest. The Superintendent found support from another student of the landscape, who suggested that the bison were the main factor in reducing the natural succession from aspen to spruce, for bison tended to eat young planted spruce. Such considerations helped explain the "mistaken premise" which had "guided the general philosophy of the park for a number of years."[16]

Webster's was a compelling historical thesis, but we have seen in previous chapters, bison were not just "passing through" in pre-settlement times, but were using the Beaver Hills in ways that the Aspen Parkland was normally used by such animals – as a sheltered seasonal wintering ground. The parallel result was that the hills provided good hunting range for Native peoples. In fur trade days, evidence has been cited for the presence of traditional bison pounds in the Beaver Hills, and that the hills remained a dependable source for bison into the late 1850s. It was true that bison, in their wild state, range widely and do not confine themselves to one area; but it was also true that during certain seasons, they may be more or less resident in a given locality.

Holdsworth may not have totally disagreed with Webster, but he and others were less concerned about the ideal character of Elk Island as bison range, and more with notions of suitable carrying capacity. Holdsworth contended that in much of the park, grass and shrub meadows had been maintained where forest should have succeeded. This, he thought, was due to nothing more mysterious than severe overgrazing in the past 20 years. The result had been to modify the original floral composition of the park. In some parts agricultural species had flourished by one means or another, not least of which was the presence of the regularly broken farm land in the park, traditionally used to produce winter feed. Here was the old "ranch" factor once again. Holdsworth recommended that bison be held at 400, elk at 400, and moose at 100. This would presumably lead to a revitalization of shrub and tree growth and to a higher percentage of rabbits and deer.[17]

In the end, the two parties agreed to disagree on the larger policy questions. Webster continued to argue that Elk Island was less than ideal bison landscape and that its small size could only increase its capacity to become a harbour of disease. The Canadian Wildlife Service scientists maintained that, whatever the limitations at Elk Island, it played an important role in the larger scheme of bison conservation sanctuaries. Webster was certainly successful in making the scope of bison management the main question for future management. He had clearly seen the financial implications of the wildlife administration costs incurred over the years. Staff had spent an extraordinary amount of time monitoring herd numbers, round-up activities related to slaughter and shipment to other centres, and to disease inspections. Webster had most success with his population recommendations. These were accepted and a new slaughter reduced the ungulate density by over 45 per cent, bringing numbers to their lowest since the 1920s.[18] Webster also managed to place biological considerations on the table by posing questions: what should be the relationship of bison with other large ungulates? In the absence of natural controls and feeding programmes, how were numbers to be controlled? These were important questions with which students of wildlife management had been struggling for some time.[19]

Webster was succeeded in 1965 by G.H. Ashley. The park administration now embraced a new "ecological" policy in which human influences were to be reduced, in the management sense. An example of change in this direction can be seen in 1967 when systematic production of feed crops in the park was suspended,

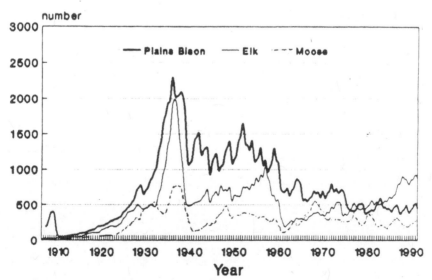

Ungulate Populations Chart, 1920s–1980s

thus bringing to a close a long-standing practice. The farm facility remained in place, however. In language beloved of planners, one park officer summarized the contradictions: "Although we are in the 'Buffalo Ranching Business' the hay farm does remain a non-conforming park use." The implication was that in a "natural setting," animal numbers should now achieve a balance based on their ability to feed themselves year round without human intervention.[20] With the adoption of such policies, the Parks Branch made a start on redressing an old bias in favour of large ungulates at Elk Island. The weight of years of accumulated practice however, determined that pursuit of this new direction would have to remain on hold for some time. History was about to repeat itself.

The singular event of the first year of Ashley's term was the introduction of 22 head of Wood Bison from vast Wood Buffalo National Park into a newly constructed Canadian Wildlife Service

Wood Bison With the establishment of a Wood Bison population in the southern reaches of Elk Island in the 1960s, history appeared to be repeating itself. Issues of ecology drove this second initiative in bison conservation.

isolation area in the south-western portion of the park. The rationale for the introduction of a number of the larger and darker coloured cousins of the Plains Bison was the endangered status of the Wood Bison, owing to the disease-compromised nature of much of the herd in Wood Buffalo Park. "The intention was to create pockets of disease-free herds in locations separate from the Mackenzie Bison Sanctuary, which at that time hosted the only relatively pure Wood Bison herd."[21]

When these animals were shipped south, they were considered to be free of disease, but testing in 1966 revealed that this was not so. By 1969 all had been slaughtered except a few calves, which were then hand-reared by wardens. This surviving group of young provided the basis for the current herd of Wood Bison in the park. Despite Webster's attempts to downplay the bison sanctuary aspects of Elk Island, by 1970 the park was right back in the thick of single species conservation, and in a new and interesting way. Efforts to establish other pockets of bison across the prairies had begun a year earlier when 50 bison taken from the Elk Island prairie population were released in the Thunder Hills, north of Prince Albert National Park, in order to improve the subsistence hunt for resident Native peoples.[22]

The various ecological balls were tossed even higher in the air in 1972 when radical reductions of the park herds were proposed by Superintendent Don MacMillan. He suggested that the Plains Bison herd should be removed entirely and be replaced by a small display herd. While this suggestion was not accepted, it was representative of the thinking displayed in a number of contemporary studies, which sought to define the optimum carrying capacity for the park and to better understand the general relationships between ungulate populations and other aspects of the park.[23]

The notion that all the Wood Bison should now be removed from the park became the occasion for more controversy in the mid-1970s. Policies on behalf of single species were clearly under assault, for the fly of ecology had been let out of the bottle by prominent headquarters staff back in the 1940s. Recent Ottawa policies indicated that the Parks Branch had been soundly infected with the new thinking and were considering its broader applications. The shift in thinking extended to a greater respect for the role of all species in a given ecosystem. The coyote, for example, consistently hunted down in the hills in the 1920s, might now find defenders such as Elk Island naturalist Ross Chapman, who wrote of its utilitarian value and adaptability.[24]

A comprehensive and progressive management plan was approved for Elk Island in 1978. The "island anomaly" idea was played up, in which the park was recognized as an "outlier" of the northern boreal forest. It was a "transitional" landscape, as described earlier. If there was a ghost in this plan, it was surely that of Webster. At the same time, room was still made for the recent preoccupation with the fate of the great northern herds of Wood Bison. Elk Island, having played an important role in the conservation of the Plains Bison, was now being asked to contribute to salvaging its cousins.[25]

After 1980, the bison programme at Elk Island became one of "purification" and shipping out of healthy specimens to other centres of conservation to further establish healthy gene pools outside of the widely infected home territory of the Wood Bison.[26] Population surveys done in 1999 revealed that Elk Island sheltered 600 Plains Bison, 350 Wood Bison, and sizable numbers of elk, deer and moose. There was now a special area set aside for monitoring and treating elk as well as bison. Wildlife populations were highly controlled populations and the word "natural" no longer had a self-evident meaning at Elk Island.[27]

Vanishing Waters

At a gathering in 1971, Alberta legislator Walter Buck recalled a parade in New Sarepta in which he noticed a Community Association float proclaiming: "Save the lowering water levels in Cooking Lake."[28] This episode was symptomatic of the reverse side of postwar trends towards land use in the Beaver Hills. What should be the approach taken to the extensive mosaic of lakes, ponds and streams in those parts? Specific designations had been given to some of these wetlands early in the century, such as Ministik Lake being recognized as a bird sanctuary in 1911. By 1971, however, there was a widespread concern that the water regimes of the hills were in trouble. There was a broadly held sentiment that over the previous 70 years forces had been at work favouring a select number of species, increased uniformity in the vegetation cover, and a lowering of water levels, with attendant decline in aquatic species and recreational opportunities. A variety of reasons for these fluctuations in the water tables have been offered over the years. A 1976 planning report made special mention of the narrow watersheds surrounding most of the individual lakes, suggesting that "the lake levels are sensitive to small variations in climatic patterns" and these influence precipitation, evaporation and runoff. Miquelon, Beaverhills, and Cooking Lakes presented the most visible measures of these environmental events.[29]

The first record of a Beaverhills Lake water level dates from 1865 "when a traveller saw bison mired in the mud of the exposed lake bottom." Edo Nyland documented the rise and fall of the levels from that early date until 1970, offering his views on the reasons for the shifts. These included fluctuations brought on by wet and dry seasons, the general clearing of the land, and human engineering modifications such as the 1926 canal which took water south from Miquelon Lake to Camrose for that city's municipal needs. An authority on Beaverhills Lake, Dick Dekker, acknowledged these influences as adversely affecting "nature's water regulatory system." Water, snow-melt and summer rains, instead of "percolating through a mossy forest floor, now cascade across cleared ground or are wasted by increased evaporation in surface pools and puddles." Even in its current diminished state, this wetland presents a dramatic visual aspect. Dekker observed that looking across its 18-kilometre expanse it becomes "the closest thing to an ocean view in land-locked Alberta."[30]

From the standpoint of waterfowl habitat, a certain amount of fluctuation in the levels of a large wetland is desirable, but too

much unpredictability is naturally a frustration to local farmers at
the wetland's edge. It is also a frustration to nesting birds. As early
as 1917, proposals were being made to construct engineering works
on the lake to help control radical rises of water in wet years, although
these ideas were not carried out. Ever since, local agriculturalists
have adopted an ambiguous attitude to the lake's movements.
Proposals for outright stabilization of water levels, or for total
drainage, have come and gone with some regularity. These proposals
have been supplemented by other ideas, such as mining the coal
seams beneath the lake, conversion of the drained lake into more
community pasture, or establishment of a shooting range for the
Air Force.[31] All of these developmental proposals were passed over
in favour of more environmentally pleasing ideas.

By the end of the 1960s, concern about the steady decline in
lake levels in the Beaver Hills moved a body of citizens to submit
a pointed petition: "The undersigned are petitioning for Alberta
Government action on the reclamation of the Beaverhill Watershed
(Miquelon, Ministik, Hastings, Cooking and Beaverhill Lakes).
Let's get some water back in our lakes."[32] An extensive and interesting body of information grew out of the subsequent commission
and its hearings. If opinions expressed were wide ranging, with
much disagreement on specifics, it was nevertheless an important
example of intelligent citizen engagement and civility.[33]

The scientific poles of the debate were defined by two distinct
views. At one end was Edo Nyland's contention that the essential
dynamic of the disappearing water involved the sustained burning
and clearing of the forest cover after 1880. This view was opposed
by University of Alberta hydrographer Aleigh Laycock, who argued
"that climatic patterns have been more than adequate explanations
for water level declines, and it is likely that man has inadvertently
reduced the rate of decline rather than accelerated it." This assertion
was based on his claim that, in the parkland, trees actually returned
more moisture to the atmosphere, in most years, than did open
grassland and cultivated land. Forests represented a kind of long
term drain on groundwater rather than a support for it.[34] Suffice

to say, this was not a conclusion that many veterans of the land were prepared to accept.

Regardless of the lack of consensus on the actual causes of water decline, there was a general agreement reached that massive expenditures on water diversions for the limited purpose of raising Cooking and Hastings Lake levels was not a sound strategy. A broader proposal in the tabled consultant's report was favoured. This alternative argued that any substantial engineering actions taken should be oriented to the overall problems of the several linked watersheds of the Cooking Lake Moraine area. The formidable costs projected and the tentative nature of long-term effects assured that the plans for piping in water to Cooking Lake remained on the shelf.[35]

Exercises such as the Cooking-Hastings Lakes hearings helped usher in a more rigorous effort at integrated land use planning by the various Crown and municipal agencies. Such an exercise was subsequently taken for the Beaverhills lake area.[36] Special status was also achieved at this location when the lake was recognized

Trumpeter Swans   This once acutely endangered species has come back in the Beaver Hills owing to active conservation programmes sponsored by public and private bodies.

in 1982 as a National Nature Viewpoint, following much joint advocacy by the Canadian Nature Federation, the Edmonton Bird Club and the Federation of Alberta Naturalists. Two provincially designated natural areas at Beaver Hills Lake were added in 1987, through the nomination of Pelican Island and Dekker Island. In 1987, under the Ramsar Convention, Beaverhills Lake was included on the world list of Wetlands of International Importance.[37] By the late 1980s, returns on these investments were noticeable. The threatened Trumpeter Swans, a species that was almost wiped out by 1900, were again seen on the lake, as they were at Elk Island. Also returning were Tundra Swans and Sandhill Cranes. In the view of naturalist Peter Dunn, we "probably had more birds at Beaverhills Lake than any other area in Alberta."[38]

Successes in the conservation of avian and large game species were not the only wildlife stories in the Beaver Hills in the postwar years. Images of the historic commercial character of the region, as understood in fur trade days, were visible once again by the mid-1970s. By virtue of a certain stabilization of water bodies and the regeneration of the aspen forest through long-term fire suppression, the namesake animal of this region, the beaver, was back in numbers, with much attendant flooding. This was no doubt noticed with some pleasure by those who had argued in 1971 that the return of the beaver would do much to help restore low lake levels. Their appearance now necessitated control on occasion and sometimes this "was dealt with by shooting beavers." By the early 1990s there were several hundred active beaver lodges in Elk Island Park alone, a terrain well suited to them owing to the rolling nature of the land and frequency of small ponds.[39]

South of Cooking Lake, the Reirson homestead was purchased by the Lion's Club of Camrose and then donated to the province in 1958, providing the core land for Miquelon Lake Provincial Park. Other lakes, such as Oliver and Joseph, both notable in earlier years as fish and wildlife areas, have lost much of their character owing to local industrial activities and redirected watershed flows.[40]

The Architectural and Landscape Heritage
of the Beaver Hills

By 1950 the conditions of postwar civilian financial restraint were coming to an end. A decline in rail travel, occasioned by increased automobile ownership, initiated a great blurring of the boundaries between town and country. The automobile and long-distance trucking slowly started to transform social and working arrangements in Alberta. The farm itself was mechanizing at a great rate, with labour being replaced by expensive machinery. The founding of Sherwood Park as a community in 1951 and the construction of a refinery at Clover Bar brought Edmonton to the very western edge of the hills. Group outings by train to Cooking Lake or Elk Island or Hay Lakes had been replaced by more frequent and predictable journeys by car.[41]

These trends did not go unnoticed by the older generation of Beaver Hills residents. We have already seen that in the late 1940s, Dr. A.C. Archer and his associates were aware that the old agricultural world of the pioneer was rapidly disappearing. Through

Restored Superintendent's Residence, Elk Island National Park, 1985   The growing community interest in preserving the pioneer heritage extended to long serving public buildings.

community effort, they worked to see that the values of the local pioneer community gained some recognition at Elk Island. Their achievement was a harbinger of the establishment of the ambitious Ukrainian Heritage Cultural Village, a few miles east of the park, for which planning commenced in the mid-1970s.[42] Similarly, federal agencies began to look to their own properties and undertake appropriate restorations and designations.

Interest in the built heritage of the hills was fostered by the mounting economic dominance of cities such as Edmonton, Red Deer and Calgary, which came at a price with respect to smaller communities. The main street of many rural Alberta towns came to display signs of lost economic vibrancy. The occasion of the public hearings on Cooking and Hastings Lakes Water Levels in 1971 provided a stimulus for a limited assessment of some of the older stock of pioneer buildings and commercial structures in the hills, revealing how few and fragile were the reminders of the

Ukrainian Heritage Cultural Village   In the early 1980s the Alberta Government helped further local initiatives aimed at establishing an outdoor museum between Elk Island and Mundare.

pre-1920 period.[43] What commercial migration to larger centres had not quite destroyed through abandonment was too often completed by the appearance of a new mall on the edge of a town. The outward migration of the young to the cities and changing social values resulted in declining memberships in churches, causing some striking older church structures to be boarded up. This trend was already noticeable in the 1960s.

In 1971, the Ukrainian Cultural Heritage Village Society was formed, to salvage and relocate regional heritage buildings to an architectural sanctuary near Elk Island National Park.[44] In 1975, the Province of Alberta purchased the site of some 320 acres, and continued the effort to rescue some of the best examples of vernacular and sacred architecture from the Ukrainian bloc settlements.[45] With a view to illustrating the pre-1930 heritage of Ukrainian town and farm life, a substantial number of structures were moved and professionally restored. The objectives went beyond mere architectural rescue. The structures were furnished and made the focus of museum treatments and first-person interpretation of the ways of life.[46] The village provides a kaleidoscopic view of the various aspects of early twentieth-century rural life in east central Alberta's Ukrainian bloc settlement and is today an important tourist attraction and educational resource.

The initiative was timely, for in recent years, North American urban planners have come to speak of "rurbanization" as a developing phenomenon. The term describes a trend visible around many cities in which urban forms, values and expectations extend into the countryside. In some cases, cities have merged into a larger "conurbation," such as the Toronto-Hamilton area.[47]

In less congested regions, the "back to the land" movement of the 1960s, which appealed to a mix of the romantic, retired, wealthy, and environmentally sensitive, transformed itself substantially in the 1990s. The original impulses, if not totally absent, had been replaced on a grander scale by a greyer, gentrified version of the countryside in which large estates and a demand for urban service facilities prevailed, as though there were no logical inconsistencies in expecting of the countryside what only the city can provide economically. In some extreme cases, golf courses encroach imprudently upon grizzly habitat. Many a quiet village outside of the normal range of the nearest city suddenly became "a bedroom community." Thus Tofield, long a quiet agricultural service centre beyond the reach of Edmonton's daily life, has undergone a rapid housing expansion and revitalization. Similarly, the small cottage community of Antler Lake, a short distance south-west of the boundary of Elk Island National Park, has become a year-round outreach of Edmonton. "Acreages" became the cry of the new North American urban pioneer, indicating that the last frontier to be subdued was the old countryside.

With this phenomenon came mounting pressures on special land reserves or traditional resource use areas. The Beaver Hills have not been immune. Local land administrators have had to adjust to new land use conflicts within the rural-urban fringe portions of the continent. The proximity of Elk Island to Edmonton supported this trend and led one sportsman to refer to it as a "Wilderness

Beaverhills Lake near Tofield One of the largest freshwater bodies in Central and Southern Alberta, the lake flanks the eastern side of the hills and remains an important focus of wildlife conservation.

Park in the Suburbs."[48] Recognizing a need to reassess the pressures
on the boundaries of Elk Island, park officers prepared a new
management plan in the early 1990s, one which sought to facilitate
greater integration with regional patterns of land use.[49] Other
parties, such as the Beaver Hills Initiative group and independent
scholars, have made substantial contributions to assessing the
extent of long-term "fragmentation" of the forest communities and
habitat in the Beaver Hills.[50] Similarly, the guardians and clients
of the Blackfoot Community Pasture completed a comprehensive
management plan in 1997. Elk Island, Miquelon Lake, the Parkland
Natural Area, and other local land use areas now form a patchwork
of special areas.[51]

Since the initial establishment of a forest reserve in the Beaver
Hills in the 1890s, there has been a certain stumbling towards a
pattern of land use similar to that recently advocated as "biosphere
reserves," an approach to landscape conservation first defined in
1968 through the United Nations with its "Man and the Biosphere"
programme, and by the International Union for the Conservation
of Nature. A network of such reserves is slowly being established
around the globe.[52] In the late 1970s, the model was adopted at
Riding Mountain National Park in Manitoba and at Waterton and
Glacier, the large international peace park on the border of Alberta
and Montana.[53] A biosphere reserve usually has three main components: a central core area of land considered worthy of conservation
for its landscape values and biological diversity; a surrounding
"buffer area" of natural resource use areas; and a third outer ring
constituting a "transition zone" in which a fuller range of industrial
and civic facilities are accommodated.[54] The core zone often provides
for the fundamental protection of regional headwaters, an aspect
shared with many national and provincial parks. Looking at the
Beaver Hills as a biosphere, Elk Island is the core zone. Several
other phases of the old Cooking Lake Forest Reserve, now under new
identities, represent aspects of a surrounding buffer zone. The fringe
farm lands and smaller communities may be taken as the transition
zone, which hosts open land and normal working enterprises.

The prospect of controlling encroaching land use and subdivision in favour of a "land ethic," to use Aldo Leopold's memorable term, requires broad civic commitment toward allowing land to serve its best purpose.[55] The difficulties often come at the boundaries of land classification where land may be considered, from some points of view, as marginal. Where pressures are strong, as in the Niagara fruit belt, the best use may be completely overlooked. Norman Conrad has suggested that in the early 1990s, it was suddenly convenient for politicians to promote the abstractions of "green plans," "vision statements," notions of "ecological integrity" and other high-sounding procedures as foils for carrying on business as usual rather than budgeting and dealing with the hard work of legislated land-use planning.[56] At the same time, a too-rigid understanding is a disadvantage in matters where nature is often the hidden player at the table. In the crucible of legislative tinkering, allowance needs to be made for trial and error and for the unexpected, and for what Kevin Lynch called "rooted information" – that great reservoir of local, but not necessarily uniform, knowledge.[57] As we have seen in the case of the water levels issue of the early 1970s, there are collective traditions of land use reform in the Beaver Hills to draw upon. It found its early reflection when Native peoples cooperated in the construction and operation of a buffalo pound; and it had a more recent manifestation when an early twentieth-century politician listened to what some of his constituents were saying about a threatened group of elk, took up the matter, and then had the courage to change his mind.

NOTES

Introduction

1. See Ralph D. Bird's Ecology of the Aspen Parkland of Western Canada in Relation to Land Use (Ottawa: Department of Agriculture, 1961) and S.C. Zoltai, Southern Limit of coniferous trees on the Canadian Prairies, Northern Forest Research Centre Nor-X-128 (Edmonton: Environment Canada, 1975). On species characteristic of the Beaver Hills, see Ross Chapman, *The Discoverer's Guide to Elk Island National Park* (Edmonton: Lone Pine, 1991).

2. Dale R. Russell, The Eighteenth Century Western Cree and their Neighbours, Archaeological Survey of Canada, Mercury Series 143 (Ottawa: Canadian Museum of Civilization, 1991), 96, 150; John Warkentin and Richard I. Ruggles, *Historical Atlas of Manitoba* (Winnipeg: Manitoba Historical Society, 1970), 88–89.

3. Richard I. Ruggles, *A Country So Interesting: The Hudson's Bay Company and Two Centuries of Mapping, 1670–1870* (Montreal/Kingston: McGill-Queen's University Press, 1991), 41–45 and Plates 6 and 8.

4. Elliott Coues, ed., *The Manuscript Journals of Alexander Henry and David Thompson, 1799–1814* (Minneapolis: Ross and Haines, 1965) 566, 594; J.B. Tyrrell, ed. *David Thompson's Narrativ* (Toronto: 1916), lxviii.

5. J.B. Tyrrell, Report on a Part of Northern Alberta and Portion of Adjacent Districts of Assiniboia and Saskatchewan, Part E, Annual Report, 1886 Geological and Natural History Survey of Canada (Montreal: Dawson Bros., 1887), 44–45, 173.

6. James Hector, Journal, 29 December 1857 and 22 October 1858, in *The Palliser Papers*, ed. Irene M. Spry (Toronto: Champlain Society, 1968), 200, 345.

7. Tyrrell, Report on a Part of Northern Alberta and Portion of Adjacent Districts of Assiniboia and Saskatchewan, 44–45.

8. Grace A. Phillips, ed., *Tales of Tofield* (Leduc: Tofield Historical Society, 1969), 20 f.

9. James W. Van Stone, "The Isaac Cowie Collection of Plains Cree Material Culture from Central Alberta," *Fieldiana: Anthropology*, New Series no. 17 (30 September 1991): 1–56.

10. Phillips, *Tales of Tofield*, 192–93.

11. Ibid., 20.

Chapter 1

1. John Shaw, "Geomorphology," in *Edmonton Beneath Our Feet*, ed. John D. Godfrey (Edmonton: Edmonton Geological Society, 1993), 25.

2. Roger D. Morton, "The Edmonton Region Through Time," in Godfrey, *Edmonton Beneath Our Feet*, 17.

3. Deirdre Griffiths, *Island Forest Year: Elk Island National Park* (Edmonton: University of Alberta Press, 1979), 4.

4. See Ralph D. Bird, Ecology of the Aspen Parkland of Western Canada (Ottawa: Department of Agriculture, 1961).

5. See R.A. Bryson and T.J. Murray, *Climates of Hunger* (Madison: University of Wisconsin Press, 1977), 171 f.

6. For literature useful as aids to reconstructing past environments in Alberta, see Alwynne B. Beaudoin, Annotated Bibliography: Late Quaternary Studies in Alberta's Western Corridor, 1950–1988, Archaeological Survey of Alberta, Manuscript Series no. 15 (Edmonton: Alberta Culture and Multiculturalism, 1989).

7. A short and readable account of the main types of projectile points found on the prairies is provided in James T. Humphreys and Michael C. Wilson, *Record in Stone: Familiar Projectile Points from Alberta* (Lethbridge: Archaeological Society of Alberta, 1987). Also see Brian Kooyman and Jane. H. Kelley, eds., *Archaeology at the Edge: New Perspectives from the Northern Plains* (Calgary: University of Calgary Press, 2001).

8. The technique was ancient first in the Old World. See Henri Breuil, *Beyond the Bounds of History: Scenes from the Old Stone Age*, trans. Mary E. Boyle, (London: P.R. Gawthorn, 1949). For the New World see Bryan C. Gordon, "World Rangifer communal hunting," in *Hunters of the Recent Past*, ed. L.B. Davis and B.O.K. Reeves (London: Unwin Hyman, 1990), 281–91; also see Donald Savoie, ed., *The Amerindians of the Canadian Northwest in the Nineteenth Century as seen by Emile Petitot*. Vol. 2. *The Loucheaux Indians*. MacKenzie Delta Research Project. (Ottawa: DIAND, Northern Science Research Group, 1970), 101, 114.

9. See L.A. Bayrock and G.M. Hughes, Surficial Geology of the Edmonton District, Alberta, Earth Sciences Report 62-6 (Edmonton: Alberta Geological Survey, Research Council of Alberta, 1962).

10. S.C. Zoltai, Southern Limits of Coniferous Trees on the Canadian Prairies, Information Report NOR-Ex-128, Northern Forest Research Centre (Edmonton: Environment Canada, Forestry Service, 1975).

11. Monrad E. Kjorlien, "A Review of historical information on fire history and vegetation description of Elk Island and the Beaver Hills," paper on file at Elk Island National Park Warden's Office (1977), 1.

12. See Griffiths, *Island Forest Year*, 4–5; Ross Chapman, *The Discoverer's Guide to Elk Island National Park* (Edmonton: Lone Pine, 1991). For a thorough discussion of the historic dimensions of the parkland succession around Elk Island see C.B. Blyth and C.J. Hudson, A Plan for the Management of Vegetation and Ungulates (Environment Canada, Parks. Elk Island National Park, 1991).

13. An attempt to chart the movements of Native peoples across the prairies and out of the Shield country was made by the Manitoba archaeologist Walter M. Hlady in 1961. See "Indian Migrations in Manitoba and the West," Historical and Scientific Society of Manitoba Papers, Series III, nos. 17 and 18 (Winnipeg, 1964), 24–53. Such ideas have been regularly updated by scholars. A review of the literature was provided by Roderick J.

Vickers in Alberta Plains Prehistory: A Review, in Archaeological Survey of Alberta, Occasional Papers no. 27 (Edmonton: Alberta Culture, 1986).

14. Jack Brink, "Dog Days in Southern Alberta, in Archaeological Survey of Alberta, Occasional Papers no. 28 (Edmonton: Alberta Culture, 1986).

15. The Head-Smashed-In UNESCO World Heritage Site near Lethbridge is a famous example, one accessible to visitors.

16. See the general comments made on this subject in Diamond Jenness, *The Indians of Canada*, 5th ed. (Ottawa: National Museum of Canada, 1960), 54 f.

17. Geographic Board of Canada, *Place-Names of Alberta* (Ottawa: 1928), 16; J.G. MacGregor, *The Battle River Valley* (Saskatoon: Western Producer, 1976), 8 f.; John S. Milloy, *The Plains Cree: Trade, Diplomacy and War, 1790 to 1870* (Winnipeg: University of Manitoba Press, 1988); *Fidler's Journal*, 10 March 1793. Bruce Haig, ed., *Journal of a Journey over Land from Buckingham House to the Rocky Mountains in 1792–93* (Lethbridge: Historical Research Centre, 1991), 88–89.

18. See Omer C. Stewart, "Fire as the Great Force Employed by Man," in *Man's Role in Changing the Face of the Earth*, ed. William L. Thomas Jr., vol. 1 (Chicago: University of Chicago Press, 1956), 115–33; and "Why the Great Plains are Treeless," *Colorado Quarterly* II (1953): 40–50.

19. Henry T. Lewis, *A Time for Burning*, Boreal Institute of North America, Occasional Publication no. 17 (Edmonton: University of Alberta, 1982).

20. Albert Tate, "A Winter Buffalo Hunt," *Alberta Historical Review* 6, no. 4 (1958): 25–26.

21. David Thompson in 1798. Cited in Charles D. Bird and Ralph D. Bird, "The Aspen Parkland," in *Alberta: A Natural History*, ed. W.G. Hardy (Edmonton: Hurtig, 1967), 135.

22. Ibid., 136.

23. MacGregor, *The Battle River Valley*, 163.

24. For the Beaver Hills region, see Kjorlien, "A Review of historical information on fire history and vegetation description of Elk Island and the Beaver Hills."

25. Editorial, *Edmonton Bulletin*, 9 May 1895.

Chapter 2

1. Gail Helgason, *The First Albertans: An Archaeological Search* (Edmonton: Lone Pine, 1987), 34–35, 52–59. The Fletcher Site south-east of Lethbridge was the first important Paleo-Indian site confirmed in Alberta, one at which the now extinct Pleistocene bison had been taken by a communal hunting effort. See also John W. Ives, "13,001 Years Ago: Human Beginnings in Alberta," in *Alberta Formed Alberta Transformed*, ed. Michael Payne, Donald Wetherell and Catherine Cavanaugh, vol. 1 (Edmonton/Calgary: University of Alberta, University of Calgary Press, 2006), 1–36; E.C. Pielou, *After the Ice: The Return of Life to Glaciated North America* (Chicago: University of Chicago Press, 1991), 156–60.

2. By the mid-1950s, efforts by the Glenbow Foundation under Douglas Leechman were underway to survey the fragments of prehistory that had accumulated in various rural collections. See H. M. Wormington and Richard G. Forbis, An Introduction to the Archaeology of Alberta, Canada, Denver Museum of Natural History, Proceedings no. 11 (Denver: 1965), 1–4; see also J. Roderick Vickers, Alberta Plains Prehistory: A Review, in Archaeological Survey of Alberta, Occasional Paper no. 27 (Edmonton: Alberta Culture, 1986), 41–44.

3. Wormington and Forbis (1965), *An Introduction*, 150; Ian R. Wilson and Thomas H. Head, Archaeology Inventory, Elk Island National Park, Parks Canada, MR No. 318 (Calgary: Indian and Northern Affairs, 1978), 19; B.O.K. Reeves, Elk Island National Park Management Plan. Cultural Resource, (Calgary: Parks Canada, 1991); Cultural Resources Assessment: Elk Island National Park, Report on File, Archaeological Research Unit (Calgary: Parks Canada, 1994), 35–40.

4. B. Newton et al., Strathcona Site (FjPi-29): Excavations, 1978, 1979 and 1980, Archaeological Survey of Alberta, Manuscript Series, nos. 2, 3 and 4 (Edmonton: Alberta Culture: Historic Resources Division, 1981).

5. Reeves, Elk Island National Park Management Plan and Alison Landals, "The Maple Leaf Site: implications of the analysis of small-scale bison kills," in *Hunters of the Recent Past*, ed. L.B. Davis and B.O.K. Reeves (London: Unwin Hyman, 1990), 122–51.

6. See B.H.C. Gordon, *Of Men and Herds In Canadian Plains Prehistory* (Ottawa: National Museums of Canada, 1979).

7. A discussion of cultural dynamics on the plains may be found in Liz Bryan, *The Buffalo People: Prehistoric Archaeology on the Canadian Plains* (Edmonton: University of Alberta Press, 1991); for the period under discussion, see Chapter 8. See also Thomas Head, "Northern Plains Prehistory: The Late Prehistoric Period as Viewed from the H.M.S. Balzac Site," in David Burley, ed., Contributions to Plains Prehistory. Archaeological Survey of Alberta, Occasional Paper no. 26 (Edmonton: Alberta Culture, 1985), 100–15; Bryan, *The Buffalo People*, 104 f.

8. See B.O.K Reeves, Culture Change in the Northern Plains, 1,000 B.C.– A.D. 1000. Archaeological Survey of Alberta, Occasional Paper no. 20 (Edmonton: Alberta Culture, 1983) and E. Leigh Syms, "The Co-influence Sphere Model: A New Paradigm for Plains Developments and Plains- Parkland-Woodland Processural Interrelationships," in Directions in Manitoba Prehistory; Papers in Honour of Chris Vickers, ed. Leo Pettipas (Winnipeg: Association of Manitoba Archaeologists and Manitoba Archaeological Society, 1980), 111–40

9. Reeves, Elk Island National Park Management Plan, 10 f.

10. Mildred Stefiszyn, ed., *Land Among the Lakes: A History of the Deville and North Cooking Lake Area* (Edmonton: Deville-North Cooking Lake Historical Society, 1983), 11, 263; Edo Nyland, "This Dying Watershed," Alberta- Forests-Parks-Wildlife 12:3 (1969), 23.

11. Wilson and Head, Archaeology Inventory, Elk Island National Park, 79, 141, 147. For reviews of work undertaken at Elk Island after 1978 see Reeves, Elk Island National Park Management Plan and Cultural Resources.

12. Wilson and Head, Archaeology Inventory, Elk Island National Park, 78–82.

13. Reeves, Elk Island National Park Management Plan, 11. While Avonlea sites have been previously associated with the southern Canadian plains, subsequent work in Saskatchewan has identified an increasing presence of Avonlea peoples in the Aspen Parkland belt. See Olga Klimko, "New Perspectives on Avonlea: A View from the Saskatchewan Forest," in Burley, *Contributions to Plains Prehistory*, 64–81.

14. See David Mendelbaum, *The Plains Cree: An Ethnographic, Historical and Comparative Study* (Regina: Canadian Plains Research Center, 1979), 13 (Map); see also the maps in Arthur J. Ray, *The Indians and the Fur Trade* (Toronto: University of Toronto Press, 1974).

15. The character of these changes is the subject of J.S. Milloy's study, *The Plains Cree: Trade War and Diplomacy, 1790–1870* (Winnipeg: University of Manitoba Press, 1990); see also Dale Russell, *The Eighteenth Century Western Cree and Their Neighbours* (Ottawa: National Museum of Civilization, 1991).

16. Mendelbaum, *The Plains Cree*; Milloy (1990).

17. See Alison Landals, "Horse Heaven: Change in Precontact to Contact Period Landscape Use in Southern Alberta," in *Archaeology on the Edge: New Perspectives from the Northern Plains*, ed. Brian Kooyman and Jane Kelley (Calgary: University of Calgary Press, 2004).

18. F.G. Roe, *The Indian and the Horse* (Norman: University of Oklahoma Press, 1955), 24–26; John C. Ewers, *The Horse in Blackfoot Indian Culture* (Washington, DC: Smithsonian Institution, 1955), 7–19.

19. See Trevor J. Peck and J. Rod Vickers, "Buffalo and Dogs: The Prehistoric Lifeways of Aboriginal People on the Alberta Plains, 1004–1005," in Payne, Wetherell and Cavanaugh, *Alberta Formed Alberta Transformed*, 55–86.

20. University of Victoria Archives, Frank Gilbert Roe Fonds, 04/02/66a, "The Indian Trail in Myth and History"; see also Roe, *The Indian and the Horse*, 299–306

21. L.J. Burpee, ed., *The Journals of La Vérendrye* (Toronto: The Champlain Society, 1927), 319; Journal of July 20, 1738 to May, 1739, 290 Larry J. Zimmerman, *Peoples of Prehistoric South Dakota* (Lincoln: University of Nebraska Press, 1985), chs. 10–14; Milloy, (1990), Map 1.

22. Tracey Harrison, *Place Names of Alberta, Central Alberta* (Calgary: University of Calgary Press, 1994), 179; Milloy (1990); J.C. Ewers, *The Blackfoot People* (Washington: United States Department of the Interior, 1944), 9–21

23. There are many references to the friction occasioned by these adjustments in the Fort Edmonton Journals of the Hudson's Bay Company between 1856 and 1864. See HBCA, B/60/A/29B and B60/a/31, Reel IM50. A few journal dates of particular interest: June 26, 1857; July 6, 1857; Sept. 2, 1857; Sept. 25–6, 1860. Feb. 9, 1861; Sept. 8–12, 1861; June 26, 1862; March 6, 1862; Dec. 7–10, 1862; Sept. 29, 1863; Oct. 2, 1863.

24. David Mendelbaum, *The Plains Cree: An Ethnographic, Historical and Comparative Study* (Regina: Canadian Plains Research Center, 1979), 11.

Chapter 3

1. See Alison Landals, "Horse Heaven: Change in Precontact to Contact Period Landscape Use in Southern Alberta," in *Archaeology on the Edge: New Perspectives from the Northern Plains*, ed. Brian Kooyman and Jane Kelley (Calgary: University of Calgary Press, 2004), 231–62.

2. Fur trade history became something of a growth industry in the 1970s, responding to some of the more general interpretations that had been established by an earlier generation of scholars such as Harold Innis and A.S. Morton. The main reinterpretation for the Canadian context was Arthur J. Ray's *Indians and the Fur Trade* (Toronto: University of Toronto Press, 1974), which examined the trade to assess more thoroughly the economic and cultural interest of Native peoples.

3. See W.J. Eccles, "La Mer de l'Ouest: Outpost of Empire," in *Aspects of the Fur Trade: Papers of the First Fur Trade Conference* (St. Paul: Minnesota Historical Society, 1967), 1–14.

4. L.J. Burpee, ed., *Journals and Letters of Pierre Gaultier de Varennes de La Vérendrye and His Sons* (Toronto: Champlain Society, 1927), 446–48, 483–88; Alexander Henry, *Travels and Adventures In Canada and the Indian Territories*, ed. James Bain (Edmonton: M.G. Hurtig, 1969), 255.

5. A.S. Morton, *A History of the Canadian West to 1870–71*, rev. ed. (Toronto: University of Toronto Press, 1973), 11–13, 237–79, 300–304; James G. MacGregor, *Blankets and Beads: A History of the Saskatchewan River* (Edmonton: Institute of Applied Arts Ltd., 1949), 70–71. An important critical addition to the literature on Henday is Barbara Belyea, ed., *A Year Inland: The Journal of a Hudson's Bay Company Winterer* (Waterloo: Wilfrid Laurier Press, 2000).

6. See James Parker, *Emporium of the North: Fort Chipewyan and the Fur Trade to 1835* (Edmonton: Alberta Culture and Multiculturalism/Canadian Plains Research Center, 1987). On Pond's extension of the fur trade into Athabasca and the violence associated with his name, see H. I. Innis, *Peter Pond: Fur Trader and Adventurer* (Toronto: Irwin and Gordon, 1930), ch. 4; Henry R. Wagner, *Peter Pond: Fur Trader and Explorer* (New Haven: Yale University Press, 1955), 10–15; W. Stewart Wallace, "Was Peter Pond a Murderer?" in *The Pedlars from Quebec* (Toronto: Ryerson Press, 1954), 19–26. On Pink, see Morton, *A History of the Canadian West to 1870–71*, 275–85; Dale Russell, The Eighteenth Century Western Cree and their Neighbours, Archaeological

Survey of Canada, Mercury Series Report 143 (Ottawa: Canadian Museum of Civilization, 1991), 97–98, 101–102. On buffalo pounds see Frank G. Roe, *The North American Buffalo: A Critical Study of the Species in its Wild State*, 2nd ed. (Toronto: University of Toronto Press, 1970), Appendix AA.

7. Cocking's account of his travels was eventually published, and is one of the important documentary references for the later eighteenth-century history of the plains. See L. J. Burpee, ed., "Matthew Cocking's Journal," Proceedings and Transactions of the Royal Society of Canada, 3rd series, vol. II, pt. 2 (Ottawa: 1908), 91–121; but see also Russell, The Eighteenth Century Western Cree and their Neighbours, 106–107.

8. Burpee, "Matthew Cocking's Journal," 92. An important bearer of this message was William Tomison, the long-serving veteran of the HBC based at York Factory. See John Nix, "William Tomison," in *Dictionary of Canadian Biography*, vol. 6 (Toronto: University of Toronto Press, 1987); and J.B. Tyrrell, ed., *The Journals of Hearne and Turnor* (Toronto: Champlain Society, 1934), Appendix A.

9. J.B. Tyrrell, ed., *David Thompson's Narrative of his Explorations in Western America, 1784–1812* (Toronto: Champlain Society, 1916), 318–20; Morton, *A History of the Canadian West to 1870–71*, 319–31.

10. E. Rich, ed., *Cumberland House Journals and Inland Journals, 1775–82*, Second Series, 1779–82, "Introduction" by Richard Glover (London: Hudson's Bay Record Society, 1952), 225 f.

11. Ibid., 181, Feb. 27, 1781; Frank Gilbert Roe, *The Indian and the Horse* (Norman: University of Oklahoma Press, 1955), 31.

12. Morton, *A History of the Canadian West to 1870–71*, 331–33.

13. J.G. MacGregor, *The Battle River Valley* (Saskatoon: Western Producer Prairie Books, 1976), 18; Tyrrell, *David Thompson's Narrative of his Explorations in Western America, 1784–1812*, 328.

14. Fidler, quoted in Peter T. Ream, *The Fort on the Saskatchewan*, 2nd ed. (Fort Saskatchewan: Metropolitan Printing, 1974), 12; see also John Nix, "William Tomison," *Dictionary of Canadian Biography*, vol. 6 (Toronto: University of Toronto Press, 1987); Roe, *The Indian and the Horse*, 31. J.G. MacGregor, *Edmonton: A History* (Edmonton: M.G. Hurtig, 1969), 23.

15. See Ream, *The Fort on the Saskatchewan*, 13–15; see also Duncan McGillivray, Journal, Dec. 11, 1894, in A.S. Morton, ed. (Toronto: Champlain Society, 1929), 49.

16. Ibid. Entry for Feb. 22, 1795

17. Cited in Ream, *The Fort on the Saskatchewan*, 15–16; MacGregor, *Edmonton: A History*, 23.

18. Bruce Haig, ed., Peter Fidler, *Journal of a Journey Overland from Buckingham House to the Rocky Mountains in 1792–3* (Lethbridge: HRC, 1991), 61.

19. Ibid., 74. Entry for Feb. 12, 1793.

20. Entry for May 2, 1797. Alice M. Johnson, ed., *Saskatchewan Journals and Correspondence, 1795–1802* (London: Hudson's Bay Record Society, 1967), 92.

21. Ibid., 24, 160; see also Barry M. Gough, ed., *The Journals of Alexander Henry the Younger: 1799–1814*, vol. 2 (Toronto: Champlain Society, 1992), 546.

22. Ibid., Henry's journal, July 8, 1810 and July 15, 1810.

23. Jack Brink, Dog Days in Southern Alberta, Archaeological Survey of Alberta, Occasional Papers no. 28 (Edmonton: Alberta Culture, 1986), 4–13; Ray, *Indians and the Fur Trade*, 22.

24. This thesis is argued in John S. Milloy, *The Plains Cree: Trade, Diplomacy and War, 1790 to 1870* (Winnipeg: University of Manitoba Press, 1988). Russell takes a somewhat different view of the reasons and timing for the arrival of Cree peoples on the plains, but his view of essentially peaceful relations between the Cree and Blackfoot up until at least 1800 parallels that of Milloy. See Russell, *The Eighteenth Century Cree*, 108–109.

25. Robert Scace, Elk Island: A Cultural History, Manuscript History Report (Ottawa: Parks Canada, 1977), 18–20, and H.J. Moberly, *When Fur Was King* (London: J.M Dent, 1929), 67–68.

26. See Peter Walker, "The Origins, Organization and Role of the Bison Hunt in the Red River Valley," *Manitoba Archaeological Quarterly* 6, no. 3 (1982): 62–68.

27. See J.G. MacGregor, *John Rowan: Czar of the Prairies* (Saskatoon: Western Producer Prairie Books, 1978), ch. 10.

28. See Frits Pannekoek, "The Rev. James Evans and the Social Antagonisms of the Fur Trade Society, 1840–1846," in *Religion and Society in the Prairie*

West, ed. Richard Allen (Regina: Canadian Plains Research Center, 1974), 3–6.

29. Hugh A. Dempsey, ed., *The Rundle Journals: 1840–1848*, Alberta Records Publication Board (Calgary: Historical Society of Alberta and Glenbow Alberta Institute, 1979), xxiv, 50, 316.

30. Ibid., 49. Entry for Jan. 14, 1841.

31. Ibid., 48–49.

32. Ibid., 49. Entry for Jan. 16, 1841.

33. Ibid., 50. Entry for Jan. 17, 1841.

34. Ibid., 118. Entries for Aug. 18 and 20, 1842.

35. Ibid., 50. Entry for Aug. 29, 1842.

36. Ibid., 151. Entry for Feb. 22, 1844.

37. See H.H. Lamb, *Climate, History and the Modern World* (London: Methuen, 1982), chs. 10–12.

38. Dempsey, *The Rundle Journals*, 49. Entry for Jan. 14, 1841. See also Timothy S. Ball, "'As Cold as I ever Knew It': Joseph Colon's Observations at York Factory," *Transactions, Manitoba Historical and Scientific Society* (1976–77), 61–66.

39. Dempsey, *The Rundle Journals*, 125. Entry for Apr. 27, 1843.

40. J.G. MacGregor, *Father Lacombe* (Edmonton: Hurtig, 1975), 34.

41. Fr. Alexis Tetreault, "Historic St. Albert," The Pioneer West, no. 3, Reprints from the *Alberta Historical Review*, 9; MacGregor, *Father Lacombe*, 28–31.

42. Michael R.A. Forsman, The Archaeology of Victoria Post, 1864–1897, Archaeological Survey of Alberta, Manuscript Series, no. 6 (Edmonton: Alberta Culture, Historical Resources Division, 1982.) 10; see also Leslie J. Hurt, The Victoria Settlement, 1862–1922, Occasional Paper no. 7, Historic Sites Service (Edmonton: Alberta Culture, 1979), 4.

43. Peter Erasmus, *Buffalo Days and Nights*, ed. Irene Spry (Calgary: Glenbow Alberta Institute, 1976), 35.

44. Hector's Journal, Mar. 16, 1858, in Irene Spry, ed., *The Palliser Papers* (Toronto: Champlain Society, 1968), 223.

45. See Frits Pannekoek, "On the Edge of the Great Transformation," in *Alberta Formed Alberta Transformed*, ed. Michael Payne, Donald Wetherell

and Catherine Cavanaugh, Edmonton/Calgary: University of Alberta, University of Calgary Press. 2006), 181–208. See also *Report From the Select Committee on the Hudson's Bay Company* (London: British Parliamentary Papers, 1857), and Chester Martin, *Dominion Lands Policy*, ed. Lewis H. Thomas (Toronto: McClelland and Stewart, 1973), 3–6.

46. Spry, *Palliser Papers*, 88–90, and Hector's Journal, Feb. 25, 1858, 22.

47. Ibid., 220–21.

48. Ibid., 221.

49. See Ray, *Indians and the Fur Trade*, 185–86.

50. Hugh Dempsey, *Big Bear: The End of Freedom* (Vancouver: Greystone Books, 1984), 28, and Dempsey, "Maskepetoon," in *Dictionary of Canadian Biography*, vol. 9 (1976), 537–38; The Victoria Settlement as it was called (now Pakan), was active until 1871 when it was relocated to Edmonton, although the HBC post operated sporadically until 1898. See R.G. Ironside and E. Tomasky, "Development of Victoria Settlement," *Alberta Historical Review* 19, no. 2 (1971): 20–30; Hurt, *The Victoria Settlement*, and Forsman, *The Archaeology of Victoria Post*, 1–5

51. John Maclean, *Vanguards of Canada* (Toronto: The Missionary Society of the Methodist Church, 1918), 202; James E. Nix, "John Chantler McDougall," *Dictionary of Canadian Biography*, vol. 14 (Toronto: University of Toronto Press, 1998), 695.

52. Dempsey, "Maskepetoon," 28.

53. Grace A. Phillips, ed., *Tales of Tofield* (Leduc: Tofield Historical Society, 1969), 20–21.

54. Henry Thompson, Letter to the *Tofield Mercury*, Jan. 23, 1958. The letter is reproduced in Phillips, *Tales of Tofield*, 29; see also "Old Timer," "War at Beaver Hills," *Edmonton Journal*, Aug. 10, 1957. (The author is undoubtedly Thompson.)

55. HBC, B60/a/31, Apr. 2, 1861. Cited in J.G. MacGregor, *Senator Hardisty's Prairies, 1840/1889* (Saskatoon: Western Producer Prairie Books, 1979), 37; see also the citation from John Sellar's Journal, quoted in Thomas McMicking, *Overland From Canada to British Columbia*, ed. Joanne Leduc (Vancouver: University of British Columbia Press, 1981), 98–99, n. 47.

56. Viscount Milton and Dr. Cheadle, *The North-West Passage by Land*, 8th ed. (London: 1875), 169–72.

57. Frank L. Farley, "Changes in the Status of Certain Animals and Birds During the Past Fifty Years in Central Alberta," *Canadian Field Naturalist* 39 (Dec. 1925), 200–202.

58. Ibid., 178; on fires on the prairies in the fur trade period, see Greg Thomas, "Fire and the Fur Trade: The Saskatchewan District, 1790–1840," *The Beaver* 308, no. 2 (1977), 32–39.

59. See Johnson, *Saskatchewan Journals*, xxxi; J.G. MacGregor, *Edmonton: A History* (Edmonton: M.G. Hurtig, 1967), 19; John Nix, "William Tomison," *Dictionary of Canadian Biography*, vol. 6 (Toronto: University of Toronto Press, 1987); Brock Silversides, *Fort de Prairies: The Story of Fort Edmonton* (Victoria: Heritage House, 2005), 2–3.

60. George Simpson, "Character Book" 2nd Class, Entry no. 4, in Glyndwr Williams, ed., *Hudson's Bay Miscellany, 1670–1870* (Winnipeg: Hudson's Bay Record Society, 1975), 188.

61. Ibid., 188, n. 3.

62. See Jennifer S.H. Brown, *Strangers in Blood: Fur Trade Families in Indian Country* (Vancouver: University of British Columbia Press, 1980), 140–41; and Sylvia Van Kirk, *Many Tender Ties: Women in Fur Trade Society, 1670–1870* (Winnipeg: Watson and Dwyer, 1980), 189–90.

63. "Two versions of origins of cemetery," *Tofield Mercury*, Jan. 10, 1963. On the St. James the Apostle, Newton-Logan Cemetery and its modern restoration, see Tofield Public Library, Logan Cemetery Restoration Project Binder and www.tofieldalberta.ca/logancem.htm. St. James the Apostle-Newton-Logan. The cemetery is located in Sec. 31, Twp. 51, Range 18, West of the 4th. In 1896 it was consecrated by the Anglican Church as St. James the Apostle-Newton-Logan. On burials see ibid., Transcript of the Funeral Register, 1896–1936.

64. Etat Trebla [Albert Tate] Letter to the *Tofield Standard*, Nov. 5, 1907. Reproduced in Phillips, *Tales of Tofield*, 29–31. Albert Tate was the son of Chief Factor Philip Tate, of Victoria Post.

65. Earl of Southesk, *Saskatchewan and the Rocky Mountains* (Edinburgh: Edmonston and Douglas, 1875), 140–41.

66. Phillips, *Tales of Tofield*, 10, 278.

67. Canada, Department of the Interior, *Lands and Forest Survey Map, Edmonton District* (Ottawa: 1894).

68. Phillips, *Tales of Tofield*, 133.

69. A large literature now exists on the origins and dispersal of the Métis on the prairies. See Jacqueline Peterson and Jennifer S.H. Brown, eds., *The New Peoples: Being and Becoming Métis in North America* (Winnipeg: University of Manitoba Press, 1985); Joe Sawchuk, et al., *Métis Land Rights in Alberta: A Political History* (Edmonton: Métis Association of Alberta, 1981), ch. 1; Gerhard Ens, *Homeland to Hinterland: The Changing Worlds of the Red River Métis in the Nineteenth Century* (Toronto: University of Toronto Press, 1996).

70. Walker, "The Origins, Organization and Role of the Bison Hunt in the Red River Valley," 62–68; Joanne Pelletier, *The Buffalo Hunt* (Regina: Gabriel Dumont Institute of Native Studies, 1985).

71. Milton and Cheadle, *The Northwest Passage*, 180.

72. Gerhard Ens, "Dispossession or Adaptation? Migration and Persistence of the Red River Métis, 1835–1890" (paper presented at the Canadian Historical Association Annual Meeting, Windsor, 1988), 17.

73. Ens, *Homeland to Hinterland*.

Chapter 4

1. Douglas MacKay, *The Honourable Company* (Toronto: Musson Book Co. 1938), 296–97; W.L. Morton, *The Critical Years: The Union of British North America, 1857–1873* (Toronto: McClelland and Stewart, 1964), 237–40.

2. See Elizabeth A. Fenn, *Pox Americana: The Great Smallpox Epidemic of 1775–82* (New York: Farrar, Straus and Giroux, 2001), ch. 6; Arthur J. Ray, "Diffusion of Diseases in the Western Interior of Canada: 1830–1850," in *People, Places, Patterns, Processes: Geographical Perspectives on the Canadian Past*, ed. Graeme Wynn (Toronto: Copp Clark Pitman Ltd., 1990), 68–87; John S. Milloy, *The Plains Cree: Trade, Diplomacy and War, 1790–1870* (Winnipeg: University of Manitoba Press, 1988), 116; J.G. MacGregor, *Senator Hardisty's Prairies, 1840–1889* (Saskatoon: Western Producer Prairie Books, 1978), ch. 6.

3. Grace A. Phillips, ed., *Tales of Tofield* (Leduc: Tofield Historical Society, 1969), 67.

4. Bobtail and Sampson, Chiefs of Cree bands, were both sons of Louis Piché, the Métis fur trader connected to Fort Edmonton, notable for his appeal to the Roman Catholic Church in St. Boniface, requesting priests be sent to the upper Saskatchewan. See Fr. P.-E. Breton, O.M.I. and E.O. Drouin, O.M.I., *Hobbema: Ongoing Mission of Central Alberta* (Cardston: 1968), 5–6. And see David Lupul, "The Bobtail Land Surrender," *Alberta Historical Review* 26, no. 1 (1978): 29–39.

5. Phillips, *Tales of Tofield*, 7.

6. George McDougall, *In the Days of the Red River Rebellion* (Toronto: William Briggs, 1903), 116; Hugh Dempsey, *Big Bear: The End of Freedom* (Vancouver: Greystone Books, 1984), 39–40.

7. Robert Scace, Elk Island National Park: A Cultural History, draft manuscript history (Calgary: Parks Canada, 1975), 14–15; Dempsey, *Big Bear: The End of Freedom*, 57–59, 106–108; Milloy, *The Plains Cree*, 71, 116.

8. See Walter Hildebrandt and Brian Hubner, *The Cypress Hills: The Land and Its People* (Saskatoon: Purich, 1994), 35 f.

9. See Paul Sharpe, *Whoop Up Country* (Helena: Montana Historical Society, 1960) and J.G. Nelson, *The Last Refuge* (Montreal: Harvest House, 1973), ch. 10.

10. The earlier relationships of the Blackfoot with the American Missouri fur trade have been well discussed in David Smyth, "The Struggle for the Piegan Trade: The Saskatchewan Versus the Missouri," *Montana: The Magazine of Western History*, 34, no. 2 (1984): 2–15.

11. Joseph F. Dion, *My Tribe The Crees* (Calgary: Glenbow Alberta Institute, 1979), 69–70. See the comments of David Thompson in J.B. Tyrrell, ed., *David Thompson's Narrative of his Explorations in Western America, 1784–1812* (Toronto: Champlain Society, 1916), 125; see also Willie Traill to Catherine Parr Traill, May 28, 1879, in K. Douglas Munro, ed., *Fur Trade Letters of Willie Traill, 1864–1894* (Edmonton: University of Alberta Press, 2006), 163; and Moberly (1929), 113–14.

12. Dion, *My Tribe The Crees*, 70–71.

13. Ibid., 72–73.

14. Ibid., 73–75.

15. See John Foster, "The Métis and the End of Plains Buffalo in Alberta," *Alberta* 3, no. 1 (1992): 61–77; Willie Traill to Catherine Parr Traill, Aug. 3, 1879, in Munro, *Fur Trade Letters of Willie Traill*, 162.

16. See Philip Goldring, "The Cypress Hills Massacre–A Century's Retrospect," *Saskatchewan History*, 26 no. 3 (1973): 89–120, and Philip Goldring, Whisky, Horses and Death: The Cypress Hills Massacre and its Sequel, Occasional Papers in Archaeology and History, no. 21 (Ottawa: National Historic Site Service, 1973). For detailed field reports for the actions of the NWMP in its early years see North West Mounted Police, Commissioners, *Opening Up the West: 1874–1881*, introduction by W.L. Higgitt (Toronto: Coles, 1973).

17. Peter T. Ream, *The Fort on the Saskatchewan*, 2nd ed. (N.P. 1974), ch. 2, and Russell W. Hanson, "The Mounted Police Patrolled Early Settlements," in Kingman Silver Club, *Harvest of Memories: History of Kingman and Districts* (Edmonton: D. Friesen, 1981), 6.

18. For the original text see Canada, *Indian Treaties and Surrenders* (Ottawa: Queen's Printer, 1891), vols. 2, 35. On Treaty 6, see Arthur J. Ray, Jim Miller, and Frank Tough, *Bounty and Benevolence: A History of Saskatchewan Treaties* (Montreal: McGill-Queens, 2000).

19. Peter Erasmus, *Buffalo Days and Nights*, ed. Irene Spry (Calgary: Glenbow Alberta Institute, 1976), ch. 14; David Lupul, "The Bobtail Land Surrender," *Alberta History*, 26 no. 1 (1978): 29; for the original text, see Canada, *Indian Treaties and Surrenders*, vol. 2, 45–46; Verne Dusenberry, *The Montana Cree: A Study in Religious Persistence* (Norman: University of Oklahoma Press, 1998), 28 f; Gary Botting, *Chief Smallboy* (Calgary: Fifth House, 2005), ch. 3.

20. Dempsey, *Big Bear: The End of Freedom*, 30–31, 160–61; G.F.G. Stanley, *The Birth of Western Canada: A History of the Riel Rebellions* (Toronto: University of Toronto Press, 1961), 343–45.

21. Canada, *Indian Treaties and Surrenders*, vol. 2, 44–45.

22. Robert Todd, "Supreme Court rejects massive land claim," http://www.lawtimes-news.com; "Court rejects Edmonton land claim," http://www.thestar.com/News/Canada/article/409844. Also see Botting, *Chief Smallboy*, 128–35.

23. See Dwayne Trevor Donald, "Edmonton Pentimento: Re-Reading History in the Case of the Papaschase Cree," *Journal of the Canadian Association for Curriculum Studies* 2, no. 1 (Spring 2004): 40–43; "A City Called Home – Memories. Interview with Fran Gosche. Papaschase and Metis History in Edmonton." http://www.epl.ca/edmontonacitycalledhome.

24. Erasmus, *Buffalo Days and Nights*, 269–70.

25. Dempsey, *Big Bear: The End of Freedom*, 71, 106 f.

26. Gerhard Ens, *Homeland to Hinterland: The Changing Worlds of the Red River Métis in the Nineteenth Century* (Toronto: University of Toronto Press, 1996); Stanley, *The Birth of Western Canada*, 13, 179–88; Diane Payment, *The Free People–Les Gens Libres: A History of the Métis Community of Batoche, Saskatchewan*, 2nd ed. (Calgary: University of Calgary Press, 2008); T.C. Pocklington, *The Government and Politics of the Alberta Métis Settlements* (Regina: Canadian Plains Research Center, 1991), 3; Stuart Baldwin, "Wintering Villages of the Hivernants: Documentary and Archaeological Evidence," in *The Métis and the Land In Alberta: Land Claims Research Project, 1979–80* (Edmonton: Métis Association of Alberta, 1980).

27. D.W. Moodie, "Alberta Settlement Surveys," *Alberta History* 12, no. 4 (1964): 1–7. An interview conducted at Tofield in 1933 with Pascal Dumont, a son of François, recounted details of the family history. See also J.R.S Hambly, ed., *The Battle River Country: An Historical Sketch of Duhamel and District* (Calgary: Duhamel Historical Society, D. Friesen, 1974), 11–12.

28. Ibid., 12; J.G. MacGregor, *The Battle River Valley* (Saskatoon: Western Producer Prairie Books, 1976), 60; and Barry M. Gough, ed., *The Journals of Alexander Henry the Younger 1799–1814* (Toronto: Champlain Society, 1992), V. 2, 456.

29. Elizabeth M. McCrum, ed., Letters of Louisa McDougall, 1878–1887. Provincial Archives of Alberta. Occasional Papers No. 1 (Edmonton: Alberta Culture, 1978), 85, n. 68.

30. MacGregor, *The Battle River Valley*, 60; Moodie, "Alberta Land Surveys," 3; Alberta Culture, Historic Sites, Heritage Resource Inventory of the Cooking Lake Study Area (Jan. 1976), in AEPD, vol. 5, appendix 10, 2.

31. Phillips, *Tales of Tofield*, 22.

32. Erasmus, *Buffalo Days and Nights*, 201–209, 223.

33. A. Whitford to R. Douglas, Secretary of the Geographic Board of Canada. May 8, 1916. Cited in Tracey Harrison, *Place Names of Alberta, Vol. III. Central Alberta* (Calgary: University of Calgary Press, 1994), 266.

34. Phillips, *Tales of Tofield*, 21.

35. Erasmus, *Buffalo Days and Nights*, 201.

36. See Fr. P.-E. Breton, O.M.I. and E.O. Drouin, O.M.I., *Hobbema: Ongoing Mission of Central Alberta* (Cardston: 1968), 5–6; and 'Rapport...de la Propagation de la Foi' (Quebec, Jan.1942, no. 4), 14–17; Botting, Chief Smallboy, 29.

37. Erasmus, *Buffalo Days and Nights*, 275; *Edmonton Bulletin*, Apr. 18, 1885.

38. J.G. MacGregor, *Edmonton Trader* (Toronto: McClelland and Stewart, 1963), 163; F.C. Jamieson, ed., *The Alberta Field Force of 1885*, Canadian North-West Historical Society Publications vol. 1, no. 7 (Battleford: 1931); Kingman Silver Club, *Harvest of Memories: A History of Kingman and District* (Edmonton: D. Friesen, 1981), 8–9.

39. Henry G. Tyrrell, "Down the Battle River," *Alberta History* 29, no. 3 (1981): 27.

40. Howard and Tamara Palmer, *Alberta: A New History* (Edmonton: Hurtig, 1990), 44–45.

41. See D.W. Moodie, "The St. Albert Settlement: A Study in Historical Geography" (M.A. thesis, University of Alberta, 1965). For a discussion of scrip as a term, see Joe Sawchuk et al. *Métis Land Rights in Alberta: A Political History* (Edmonton; Métis Association of Alberta, 1981), ch. 4, and Donald Purich, *The Métis* (Toronto: James Lorimer, 1988), ch. 5.

42. Edo Nyland, "This Dying Watershed," Alberta Lands Parks Wildlife 12, no. 3 (1969): 24.

43. J.B. Tyrrell, Report on a Part of Alberta and Portions of Adjacent Districts of Assiniboia and Saskatchewan, Part E, Annual Report, 1886 (Montreal: Dawson Bros., 1887), 38 E.

44. Linda Redekop and Wilfred Gilchrist, *Strathcona County: A Brief History* (Edmonton: University of Alberta Printing Services, 1981), 23.

45. Moodie, "Alberta Settlement Surveys," 1–7; MacGregor, *Edmonton Trader*, 167–70; R.G. Ironside and E. Tomasky, "Development of Victoria Settlement," *Alberta Historical Review* 19, no. 2 (1971): 20–30; John Grigsby Geiger,

"River Lot Three: Settlement Life on the North Saskatchewan," *Alberta History* (Winter 1996): 15–25.

46. Lupul, "The Bobtail Land Surrender," 29.

47. The last vestiges of British hereditary privilege were put to rest between 1919 and 1931. See G.F.G. Stanley, *A Short History of the Canadian Constitution* (Toronto: Ryerson Press, 1969), 37–38, 195–96, 202.

48. On the Hudson's Bay Company's early years as a land agent in the new Dominion, see Duane C. Tway, "The Influence of the Hudson's Bay Company upon Canada, 1870–1879" (Ph.D. dissertation, University of California, 1963).

49. A.S. Morton, *A History of the Canadian West to 1870–71*, 2nd ed. (Toronto: University of Toronto Press, 1973), 814–17; Stanley, The Birth of Western Canada, ch. 3; James B. Hedges, *Building the Canadian West: The Land and Colonization Policies of the Canadian Pacific Railway* (New York: Macmillan, 1939); Alan Wilson, "Introduction" in *The Letters of Charles James Bridges, 1879–1882*, ed. H. Bowsfield (Winnipeg: Hudson's Bay Record Society, 1977), xi–xvii. For a review of the conditions for homestead filing in the West after 1870 see Martin, *Dominion Lands Policy* (Toronto: McClelland and Stewart, 1973), ch. 9.

50. Redekop and Gilchrist, *Strathcona County: A Brief History*, 8.

51. "Clover Bar to Celebrate Golden Jubilee," *Edmonton Journal*, Aug. 1, 1931; John F. Gilpin, "The Edmonton and District Settlers' Rights Movement," in *Swords and Ploughshares: War and Agriculture in Western Canada*, ed. R.C. MacLeod (Edmonton: University of Alberta Press, 1993), 149–72.

52. Ragna Steen and Magda Hendrickson, *Pioneer Days in Bardo* (Tofield: Historical Society of Beaver Hills Lake, 1944), 21; Brydges to William Armit, Sept. 19, 1887, in *The Letters of Charles John Brydges, 1883–1889*, ed. Hartwell Bowsfield (Winnipeg: Hudson's Bay Record Society, 1981), 287

53. See Hugh Dempsey, "The Calgary-Edmonton Trail," *Alberta Historical Review 7*, no. 4 (1959): 16–21.

54. Josephburg Historical Committee, *South of the North Saskatchewan* (Fort Saskatchewan: 1984), 11.

55. Ibid., 6–12.

56. Scace, Elk Island National Park: A Cultural History, 68.

57. *Edmonton Bulletin*, Nov. 2, 1893. Cited in Ream, *The Fort on the Saskatchewan*, 155.

58. On the early families around Josephburg, see Mrs. Albert Mohr, "The great pioneers who cleared and broke the virgin land of Josephburg" (typescript in possession of Josephburg Historical Committee, c. 1967).

59. W.S. Waddell, "Frank Oliver and the Bulletin," *Alberta Historical Review* 5, no. 3 (1957): 8; and W.S. Waddell, "The Honourable Frank Oliver" (M.A. thesis, University of Alberta, 1950), chs. 6 and 7.

60. The story is told by W.C. Pollard, the son of one of the early Parry Sounders. See W.C. Pollard, *Pioneering in the Prairie West* (Toronto: Thomas Nelson, 1926), chs. 5 and 6. See also R. Douglas Francis, "Establishment of the Parry Sound Colony," *Alberta History* 29, no. 1 (1981): 23–30.

61. Lawrence M. Rye, "Reminiscences of a Parry Sound Colonist," *Alberta Historical Review* 10, no. 4 (1962): 19.

62. Pollard, *Pioneering in the Prairie West*, 50–52.

63. Ibid., 51.

64. Canada, Department of Interior, Departmental Order, June 5, 1899.

65. Steen and Hendrickson, *Pioneer Days in Bardo*, 15; Hay Lakes History Book Committee, *Each Step Left Its Mark: A History of Hay Lakes and Surrounding Area* (Edmonton: D. Friesen, 1982), 18–36; Elvira Backstrom, "Pioneer Parents," *Alberta Historical Review* 9, no. 4 (1964): 10–21; Phillips, *Tales of Tofield*, 69–70; Kingman Silver Club, *Harvest of Memories: History of Kingman and Districts* (Edmonton: D. Friesen, 1981), 89 f; Ryley Ladies Auxiliary, Royal Canadian Legion Book Committee, *Beaver Tales: A History of Ryley and District* (Calgary: D. Friesen, 1978), 94–96.

66. Steen and Hendrickson, *Pioneer Days in Bardo*, 23.

67. Ibid., 228.

68. William C. Wonders, "Scandinavian Settlement in Central Alberta," in *The New Provinces: Alberta and Saskatchewan, 1905–1980*, ed. Howard Palmer and Donald Smith, B.C. Geographical Series, no. 30 (Vancouver: Tantalus Research Ltd., 1980), 131–71. On the traits of culture introduced by the Norwegians in central Alberta, see Jan H. Brunvand, Norwegian Settlers in Alberta, Mercury Series, Canadian Centre for Folk Culture Studies, Paper no. 9 (Ottawa: National Museums of Canada, 1974).

69. See David R. Miller, introduction to *Isaac Cowie, The Company of Adventurers* (Lincoln: University of Nebraska Press, 1993), 13 f.

70. Isaac Cowie, *The Agricultural and Mineral Resources of the Edmonton Country, Alberta, Canada* (Edmonton: 1897; Rev. 1901); and Isaac Cowie, *The Grain, Grass and Gold Fields of South-Western Canada* (Edmonton: 1897).

71. Cowie, *The Agricultural and Mineral Resources of the Edmonton Country*, 6 f.

72. For a review of the process see Orest T. Martynowych, The Ukrainian Bloc Settlement in East Central Alberta, 1890–1930: A History, Historic Sites Service, Occasional Paper no. 10 (Edmonton: Alberta Culture, 1985); a more popular treatment is found in J.G. MacGregor, *Vilni Zemli (Free Lands): The Ukrainian Settlement of Alberta* (Toronto: McClelland and Stewart, 1969).

73. MacGregor, *Vilni Zemli*, 11.

74. Ibid., 21–23, 39.

75. *Polish Settlers in Alberta* (Toronto: Drukiem Polish Alliance Press, 1979), 270–72; Joanna Metejlo, "The Polish Experience in Alberta," in *Peoples of Alberta*, eds. Howard and Tamara Palmer (Saskatoon: Western Producer Books, 1985), 279–80.

76. The history of the Mennonites is illustrative of periodic group peregrinations in search of a suitable prince. See Cornelius J. Dyck, ed., *An Introduction to Mennonite History* (Scottdale: Herald Press, 1967). The Doukhobor settlements in Western Canada beg some comparison with the special land grants to Mennonites and Hutterites, but their search was for even greater liberties from the state, a quest which did not impress Frank Oliver during his tenure as federal Minister of the Interior. See William Janzen, "The Doukhobor Challenge to Canadian Liberties," in *Spirit Wrestlers: Centennial Papers in Honour of Canada's Doukhobor Heritage*, ed. K.J. Tarassoff and R.B. Klymasz (Ottawa: Canadian Museum of Civilization, 1995), 167–82.

77. Gillian L. Gollin, *Moravians in Two Worlds* (New York: Columbia University Press, 1967), 4.

78. See Georges Pages, *The Thirty Years War, 1618–1648*, trans. D. Maland (New York: Harper and Row, 1971).

79. Gollin, *Moravians in Two Worlds*, 5; see also J. Taylor Hamilton, *A History of the Church Known as the Moravian Church or the Unitas Fratrum* (Bethlehem, PA: Times Publishing Co., 1900), ch. 1.

80. M.W. Liebert, *Bruderfeld and Bruderheim: Moravian Settlements in Alberta, Canada* (Bethlehem, PA: Moravian Publications Concern, 1896), 7–8.

81. Redekop and Gilchrist, *Strathcona County: A Brief History*, 20; Canada, (1971) vol. 3, 119.

82. "Grass on the Roof," *Edmonton Journal*, Nov. 5, 1960.

83. Redekop and Gilchrist, *Strathcona County: A Brief History*, 18, 24; Bruderheim Historical Committee, *From Bush to Bushels: A History of Bruderheim and District* (Edmonton: D. Friesen, 1983), 6–15.

84. D.J. Hall, *Clifford Sifton*, vol. 1 (Vancouver: University of British Columbia Press, 1981), 253.

85. Ibid., vol. 2, 58–60.

86. *Manitoba Free Press*, Feb. 29, 1896. Cited in Hall, *Clifford Sifton*, vol. 1, 132.

87. Ibid., vol. 1, 261–62.

88. Ibid., 132, 253 f.

89. The social background to many of the religious groups that came to the West after 1870 is reviewed in Benjamin J. Smillie, ed., *Visions of the New Jerusalem: Religious Settlement on the Prairies* (Edmonton: NeWest Press, 1983).

90. Hall, *Clifford Sifton*, 262–65 on Oliver's performance as a politician, see Waddell, "The Honourable Frank Oliver" and "Frank Oliver and the Bulletin."

91. Myrna Kostash, *All of Baba's Children* (Edmonton: NeWest Publishers, 1992), 3–4.

92. Anne B. Woywitka, "A Rumanian Pioneer," *Alberta Historical Review* 21, no. 4 (1973): 20–27.

93. See Vladimir J. Kaye, *Early Ukrainian Settlements in Canada: 1895–1900* (Toronto: University of Toronto Press, 1964); Martynowych, The Ukrainian Bloc Settlement in East Central Alberta; Palmer, *Peoples of Alberta*, 16–23, 214–96.

94. John W. Friesen and Michael M. Verigin, *The Community Doukhobors: A People in Transition* (Ottawa: Borealis Press, 1996), xix–xx; George Woodcock and Ivan Avakumovic, *The Doukhobors* (Toronto: Oxford University Press, 1968), 132–33, 204.

95. The name appeared on a 1903 map. Mundare may commemorate a French Catholic priest named Mundare; it may be a corruption of the Ukrainian term for monestary; or it may designate a railway station master, William Mundare.

96. I. Pyskor, *Winnipeg to Basilian Fathers' Monastery* (Zolkwa, Western Ukraine). Translated from the Ukrainian of Neil Savaryn, O.S.B.M. *Rolia Otsiv Vasilian v Kanadi* [The Role of the Basilian Fathers in Canada], Educational Letters no. 6. (Mundare, Alberta, Basilian Fathers, 1938). Cited in J. Skwarok, O.S.B.M., *The Ukrainian Settlers in Canada and Their Schools* (Edmonton: 1959), 24.

97. Michael Walsh, ed., *Butler's Lives of Patron Saints* (New York: Harper and Row, 1987), 67–70.

98. See generally, Mundare Historical Society, *Memories of Mundare* (Edmonton: D. Friesen, 1980).

99. Phillips, *Tales of Tofield*, 6–10.

100. Nyland, "This Dying Watershed," 11.

101. MacGregor, *The Battle River Valley*, 163.

102. Monrad E. Kjorlien, "A Review of Historical Information of Fire History and Vegetation Description of Elk Island and the Beaver Hills," unpublished paper, Elk Island National Park (April, 1977), 10; Edo Nyland, "Miquelon Lake," Alberta Lands, Forests, Parks, Wildlife, 13, no. 1 (1970): 20; Peter Murphy, History of Forest and Prairie Fire Control Policy in Alberta, ENR Report No. T-77 (Edmonton: Alberta Energy and Natural Resources, Forest Service, 1985), 86 f.

103. Nyland, "This Dying Watershed," 28.

104. Nyland, oral testimony, Alberta Environment Conservation Authority, Proceedings: Public Hearings on Proposal to Restore Water Levels in Cooking and Hastings Lakes (Edmonton: AECA, 1971), 138.

105. Robert Scace, Elk Island National Park: A Cultural History, 122.

106. Nyland, E., "This Dying Watershed," 30; Redekop and Gilchrist, *Strathcona County: A Brief History*, 24.

107. Interesting recollections of the recreational history of this area are contained in the oral and written submissions contained in the Proceedings of the Public Hearings on a Proposal to Restore Water Levels in Cooking

and Hastings Lake (Edmonton: Alberta, Environment Conservation Authority, 1971).

Chapter 5

1. See L.G. Thomas, *The Liberal Party in Alberta: A History of Politics in the Province of Alberta, 1905–1921* (Toronto: University of Toronto Press, 1959), 5–7.

2. Howard and Tamara Palmer, *Alberta: A New History* (Edmonton: University of Alberta Press, 1990), 124–25.

3. See Pierre Berton, *The Promised Land: Settling the West, 1896–1914* (Toronto: McClelland and Stewart, 1984), 57–59.

4. Robert W. Sloan, "The Canadian West: Americanization or Canadianization?" *Alberta Historical Review* 16, no. 1 (1968): 1–7; D.J. Hall, *Clifford Sifton*, vol. 2 (Vancouver: University of British Columbia Press, 1985), 192; W.S. Waddell, "Frank Oliver and the Bulletin," *Alberta Historical Review* 5, no. 3 (1957): 11.

5. Hall, *Clifford Sifton*, 192; see also LAC, RG 84, vol. 479 E.2, Boundaries, 1903–38, Oliver to Smart, Sept. 2, 1903.

6. Edo Nyland, "This Dying Watershed," Alberta Lands, Forests, Parks, Wildlife, 12, no. 3 (1969): 24–26.

7. LAC, RG 84, vol. 479 E.2, Boundaries, 1903–38, Cooper to Oliver, Aug. 15, 1903.

8. Canada, Order in Council, July 13, 1906. This Order established 16 square miles as the game reserve.

9. For background on Simmons, see Dennis P. Fjestad, ed., *South of the North Saskatchewan* (Edmonton: Josephburg Historical Committee, 1984), 725, 731–35. Minor glimpses of this period are provided by a nephew of Ellsworth Simmons in Clarence Simmons, *The Endless Reach* (Fort St. John: 1989), 179–81.

10. W.F. Lothian, *A History of Canada's National Parks*, vol. 1 (Ottawa: Parks Canada, 1976), 48; "A History of Elk Island National Park in the Province of Alberta," typescript dated May 9, 1957, on file with the Historical Services Division, Parks Canada, Calgary, File 63/1-16-5.

11. *Elk Island Triangle*, Aug. 26, 1981.

12. Ida May Reid, "Good Hope Days," *Alberta Historical Review* 9, no. 2 (1961): 24.

13. Ross Chapman, *The Discover's Guide to Elk Island National Park* (Edmonton: Lone Pine Publishing, 1991), 52; P.B. Sullivan, "Elk Park," *Edmonton Evening Bulletin*, Jan. 20, 1917. See also Robert C. Scace, Elk Island National Park: A Cultural History, Manuscript Report Series (Ottawa: National Historic Parks and Sites Branch, 1977).

14. See Irene M. Spry, "The Great Transformation: The Disappearance of the Commons in Western Canada," in *Man and Nature on the Prairies*, ed. R. Allen (Regina: Canadian Plains Research Center, University of Regina, 1976), 21–45; Frank G. Roe, *The North American Buffalo: A Critical Study of the Species in its Wild State*, 2nd ed. (Toronto: University of Toronto Press, 1970); Sheilagh C. Ogilvie, *The Park Buffalo* (Calgary-Banff: National and Provincial Parks Association, 1979); W.F. Lothian, *A History of Canada's National Parks*, vol. 4 (Ottawa: Parks Canada, 1981), 23–40. On the American experience see: David A. Dary, *The Buffalo Book* (Chicago: Sage Press, 1974); Wayne Gard, *The Great Buffalo Hunt* (New York: Alfred A. Knopf, 1960); Andrew C. Isenberg, *The Destruction of the Bison* (Cambridge: Cambridge University Press, 2000).

15. See Walter Hildebrandt and Brian Hubner, *The Cypress Hills: The Land and Its People*, 2nd ed. (Calgary: Fifth House\, 2007); and Gordon Nelson, *The Last Refuge* (Montreal: Harvest House, 1973).

16. Fred Cook, "Giants and Jesters in Public Life: How Frank Oliver Preserved the Buffalo," *Calgary Herald*, Jan. 16, 1936; Ogilvie, *The Park Buffalo*, 26–34.

17. Ibid., 30.

18. Morley A.R. Young, "An Account of the History of the Buffalo: Elk Island National Park," offprint, Northern Alberta Pioneers and Old Timers' Association, Nov. 15, 1961. This account was also reproduced in *Alberta Historical Review* 13, no. 1 (1965): 26–28; "The Last Stand of the Prairie Monarch," *Fort Saskatchewan Reporter*, June 6, 1907; John Kidder, "Montana Miracle: It Saved the Buffalo," *Montana: The Magazine of Western History* (Spring 1965): 52–67; Norman Luxton, *The Last of the Buffalo* (Cincinnati: Tom Jones, 1908).

19. Ogilvie, *The Park Buffalo*, 30.

20. Ibid., 29, 35. On the history of the park at Wainwright, see Jennifer Brower, *Lost Tracks: Buffalo National Park, 1909–1939* (Edmonton: AU Press, 2008).

21. Scace, (1976), 109.

22. *Fort Saskatchewan Reporter*, June 6, 1907, 1,8.

23. Canada. Order in Council. P.C. No. 646. March 27, 1913.

24. Edo Nyland, "Miquelon Lake," *Alberta Lands, Forests, Parks, Wildlife*, 13(1) (1970), 20.

25. Hay Lakes History Book Committee. *Each Step Left Its Mark: A History of Hay Lakes and Surrounding Area* (Edmonton: Friesen, 1982), 131–2, 4.

26. Nyland (1969), 29–30; Mildred Stefiszyn, ed., *Land Among the Lakes: A History of the Deville and North Cooking Lake Area* (Edmonton: Deville-North Cooking Lake Historical Society, 1983), 33–45.

27. Phillips, ed., (1969), 126–28; *Cooking Lake-Blackfoot Grazing, Wildlife and Provincial Recreation Area: Management Plan* (Edmonton: Environmental Protection Natural Resources Service, 1997), 14; Stefiszyn, ed.(1983), 46–54.

28. Canada. Department of the Interior, *Report of the Commissioner, 1923* (Ottawa: 1924), 24.

29. William C. Wonders, "Scandinavian Settlers in Central Alberta," in Howard Palmer and Donald Smith, eds. *The New Provinces of Alberta and Saskatchewan* (Vancouver: Tantalus, 1980), 144–50.

30. Phillips, ed., *Tales* (1969), 184; Linda Redekop and Wilfred Gilchrist, *Strathcona County: A Brief History* (Edmonton: University of Alberta Publishing, 1981), 23.

31. Alberta Culture. Historic Sites. *Heritage Resource Inventory of the Cooking Lake Study Area*, in Alberta Environment. Planning Division. Cooking Lake Area Study (Edmonton. AEPD. 1976). Vol. 5, 11–14.

32. Cited in Redekop and Gilchrist, (1981), 38.

33. *Edmonton Bulletin*, May 7, 1884, cited in Redekop and Gilchrist, (1981), 39–40. W.C. Pollard, *Pioneering in the Prairie West* (Toronto: Nelson, 1926), 40.

34. John Morrow, "The History of Deville," in Phillips, ed. (1969), 192–4.

35. Ibid., 194–5.

36. *Edmonton Journal*, March 31, 1962.

37. Cited in Leslie Lin, "Elk Island National Park. History," 1975. Typescript, Elk Island National Park Warden Office, 80.

38. Pollard (1926), 35 f; Reid, (1961), 22–24; Redekop and Gilchrist (1981), 15, 42A–43A; R. Douglas Francis, "Establishment of the Parry Sound Colony," *Alberta History*, 29 (1) (1981), 23–30.

39. Redekop and Gilchrist (1981), 23; Reid (1961), 24; Lawrence M. Rye, "Reminiscences of a Parry Sound Colonist," *Alberta Historical Review* 10(4)(1962), 21.

40. Mundare Historical Society, *Memories of Mundare* (Edmonton: Friesen Publishers, 1984), 6; Phillips, ed. (1969), 100–101.

41. Ibid. (1969), 98.

42. Ibid.

43. Ibid., 99–100.

44. James H. Gray, *Men Against the Desert* (Saskatoon: Western Producer Prairie Books, 1967), 14 f.

45. *Atlas of Alberta* (Edmonton: Government of Alberta and University of Alberta, 1969), Plates 56 and 57; Kim Mah, "Alberta's Church Country," *Westworld Alberta* (Sept. 2000), 9.

46. Pollard (1926), 60. See Frederick Jackson Turner, *The Frontier in American History* (New York: Dover, 1996), 121; Richard Allen, ed., *Religion and Society in the Prairie West*. Canadian Plains Studies, 3 (Regina: Canadian Plains Research Center, 1974).

47. See John H. Blackburn, *Land of Promise*, John Archer, ed. (Toronto: Macmillan, 1970), Ch. 3; Pollard, *Pioneering* (1926), 30 f.; Wilfred Egleston, "The Old Homestead: Romance and Reality," in Howard Palmer, ed. *The Settlement of the West* (Calgary: University of Calgary/Comprint, 1977), 114–29; David C. Jones and Ian MacPherson, eds., *Building Beyond the Homestead* (Calgary: University of Calgary Press, 1988); Lyle Dick, *Farmers "Making Good": The Development of Abernethy District, Saskatchewan, 1880–1920*, 2nd ed. (Calgary: University of Calgary Press, 2008), Ch.1.

48. In his consideration of the frontier in North American settlement, Turner saw egalitarianism as a virtue. Turner (1996), 269 f. On the halting efforts to establish a new *modus operandi* with respect to land after 1870, see the

essays in R.C. Macleod, ed. *Swords and Ploughshares: War and Agriculture in Western Canada* (Edmonton: University of Alberta Press, 1993).

49. See Waddel (1950); Lupul (1978); and Linda Goyette and Caroline Jakeway Roemmich, *Edmonton In Our Own Words* (Edmonton: University of Alberta Press, 2004), 88–106; 130–36; 150–51.

50. For details on all treaties see Canada. *Indian Treaties and Surrenders*. (Ottawa: Queen's Printer, 1891), 3 V.

51. See Simon Evans, *The Bar U and Canadian Ranching History* (Calgary: University of Calgary Press, 2004), Ch. 2.

52. See Sarah Carter, *Lost Harvests: Prairie Indian Reserve Farmers and Government Policy* (Montreal: McGill-Queens, 1990); "Demonstrating Success: The File Hills Farm Colony," *Prairie Forum*, 16 (2) (1991), 157–83.

53. Ian Sumpter, *Report on Elk Island Park Archaeology* (Calgary: Parks Canada Regional Office. 1987), 10; Nyland, (1969), 23.

54. On the cumulative effects of government and church educational policies with respect to Native peoples, see John S. Milloy, *A National Crime: The Canadian Government and the Residential School System, 1879 to 1986.* Winnipeg: University of Manitoba Press, 1999.

55. See W.L. Morton, 'Manitoba Schools and Canadian Nationality' in: R. Craig Brown, ed., *Minorities, Schools and Politics* (Toronto: University of Toronto Press, 1969), 10–18; and see C.B. Sissons, *Bilingual Schools in Canada* (Toronto: 1917).

56. Randall J. Brown, "Hobbema Sun Dance of 1923," *Alberta Historical Review*, 30(3) (1982), 1–8; Pettipas (1994), 97- 98.

57. Peter Erasmus, *Buffalo Days and Nights.* Irene Spry, ed. (Calgary: Glenbow Institute, 1976), 268, and see Irene Spry, "Introduction," Erasmus (1976), xxix–xxxii

58. The "jingoism" associated with the Boer War and mounting tensions with Germany, helped foster an aggressive pride in the Anglo-American community. See Ronald Hyam, "The Partition of Africa," in: R. Hyam and G. Martin, *Reappraisals in British Imperial History* (London: MacMillan, 1975), 142; and Myrna Kostash, *All of Baba's Children* (Edmonton: NeWest Press, 1992), 26 f; Robert W. Sloan, "The Canadian West: Americanization or Canadianization?" *Alberta Historical Review* 16(1) (1968), 1–7; and Howard

Palmer, *Patterns of Prejudice: A History of Nativism in Alberta* (Toronto: McClelland and Stewart, 1982), 22 f.

59. Zonia Keywan, *Greater Than Kings: Ukrainian Pioneer Settlement in Canada.* (Montreal: Harvest House, 1977), 34–9; J.S. Woodsworth, *Strangers Within Our Gates* (1909). Introduction by Marilyn Barber (Toronto: University of Toronto Press, 1972), 253.

60. On the idea of progress and Macaulay, See J.H. Plumb, *The Making of an Historian* (Athens: University of Georgia Press, 1988), 253–5. On Woodsworth and his context in early 20th century Canada, see Ramsay Cook, *The Regenerators: Social Criticism in Late Victorian English Canada* (Toronto: University of Toronto Press, 1985), 213 f. And see Hugh Dempsey, *Big Bear: The End of Freedom* (Vancouver: Greystone Books, 1984), 39; Woodswoth, quoted in Fr. Boniface, *Pioneering in the West* (Vancouver: Evergreen Press, 1957), 49–50; Kostash (1992), 29 f.

61. See Frank J. Dolphin, *Indian Bishop of the West: Vital Justin Grandin, 1829–1902* (Ottawa: Novalis, 1986), 151; I.A. Silver, "French Canada and the Prairie Frontier, 1870–1890," *Canadian Historical Review* 50 (1) (1969), 11–36; J. Skwarok, *The Ukrainian Settlers in Canada and Their Schools, 1891–1921.* (Toronto: Basilian Press, 1959) 23–5.

62. See Raymond J.A. Huel, "French Speaking Bishops and the Cultural Mosaic in Western Canada," in Allen, ed., *Religion and Society* (1974), 53–64.

63. Ibid., 2,6 and Chapters 9–13.

64. Fr. Boniface (1957), 5–6; and see G.N. Emery, "Methodist Missions Among the Ukrainians," *Alberta History* 19(2) (1971), 8–19.

65. Vera Lysenko, *Men In Sheepskin Coats: A Study in Assimilation* (Toronto: Ryerson, 1947), 63.

66. J. Skwarok, *The Ukrainian Settlers In Canada and Their Schools* (Edmonton 1958), 24.

67. Nicolas Zernov, *Eastern Christendom: A Study of the Origin and Development of the Eastern Orthodox Church* (New York: G.P. Putnam's Sons, 1961), 146–8.

68. Paul Yuzyk, *The Ukrainian Orthodox Church of Canada, 1918–1951* (Ottawa: University of Ottawa Press, 1981), 7–18.

69. See Orest Martynowych, *Ukrainians in Canada: The Formative Years, 1891–1924* (Edmonton: University of Alberta Press, 1991), 3–5; and see

Geoffrey York, "Ukraine fractured along ancient fault lines'," *Globe and Mail,* (June 22, 2001), A3.

70. Martynowych, (1991), 155 f.

71. Yuzyk, (1981), 36.

72. Ibid., 36–40. The Russo-Orthodox Church of the Transfiguration, which now occupies the original site, dates from 1913. See Diana Thomas Kordan, *Historical Driving Tour: Ukrainian Churches in East Central Alberta* (Edmonton: Alberta Culture and Multiculturalism, 1988), Stop 22.

73. Yuzyk, (1981), 52; Martynowych, (1991), Ch. 11; Kostash, (1992), 272.

74. Fr. Boniface, (1957), 61. On the distinctions between urban and rural in the development of local institutions in the pioneer period, and on other factors which shaped the success or failure of cultural programs, see Martynowych, (1991), Ch. 11; Kostash (1992), 173 f; 267 f.

75. Skwarok (1959). 24–6.

76. Kordan, (1988), Stop 3.

77. Cited in Andry Makuch, *Hly's Church: A Narrative History of the Ukrainian Catholic Church at Buczacz, Alberta.* Historic Sites Service. Occasional Paper No. 19. (Edmonton: Alberta Culture, 1989), 11.

78. Howard and Tamara Palmer, eds. *Peoples of Alberta: Portraits of Cultural Diversity* (Saskatoon: Western Prairie Producers, 1985), 274 f.

79. Fr. Boniface, (1957), 65.

80. See Bill Waiser, *Park Prisoners: The Untold Story of Western Canada's National Parks, 1915–1946* (Calgary: Fifth House, 1995), 15 f.

81. See *50th Anniversary - Skaro Shrine - Star* (Edmonton: 1969). Anthony Sylla, OMI, came to Alberta in 1909 and served many of the new Polish-speaking settlements and left an important diary and memoir of his experiences. See also *Pride in Progress* (Chipman: Alberta Rose Historical Society, 1982), 142-44; and Palmer and Palmer, eds. (1985), 279–82; 516–17. On Ruh, see Basil Rotoff, et al. *Monuments to Faith: Ukrainian Churches in Manitoba* (Winnipeg: University of Manitoba Press, 1990), 106–8.

82. Kordan, (1988), Stop 3.

83. Kostash (1992), 185–87.

84. Ibid., 269.

Chapter 6

1. David P. McGinnis, "The Keynesian Revolution in Canada, 1929–1945," in *The Dirty Thirties in Prairie Canada*, ed. R.D. Francis and H. Ganzevoort (Vancouver: Tantalus, 1980), 48.

2. John H. Blackburn, *Land of Promise*, (Toronto: MacMillan, 1970), ch. 1, ch. 5, p. 188.

3. Michael Horn, *The Great Depression of the 1930s in Canada* (Ottawa: Canadian Historical Association, 1984), 3.

4. Blackburn, *Land of Promise*, 189.

5. Phillips, *Tales of Tofield*, 136.

6. Blackburn, *Land of Promise*, 189.

7. Phillips, *Tales of Tofield*, 135.

8. James Gray, *The Winter Years* (Toronto: MacMillan, n.d.), 104–105.

9. On Aberhart see Howard Palmer, with Tamara Palmer, *Alberta: A New History* (Edmonton: Hurtig, 1990), 277–78; John A. Irving, *The Social Credit Movement in Alberta* (Toronto: University of Toronto Press, 1959); C.B. MacPherson, *Democracy in Alberta: Social Credit and the Party System*, 2nd ed. (Toronto: University of Toronto Press, 1962); David Elliott and Iris Miller, *Bible Bill: A Biography of William Aberhart* (Edmonton: Reidmore, 1987); Anthony Mardiros, *William Irvine: The Life of a Prairie Radical* (Toronto: James Lorimer, 1979), 146–54.

10. Blackburn, *Land of Promise*, 191.

11. Ibid., 191–92.

12. Kostash, *All of Baba's Children* (Edmonton: NeWest Press, 1972), 126.

13. See Carl Betke, "Pioneers and Police on the Canadian Prairies, 1885–1914," in *The Mounted Police and Prairie Society, 1873–1919*, ed. William M. Baker (Regina: Canadian Plains Research Center, 1998), 217–18. 298–301; Palmer, *Alberta: A New History*, 22 f; Kostash, *All of Baba's Children*, 256–60.

14. On Bennett, see Richard Wilbur, *The Bennett Administration: 1930–1935*, CHR Booklet no. 24 (Ottawa: Canadian Historical Association,1969); H. Blair Neatby, *The Politics of Chaos: Canada in the Thirties* (Toronto: Copp Clark, 1986), 51–72; and see McGinnis, "The Keynesian Revolution in Canada," 46–63, and R.B. Bryce, "The Canadian Economy in the 1930s:

Unemployment Relief Under Bennett and Mackenzie King," in *Explorations in Canadian Economic History: Essays in Honour of Irene M. Spry*, ed. Duncan Cameron (Ottawa: University of Ottawa Press, 1985), 7–26.

15. On the experience of those in the park camps in Waterton, see Frank Goble, *The 20 Cent Men* (Cardston: Frank Goble Publishing, 2000); and see Bill Waiser, *Park Prisoners: The Untold Story of Western Canada's National Parks, 1915–1946* (Saskatoon: Fifth House, 1995), 63–64, 92.

16. *Lamont Tribune*, Nov. 10, 1932; Robert C. Scace, Elk Island National Park: A Cultural History, Manuscript Report Series (Ottawa. National Historic Parks and Sites Branch. 1977), 125.

17. Linda Redekop and Wilfred Gilchrist, *Strathcona County: A Brief History* (Edmonton: University of Alberta Publishing, 1981), 48–49; and see J.R.K. Main, *Voyageurs of the Air: A History of Civil Aviation in Canada, 1858–1967* (Ottawa: Queen's Printer, 1967), 107 f.

18. "Urge Development Elk Island Park," *Lamont Tribune*, Aug. 17, 1933.

19. Scace, Elk Island National Park, 127; Cathy Benson, "Elk Island Golf Course," *Elk Island Triangle* (Elk Island National Park: 1985).

20. Scace, Elk Island National Park, 126.

21. W.F. Lothian, *A History of Canada's National Parks*, vol. 1 (Ottawa: Parks Canada, 1976), 51.

22. LAC, RG 84, vol. 1005, E. 16. pt. 2 (1928–1941), R.S. Gibson to J.B. Harkin. Jan. 11, 1934.

23. LAC, RG 84, vol. 1020, E. 318. (Museum, 1947–57), minutes of a meeting, Lamont, Apr. 18, 194.

24. Elizabeth Carlsson, ed., *Along Victoria Trail: Lamont and Districts* (Edmonton: Lamont and District Historian, 1978), 172; LAC, RG 84, vol. 482, file E. 326, B.I. Love to B.I.M. Strong, Nov. 12, 1957; Scace, Elk Island National Park, 152.

25. Marianne G. Ainley, *Restless Energy: A Biography of William Rowan, 1891–1957* (Montreal: Vehicule Press, 1993), 101–17, and Robert Lister, *The Birds and Birders of Beaverhills Lake* (Edmonton: Edmonton Bird Club, 1979), 15.

26. Ainley, *Restless Energy*, 149–50.

27. William Rowan, "Notes on Alberta Waders included on the British List," *British Birds* 20 (1926): 2, cited in Ainley, Restless Energy, 149.

28. Lister, *The Birds and Birders of Beaverhills Lake*, 15.

29. Ainley, *Restless Energy*, 150, 164–65.

30. Ibid., 154, 172, 206–209.

31. Ibid., 154 f; W.F. Lothian, *A History of Canada's National Parks*, vol. 4 (Ottawa: Parks Canada, 1981), 34; and W.A. Fuller, The Biology and Management of the Bison of Wood Buffalo National Park, Wildlife Management Bulletin Series no. 16 (Ottawa: 1966).

32. Thomas R. Dunlap, "Ecology, Nature and Canadian National Park Policy: Wolves, Elk and Bison as a Case Study," in *To See Ourselves, To Save Ourselves: Ecology and Culture in Canada*, ed. Rowland Lorimer et al., Proceedings of an annual conference, Victoria, 1991 (Montreal: Association for Canadian Studies, 1991), 139–48.

33. Margaret Lewis, *To Conserve a Heritage* (Calgary: Alberta Fish and Game Association, 1979), 1.

34. William Rowan, "Some Effects of Settlement on Wildlife in Alberta," paper presented at the Canadian Conservation Association, June 5, 1952; William Rowan, "Canada's Premier Problem of Animal Conservation: A Question of Cycles," *New Biology* 9 (1950): 38–57. A bibliography of Rowan's writings is contained in Ainley, *Restless Energy*.

35. Ainley, *Restless Energy*, 270–71 and ch. 14.

36. Ibid., 125.

37. Lister, *The Birds and Birders of Beaverhills Lake*.

38. Ibid., 13.

39. Janet Foster, *Working for Wildlife* (Toronto: University of Toronto Press, 1978), 159 f.

40. Ian L. Getty, A History of Waterton Lakes National Park, manuscript history (Ottawa: National Historic Sites Service. 1972), 160–63; LAC, RG 84, vol. 75, U 300, no. 3, W.W. Cory, Memorandum, May 20, 1925; Dunlap, "Ecology, Nature and Canadian National Park Policy," 143.

41. Aldo Leopold (1933), 21.

42. Ainley, *Restless Energy*, chs. 14, 15: Rowan, "Canada's Premier Problem of Animal Conservation," 38–57. Another scientist advancing the study of wildlife on ecological grounds was Charles Elton. The first edition of his

Animal Ecology appeared in 1927. Significant new journals included *Animal Ecology*, appearing in 1932, and the *Journal of Wildlife Management* in 1937.

43. For background to the resource transfer agreements, see: Chester Martin, ed., *Dominion Lands Policy* (Toronto: McClelland and Stewart, 1973), ch. 12; C.B. Blyth and R.J. Hudson, A Plan for the Management of Vegetation and Ungulates, Elk Island National Park (Environment Canada: Parks, Elk Island National Park, 1987), 116; W.F. Lothian, *A History of Canada's National Parks*, vol. 2 (Ottawa: Parks Canada, 1977), 16–17.

44. LAC, RG 84, vol. 481, E. 232 pt. 1. C.M. Walker, National Parks Engineering Report on Buffalo Situation at EINP. Apr. 24, 1936; B.I. Love, Veterinarians of the North-West Territories and Alberta (NP: Alberta Veterinarians Association, 1965), 179. For a review of how ideas of carrying capacity were generally considered during the period of Love's superintendency, see R.Y. Edwards and C. David Fowle, "The Concept of Carrying Capacity," in *Transactions of the Twentieth North American Wildlife Conference*, March 14–16, 1955 (Montreal, Washington, DC: Wildlife Management Institute, 1955). On expansion, see Alberta Provincial Archives, Order in Council 933/36. June 30, 1936.

45. LAC, RG 84, vol. 268, file E210-1 (1936–1942). J. Buie, Report of the Inspector, Department of Agriculture. July 25, 1936.

46. See Graham A. MacDonald, Science and History at Elk Island: Conservation Work in a Canadian National Park, 1906–1994, MRS, 525 (Ottawa: Parks Canada, 1994), ch. 4; Blyth and Hudson, A Plan for the Management of Vegetation and Ungulates, Elk Island National Park, 135–37.

47. See Gary Wobeser, "Disease in Northern Bison: What to Do?" in *Buffalo*, ed. John Foster et al. (Edmonton: University of Alberta Press, 1992), 179–188; MacDonald, Science and History at Elk Island, 42 f.

48. Alberta Provincial Archives, Alberta Order in Council 143/48, Feb. 11, 1948.

49. See Blyth and. Hudson, A Plan for the Management of Vegetation and Ungulates, 192–93; Elk Island National Park, Resource Description and Analysis (Calgary: Natural Resource Conservation Division, 1989), fig. 123, 320.

50. LAC, RG 84, vol. 482, E. 299. Slaughter of animals.

51. Stefiszyn, Mildred, ed., *Land among the Lakes: A History of the Deville and North Cooking Lake Area* (Edmonton: Deville-North Cooking Lake Historical Society, 1983), 50–54.

52. See J. Alexander Burnett, *A Passion for Wildlife: The History of the Canadian Wildlife Service* (Vancouver: University of British Columbia Press, 2003), ch. 1.

53. Foster, *Working for Wildlife*, 159, 222.

Chapter 7

1. John F. Gilpin, *Edmonton: Gateway to the North*, (Edmonton: Windsor Publications, 1984), 168–80; J.R.K. Main, *Voyageurs of the Air: A history of Civil Aviation in Canada, 1858–1967* (Ottawa: Queen's Printer, 1967), 37, 64, 171; Oral testimony of Art Spooner, in Alberta, Environment Conservation Authority, Proceedings, Public Hearings on Proposal to Restore Water Levels in Cooking and Hastings Lakes (Edmonton: AECA,1971), 178 f; R.S. Coates, ed., *The Alaska Highway: Papers of the 40th Anniversary Symposium* (Vancouver: University of British Columbia Press, 1985); and R.J. Diubaldo, "The Canol Project in Canadian-American Relations," Canadian Historical Association, Historical Papers (Ottawa: 1977).

2. Howard Palmer, with Tamara Palmer, *Alberta: A New History* (Edmonton: Hurtig, 1990), ch. 11; Linda Redekop and Wilfred Gilchrist, *Strathcona County: A Brief History* (Edmonton: University of Alberta Printing Services, 1981). 85; Hay Lakes History Book Committee, *Each Step Left Its Mark: A History of Hay Lakes and Surrounding Area* (Edmonton: D. Friesen, 1982), 140–41; Grace Phillips, ed., *Tales of Tofield* (Leduc: Tofield Historical Society, 1969), 13; David H. Breen, *Alberta's Petroleum Industry and the Conservation Board* (Edmonton: University of Alberta Press, 1993), 49; Gilpin, *Edmonton: Gateway to the North*, 199.

3. Redekop and Gilchrist, *Strathcona County*, 25, 75–76; Phillips, *Tales of Tofield*, 102–104. The question of a satisfactory definition of drought and the variability of moisture conditions on the prairies had been thoroughly reviewed in A.H. Laycock, Water Deficiency and Surplus Patterns in the Prairie Provinces, Prairie Provinces Water Board, Report no. 13 (Regina: PFRA, 1967).

4. See Sarah Carter, "'An Infamous Proposal': Prairie Indian Reserve Land and Soldier Settlement after World War I," *Manitoba History* 37 (Spring/Summer 1999): 9–21.

5. Phillips, *Tales of Tofield*, 104.

6. Ibid., 127–28.

7. A plan was prepared in 1984 with assistance from the Alberta Heritage Fund. See Grazing Reserves, Northeast Region (Edmonton: Alberta Forestry, Lands and Wildlife, 1990), 6. Donna Von Hauff, ed., Alberta Parks – Our Legacy (Edmonton: Alberta Recreation, Parks and Wildlife Foundation, 1992), 102–103; Alberta Public Lands (Edmonton: Alberta Forestry, Lands and Wildlife, 1988), 36–37.

8. W.F. Lothian, "Elk Island National Park," *Canadian Geographical Journal* 20, no. 1 (1940): 325.

9. LAC, RG 84, vol. 1005, E.16 (1941–55), pt. I, J.R.B. Coleman to Superintendent, Elk Island National Park, Sept. 14, 1954.

10. Robert C. Scace, Elk Island National Park: A Cultural History, Manuscript Report Series (Ottawa: National Historic Parks and Sites Branch, 1977, 148–50.

11. Revised policies were adopted at the federal level in 1967, the outcome of the first extended discussion on park direction since the passage of the 1930 National Parks Act. See National Parks Policy (Ottawa: Queen's Printers, 1967). Scace, Elk Island National Park, 109; John Ise, *Our National Parks Policy: A Critical History* (Baltimore: Johns Hopkins Press, 1961); J.G. Nelson, ed., *Canadian Parks in Perspective* (Montreal: Harvest House, 1970), 27–31; More recent reviews may be found in Philip Dearden and Rick Rollins, eds., *Parks and Protected Areas in Canada* (Toronto: Oxford University Press, 1993).

12. Oral presentation of P.B. Lesaux, Proceedings: Public Hearings on Proposal to Restore Water Levels in Cooking and Hastings Lakes (Edmonton: Alberta Environment Conservation Authority, 1971), 19–22; C.B. Blyth and R.J. Hudson, A Plan for the Management of Vegetation and Ungulates, Elk Island National Park (Environment Canada: Parks, Elk Island National Park, 1987), 195.

13. LAC, RG 84, vol. 482, E. 299, Slaughter of Animals.

14. LAC, RG 84, vol. 482, E. 299, vol. 9, Slaughter of Animals (1961–64), Webster to Chief, Dec. 21, 1961.

15. LAC, RG 84, vol. 482, E. 299, vol. 9, Slaughter of Animals (1961–64). DIANR, News Release, Jan. 16, 1962; Price List for Animal By-Products, May 14, 1962; H.R. Webster to Director National Parks Branch, Jan. 4, 1965.

16. Blyth and Hudson, Elk Island National Park, 196; K.W. Reid Limited, "Study of Bison Behaviour with Respect to Spruce Trees" Canadian Wildlife Service unpublished report (1964), cited in Blyth and Hudson, Elk Island National Park , 45 and 198–99.

17. Blyth and Hudson, Elk Island National Park, 197–98.

18. Ibid., 199.

19. R.Y. Edwards and C. David Fowle, "The Concept of Carrying Capacity," in *Transactions of the Twentieth North American Wildlife Conference*, March 14–16, 1955 (Montreal and Washington, D.C.: Wildlife Management Institute, 1955).

20. LAC, RG 84, vol. 1011, E. 41 (1966–67), Lloyd Brooks to R.T. Flanagan, May 9, 1968; Blyth and Hudson, Elk Island National Park, 68–69.

21. Blyth and Hudson, Elk Island National Park, 202.

22. Ibid., 168. The complete story is told by C. Gates et al., "Wood Buffalo at the Crossroads," in *Buffalo*, ed. John Foster et al. (Edmonton: University of Alberta Press, 1992), 139–65. As of 2008, the Thunder Hills herd had ranged south into Prince Albert National Park and become a free-ranging herd based on the Sturgeon River. It is cooperatively managed through the efforts of public agencies and non-profit organizations. See Prince Albert National Park Management Plan (Ottawa: Canadian Heritage, 1995), 26 and Prince Albert National Park Management Plan (Ottawa: Parks Canada Agency, 2007), 8, 32. On the role of the non-profit Sturgeon River Plains Bison Stewards Inc., see panp.info.@pc.gc.ca.

23. Blyth and Hudson, Elk Island National Park, 205–207.

24. See *Edmonton Journal*, Mar. 31, Apr. 18, 25, and 29, 1975; Ross Chapman, "Coyotes able to survive man," *Fort Saskatchewan Record*, Feb. 29, 1984, 25. Scientists such as Ralph McTaggart Cowan and C.H.D. Clarke were active in the National Parks Branch in the 1940s and were important sources of new ecological thinking in Canadian National Park policy. See for example,

LAC, RG 84, vol. 15, file K-300, Wildlife General, Clarke to Lloyd, Dec. 4, 1942.

25. Elk Island National Park. Management Plan (Parks Canada: Park Planning, Western Region, Dec. 1978); National Parks Policy (Ottawa: Parks Canada, 1978); C.B. Blyth and R.J. Hudson, "Elk Island National Park, Canada – A Historical Perspective of Protected Areas Management, " in *Science and the Management of Protected Areas: Proceedings of an International Conference, Acadia University*, May 14–19, 1991; Developments in Landscape Management and Urban Planning 7 (1992): 73; and S.C. Zoltai, Southern Limit of coniferous trees on the Canadian Prairies, Northern Forest Research Centre, Nor-X-128 (Edmonton: Environment Canada, 1975).

26. This is an ongoing story. Readers are referred to Gates, "Wood Buffalo at the Crossroads," 139–65, and Gary Wobeser, "Disease in Northern Bison: What to Do?" in *Buffalo*, 179–88.

27. Elk Island National Park Visitor Guide (Parks Canada, 1999).

28. Public Hearings on a Proposal to Restore Water Levels in Cooking and Hastings Lakes, 3 vols. (Edmonton: AECA, 1971), vol. 1, 145–46.

29. Alberta Environment, Planning Division, Cooking Lake Area Study, vol. 1, Planning Report (Edmonton: AEPD, 1976), 35; Edo Nyland, "This Dying Watershed," Alberta Lands, Forests, Parks, Wildlife 12, no. 3 (1969): 22–38, and "Miquelon Lake," Alberta, Forests, Parks, Wildlife 13, no. 1 (1970): 18–25; Scace, Elk Island National Park, 88; Graham A. MacDonald, Science and History at Elk Island National Park: Conservation Work in a National Park, 1906–1994, Parks Canada, MRS no. 525 (Ottawa: Department of Canadian Heritage, 1994), 36–37; and AECA, Proceedings, 3 vols. In 1958, Miquelon Lake was established as a Provincial Park.

30. Dick Dekker, *Prairie Waters: Watchable Wildlife and Beaverhills Lake* Alberta (Edmonton: BST Publications, 1998), 13–14; Nyland, "This Dying Watershed," 22–38, and "Miquelon Lake," 18–25; and see AECA, Proceedings, 87–92; 136–39.

31. Dick Dekker, *Naturalist Painter: An Artist's Observations of Western Wildlife* (Saskatoon: Western Producer Prairie Books, 1980), 8; Dekker, *Prairie Waters*, 15–16. A range of views were expressed by farmers and farm groups during the 1971 hearings on water levels on Cooking and Hastings Lakes. See AECA, Proceedings, 149–56; 166–69; 199–202.

32. AECA, Proceedings, 4.

33. See AECA, Proceedings.

34. Oral testimony of A. H. Laycock, in AECA, Proceedings, 78–83; 212–15.

35. AECA, Proceedings, 27; Personal Communication, the author and Strathcona County. July 18, 2002.

36. Alberta Public Lands (Edmonton: Alberta Forestry, Lands and Wildlife, Public Lands, 1988), 6; Dekker, *Prairie Waters*, 126.

37. Dekker, *Prairie Waters*, 16.

38. "Trumpeter Swans," in Elk Island National Park Visitor Guide (Parks Canada, 1999), 14; Elk Island National Park, Park Management Plan Newsletter No. 1 (Canadian Parks Service, 1992), 3–5; Beaver Hills Lake Nature Centre, Tofield, Alberta, News Clipping Binder,1987.

39. Scace, Elk Island National Park, 202; and see the wildlife distribution maps for beaver in Alberta Environment, Planning Division, Cooking Lake Area Study, vol. 3, Ecology. See also Ross Chapman, *The Discover's Guide to Elk Island National Park* (Edmonton: Lone Pine and the Friends of Elk Island National Park, 1991), 15.

40. Hay Lakes History Book Committee, *Each Step Left Its Mark: A History of Hay Lakes and Surrounding Area* (Edmonton: D. Friesen, 1982), 127–32; A.J. Gilchrist, "Preliminary report on Miquelon Lake Provincial Park," unpublished report (Edmonton: Alberta Department of Lands and Forests, Parks Division, n.d.).

41. Redekop and Gilchrist, *Strathcona County*, 77 f.

42. Alberta Culture, Ukrainian Cultural Heritage Village: Historical Development Proposal (Edmonton: Alberta Culture, 1981).

43. Alberta Culture, Historic Sites, "Heritage Resource Inventory of the Cooking Lake Study Area, Jan. 1976," in AEPD, Cooking Lake Area Study, vol. 5.

44. See Ukrainian Cultural Heritage Village, Historical Development Proposal (Edmonton: Alberta Culture, 1981).

45. Ibid.

46. Ibid., 35 f.

47. Commencing in the early 1960s, it became the melancholy task of the Waterloo geographer, Ralph Krueger, to document the progressive disappearance of this important agricultural landscape. See Ralph Krueger, "The Disappearing Niagara Fruitbelt," in *Regional and Resource Planning in Canada*, ed. R. Krueger et al. (Toronto: Holt, Rinehart and Winston, 1970), 134–49.

48. In 1988, Alberta was preparing integrated resource management plans for areas where public lands are involved or fish and wildlife resources on public or private lands. See Alberta Public Lands (Edmonton: Alberta Forestry, Lands and Wildlife, Public Lands, 1988), 23–25; and see Tom Raisbeck, "Wilderness Park in the Suburbs," *Fish and Game Sportsman* 5, no. 1 (1973): 93–94.

49. Fred Bamber, "Preparing to Meet the Challenges of the 21st Century," in Elk Island National Park, Park Management Plan Review, Newsletter No. 1 (Jan. 1992), 2.

50. Guy S. Swinnerton, "Beaver Hills Initiative: Applying the Protected Landscape Approach to Bioregional Planning," SRD-Integrated Land Management Workshop, Edmonton, Jan. 23, 2007; Jason E. Young, et al., "Trends in land cover change and isolation of protected areas at the interface of the southern boreal mixedwood and aspen parkland in Alberta, Canada," Forest Ecology and Management, 230 (2006): 151–61.

51. Cooking Lake-Blackfoot Grazing, Wildlife and Provincial Recreation Area Management Plan (Edmonton: Alberta Environmental Protection, 1997). On some of the measures put in place around Beaverhills Lake, see Dekker, *Prairie Waters*, chs. 22 and 24.

52. See M.I. Dyer and M.M. Holland, "The Biosphere-reserve concept: Needs for a network design," *Bioscience* 41 (1991): 319–25; and W.P. Gregg, et al., eds., *Proceedings of the Symposium on Biosphere Reserves, Fourth World Wilderness Congress* (Atlanta: U.S. Department of the Interior, National Park Service, 1987).

53. See Graham A. MacDonald, *Where the Mountains Meet the Prairies: A History of Waterton Country* (Calgary: University of Calgary Press, 2000), 155–56.

54. See Dyer and Holland, "The Biosphere-reserve concept, " 319–25; William L. Baker, "The Landscape Ecology of Large Disturbances in the Design and Management of Nature Reserves," in *Environmental Policy and Biodiversity*, ed. R. Edward Grumbine (Washington, DC and Covelo, CA: Island Press, 1994), 34–36.

55. Many of the issues associated with efforts to achieve effective integration of landscape values with multiple-use land management objectives were vetted in 1997 at the international conference on the Science and Management of Protected Areas, held at Calgary. See Neil W.P. Munro and J.H. Martin Willison, eds., *Linking Protected Areas with Working Landscapes Conserving Biodiversity: Proceedings of the Third International Conference on Science and Management of Protected Areas* (Wolfville, NS: Science and Management of Protected Areas Association, 1998).

56. Mathis Wackernagel and William Rees, *Our Ecological Footprint: Reducing Human Impact on the Earth* (Gabriola Island: New Society Publishers, 1996); Phillip M. Hoose, *Building an Ark: Tools for the Preservation of Natural Diversity* (Covelo, CA: Island Press, 1981); Lesley P. Curthoys, *For the Love of Alberta: Ways to Save Our Natural Heritage* (Edmonton: Federation of Alberta Naturalists, 1998).

57. Wackernagel and Rees, *Our Ecological Footprint*; Hoose, *Building an Ark*; Curthoys, *For the Love of Alberta*; Kevin Lynch, *Managing the Sense of Region* (Cambridge: MIT Press, 1980), 192 f.

BIBLIOGRAPHY

Archival Sources

Provincial Archives of Alberta, Edmonton.
Township and County Survey Maps Coll.
Orders in Council.

Beaver Hills Lake Nature Centre, Tofield, Alberta.
News Clipping Binder. 1987.

Library and Archives Canada [LAC]. Ottawa.
RG 84   Parks Canada Records.
RG 85   Department of Interior Records.
RG 109   Canadian wildlife Service Records.

Hudson's Bay Company Archives.
Fort Edmonton Journals.

Town of Tofield, Alberta.
Logan Cemetery Records.

University of Victoria Archives.
Frank Gilbert Roe Fonds.

Books and Articles

Ainley, Marianne G. *Restless Energy: A Biography of William Rowan, 1891–1957.* Montreal: Vehicule Press, 1994.

Alberta. *Alberta Public Lands.* Edmonton: Alberta Forestry, Lands and Wildlife: 1988.

Alberta. *Cooking Lake-Blackfoot Grazing, Wildlife and Provincial Recreation Area Management Plan.* Edmonton: Alberta Environmental Protection, 1997.

Alberta. *Grazing Reserves: Northeast Region.* Edmonton: Alberta Forestry, Lands and Wildlife, 1990.

Allen, Richard, ed., *Religion and Society in the Prairie West.* Canadian Plains Studies, 3. Regina: Canadian Plains Research Center, 1974.

Atlas of Alberta. Edmonton: Government of Alberta and University of Alberta, 1969.

Baker, William L. "The Landscape Ecology of Large Disturbances in the Design and Management of Nature Reserves." In *Environmental Policy and Biodiversity,* ed. R. Edward Grumbine, 34–36. Washington, DC: Covelo/Island Press, 1994.

Baker, William M., ed. *The Mounted Police and Prairie Society, 1873–1919.* Regina: Canadian Plains Research Center, 1998.

Bamber, Fred. "Preparing to Meet the Challenges of the 21st Century." In *Park Management Plan Review. Newsletter No. 1,* Elk Island National Park (Jan. 1992), 2.

Barnet, Donald C. *Poundmaker.* Toronto: Fitzhenry and Whiteside, 1976.

Bayrock, L.A. and G.M. Hughes. *Surficial Geology of the Edmonton District, Alberta.* Earth Sciences Report 62-6. Edmonton: Alberta Geological Survey. Research Council of Alberta. 1962.

Beardsley, Gretchen. "Notes on Cree Medicines, Based on a collection made by I. Cowie in 1892." *Papers of the Michigan Academy of Science, Arts and Letters,* 27 (1941): 483–96.

Beaudoin, Alwynne B. *Annotated Bibliography: Late Quaternary Studies in Alberta's Western Corridor, 1950–1988.* Archaeological Survey of Alberta, Manuscript Series, No. 15. Edmonton: Alberta Culture and Multiculturalism, 1989.

— "What they Saw: The Climatic Environmental Context for Euro-Canadian Settlement in Alberta." *Prairie Forum*, 24, no. 1 (1999): 1–40.

Belyea, Barbara, ed. *A Year Inland: The Journal of a Hudson's Bay Company Winterer*. Waterloo: Wilfrid Laurier Press, 2000.

Berry, Susan and Brink, Jack. *Aboriginal Cultures in Alberta: Five Hundred Generations*. Edmonton: Provincial Museum of Alberta / Syncrude, 2004.

Binnema, Theodore. *Common and Contested Ground: A Human and Environmental History of the Northwestern Plains*. Norman: University of Oklahoma Press, 2001.

Bird, Charles D. and Ralph D. Bird. "The Aspen Parkland." In *Alberta: A Natural History*, ed. H.G. Hardy, 117–35. Edmonton: M.G. Hurtig, 1967.

Bird, Ralph D. *Ecology of the Aspen Parkland of Western Canada in Relation to Land Use*. Ottawa: Canada Department of Agriculture, 1961.

Blackburn, John H. *Land of Promise*. Edited by John Archer Toronto: MacMillan, 1970.

Blyth, C. and R.J. Hudson. "Elk Island National Park, Alberta Canada: Historical Perspective of Protected Area Management." In *Science and Management of Protected Areas. Proceedings of an International Conference*. Wolfville: Acadia University, 1991.

Boniface, Fr. *Pioneering in the West*. Vancouver: Evergreen Press, 1957.

Botting, Gary. *Chief Smallboy*. Calgary: Fifth House, 2005.

Boumez, John B. "Coyote Control in Alberta," in Internet Center for Great Plains Wildlife Damage Control, Workshop Proceedings, University of Nebraska, 1989. http://digitalcommons. unl.edu/gpwdewp/396.

Bowsfield, Hartwell, ed. *The Letters of Charles John Brydges, 1879–1882*. Winnipeg: Hudson's Bay Record Society, 1977.

— *The Letters of Charles John Brydges, 1883–1889*. Winnipeg: Hudson's Bay Record Society, 1981.

Breen, David H. *Alberta's Petroleum Industry and the Conservation Board*. Edmonton: University of Alberta Press, 1993.

Brink, Jack. *Dog Days in Southern Alberta*. Archaeological Survey of Alberta. Occasional Papers No. 28. Edmonton: Alberta Culture, 1986.

Brower, Jennifer. *Lost Tracks: Buffalo National Park, 1909–1939*. Edmonton: AU Press, 2008.

Brown, Jennifer S.H. *Strangers in Blood: Fur Trade Families in Indian Country*. Vancouver: University of British Columbia Press, 1980.

Brown, Randall J. "Hobbema Sun Dance of 1923." *Alberta Historical Review* 30, no. 3 (1982): 1–8.

Bruderheim Historical Committee. *From Bush to Bushels: A History of the Bruderheim District*. Edmonton. D.W. Friesen, 1983.

Brunvand, Jan H. *Norwegian Settlers in Alberta*. Mercury Series, Canadian Centre for Folk Culture Studies Paper No. 9. Ottawa: National Museums of Canada, 1974.

Bryan, H.C. *Of Men and Herds In Canadian Plains Prehistory*. Ottawa: National Museums of Canada, 1979.

Bryan, Liz. *The Buffalo People: Prehistoric Archaeology on the Canadian Plains*. Edmonton: University of Alberta Press, 1991.

Bryce, R.B. "The Canadian Economy in the 1930s: Unemployment Relief Under Bennett and Mackenzie King." In *Explorations in Canadian Economic History: Essays in Honour of Irene M. Spry*, ed. Duncan Cameron, 7–26. Ottawa: University of Ottawa Press, 1985.

Burley, David, ed. *Contributions to Plains Prehistory*. Archaeological Survey of Alberta, Occasional Paper No. 26. Edmonton: Alberta Culture, 1985.

Burnett, J. Alexander. *A Passion for Wildlife: The History of the Canadian Wildlife Service*. Vancouver: University of British Columbia Press, 2003.

Burpee, L.J., ed. *Journals and Letters of Pierre Gaultier de Varennes de La Vérendrye and His Sons*. Toronto: The Champlain Society, 1927.

— "Matthew Cocking's Journal." *Proceedings and Transactions of the Royal Society of Canada*. Third Series, Vol. 2, Pt. 2, 91–112. Ottawa: 1908.

— "York Factory to the Blackfoot Country: The Journal of Anthony Hendry; 1754–55," *Proceedings and Transactions of the Royal Society of Canada*, Third Series, Vol. 1, Section II, 307–364. Ottawa: 1907.

Cameron, William Bleasdell. *Blood Red the Sun*. Rev. ed. Calgary: Kenway Publishing Co., 1950.

Canada. *Indian Treaties and Surrenders*. 3 Vols. Ottawa: Queen's Printer, 1891.

Canada. *Revised Statutes* (1927). Ch. 78. Forest Reserves and Parks.

Canada. Department of the Interior. *Report of the Commissioner, 1923*. Ottawa: 1924.

Canada. Department of the Interior. *Report of the Commissioner of Dominion Parks*. Ottawa: 1911–22.

Canada. *National Parks Policy*. Ottawa: Parks Canada, 1978.

Carlsson, Elizabeth, ed. *Along Victoria Trail: Lamont and District*. Edmonton: Lamont and District Historian, 1978.

Carter, Sarah. "'An Infamous Proposal:' Prairie Indian Reserve Land and Soldier Settlement after World War I." *Manitoba History* 37 (1999): 9–21.

— "Demonstrating Success: The File Hills Farm Colony." *Prairie Forum* 16, no. 2 (1991): 157–83.

— *Lost Harvests: Prairie Indian Reserve Farmers and Government Policy*. Montreal: McGill-Queens, 1990.

Chapman, Ross. *The Discoverer's Guide to Elk Island National Park*. Edmonton: Lone Pine, 1991.

— "Coyotes able to survive man." *Fort Saskatchewan Record*, Feb. 29, 1984, 25.

Conrad, Norman C. *Reading the Entrails: An Alberta Ecohistory*. Calgary: University of Calgary Press, 1999.

Cook, Fred. "Giants and Jesters in Public Life: How Frank Oliver Preserved the Buffalo." *Calgary Herald*, Jan. 16, 1936.

Cowie, Isaac. *The Agricultural and Mineral Resources of the Edmonton Country, Alberta, Canada*. Rev. ed. Edmonton: 1905.

— *The Company of Adventurers*. Introduction by David R. Miller. Lincoln: University of Nebraska Press, 1993.

— *Information for Intending Settlers Concerning Edmonton and District*. Edmonton: Edmonton Board of Trade, 1908.

— *The Western Plains of Canada Rediscovered*. n.p., 1903.

Coxford, A. "Annual Reports of the Superintendent, Elk Island National Park." In *Report of the Commissioner of Dominion Parks*. Canada. Department of the Interior. Ottawa: 1911–22.

Curthoys, Lesley P. *For the Love of Alberta: Ways to Save Our Natural Heritage*. Edmonton: Federation of Alberta Naturalists, 1998.

Dekker, Dick. *Naturalist Painter: An Artist's Observations of Western Wildlife.* Saskatoon: Western Producer Prairie Books, 1980.

— *Prairie Waters: Wildlife at Beaverhills Lake, Alberta.* Rev. ed. Edmonton: University of Alberta Press, 1998.

Dempsey, Hugh A. *Big Bear: The End of Freedom.* Vancouver: Greystone Books, 1984.

— "Maskepetoon." In *Dictionary of Canadian Biography,* Vol. 9, 537–38 (1976).

Dempsey, Hugh A., ed. *The Rundle Journals: 1840–1848.* Introduction by Gerald M. Hutchinson. Alberta Records Publication Board. Calgary: Historical Society of Alberta and Glenbow Alberta Institute, 1977.

Dick, Lyle. *Farmers "Making Good": The Development of Abernethy District, Saskatchewan, 1880–1920.* 2nd ed. Calgary: University of Calgary Press, 2008.

Dolphin, Frank J. *Indian Bishop of the West: Vital Justin Grandin, 1829–1902.* Ottawa: Novalis, 1986.

Donald, Dwayne Trevor. "Edmonton Pentimento: Re-Reading History in the Case of the Papaschase Cree." *Journal of the Canadian Association for Curriculum Studies* 2, no. 1 (Spring 2004): 21–54.

Dunlap, Thomas R. "Ecology, Nature and Canadian National Park Policy: Wolves, Elk and Bison as a Case Study." In *To See Ourselves, To Save Ourselves: Ecology and Culture in Canada,* Proceedings of an Annual Conference, Victoria, 1991, ed. Lorimer et al., 139–48. Montreal: Association for Canadian Studies, 1991.

Dusenberry, Verne. *The Montana Cree: A Study in Religious Persistence.* Norman: University of Oklahoma Press, 1998.

Dyer, M.I. and M.M. Holland. "The Biosphere-reserve Concept: Needs for a Network Design," *Bioscience* 41 (1991): 319–25.

Eccles, W.J. "La Mer de l'Ouest: Outpost of Empire," in *Essays on New France,* 96–109. Toronto: Oxford University Press, 1984.

Edwards, R.Y. and C. David Fowle. "The Concept of Carrying Capacity." In *Transactions of the Twentieth North American Wildlife Conference,* March 14–16, 1955. Montreal/Washington, DC: Wildlife Management Institute, 1955.

Egleston, Wilfred. "The Old Homestead: Romance and Reality." In *The Settlement of the West,* ed. Howard Palmer, 114–29. Calgary: University of Calgary/ Comprint, 1977.

Elliot, David and Iris Miller. *Bible Bill: A Biography of William Aberhart*. Edmonton: Reidmore, 1987.

Emery, G.N. "Methodist Missions Among the Ukrainians." *Alberta History* 19, no. 2 (1971): 8–19.

Ens, Gerhard. *Homeland to Hinterland: The Changing Worlds of the Red River Métis in the Nineteenth Century.* Toronto: University of Toronto Press, 1996.

Erasmus, Peter. *Buffalo Days and Nights.* Edited by Irene Spry. Calgary: Glenbow Institute, 1976.

Evans, Simon. *The Bar U and Canadian Ranching History.* Calgary: University of Calgary Press, 2004.

Ewers, John C. *The Horse in Blackfoot Indian Culture.* Washington DC: Smithsonian Institution, 1955.

Farley, Frank L. "Changes in the Status of Certain Animals and Birds During the Past Fifty Years in Central Alberta." *Canadian Field Naturalist* 39 (Dec. 1925): 200–202.

Fenn, Elizabeth A. *Pox Americana: The Great Smallpox Epidemic of 1775–82.* New York: Farrar, Straus and Giroux, 2001.

Fjestad, Dennis P., ed. *South of the North Saskatchewan.* Edmonton: Josephburg Historical Committee, 1984.

Forsman, Michael R.A. *The Archaeology of Victoria Post, 1864–1897.* Archaeological Survey of Alberta, Manuscript Series No. 6. Edmonton: Alberta Culture, Historical Resources Division, 1982.

Foster, Janet. *Working for Wildlife.* Toronto: University of Toronto Press, 1978.

Foster, John. "The Métis and the End of Plains Buffalo in Alberta." *Alberta* 3, no. 1 (1992): 61–77.

Foster, John, et al., eds. *Buffalo.* Edmonton: University of Alberta Press, 1992.

Francis, R. D. "Establishment of the Parry Sound Colony," *Alberta History* 29, no. 1 (1981): 23–30.

Friesen, John W. and Michael M. Verigin. *The Community Doukhobors: A People in Transition.* Ottawa: Borealis Press, 1996

Fuller, W.A. *The Biology and Management of the Bison of Wood Buffalo National Park.* Wildlife Management Bulletin Series No. 16. Ottawa: 1966.

Gates, C., et al. "Wood Buffalo At the Crossroads." *Alberta* 3, no. 1 (1992); 139–65.

Geiger, John Grigsby. "River Lot Three: Settlement Life on the North Saskatchewan." *Alberta History* (Winter 1996): 15–25.

Gillese, John P. "The Wildlife Journals of William Rowan." *The Beaver* (Autumn 1958): 46–53.

Gilpin, John F. *Edmonton: Gateway to the North*. Edmonton: Windsor Publications, 1984.

Goble, Frank. *The 20 Cent Men*. Cardston: Frank Goble Publishing, 2000.

Godrey, John D., ed. *Edmonton Beneath Our Feet: A Guide to the Geology of the Edmonton Region*. Edmonton: Edmonton Geological Society, 1993.

Gordon, Bryan C. "World *Rangifer* Communal Hunting." In *Hunters of the Recent Past*, ed. L.B. Davis and B.O.K. Reeves, 277–303. London: Unwin Hyman, 1990.

Gough, Barry M., ed. *The Journals of Alexander Henry the Younger:1799–1814*. 2 Vols. Toronto: Champlain Society, 1992.

Goyette, Linda and Caroline Jakeway Roemmich. *Edmonton In Our Own Words*. Edmonton: University of Alberta Press, 2004.

Gray, James H. *The Winter Years*. Toronto: Macmillan, 1964.

— *Men Against the Desert*. Saskatoon: Western Prairie Producer Books, 1967.

— *The Roar of the Twenties*. Toronto: Macmillan, 1975.

United Kingdom. Parliament. *Report From the Select Committee on the Hudson's Bay Company*. 1857.

Gregg, W.P., et al., eds. *Proceedings of the Symposium on Biosphere Reserves. Fourth World Wilderness Congress*. Atlanta: U.S. Department of the Interior, National Park Service, 1987.

Haig, Bruce, ed. Peter Fidler. *Journal of a Journey Overland from Buckingham House to the Rocky Mountains in 1792–3*. Lethbridge: HRC, 1991.

Hall, D.J. *Clifford Sifton*. 2 Vols. Vancouver: University of British Columbia Press, 1985.

Hambly, J.R.S., ed. *The Battle River Country: An Historical Sketch of Duhamel and District*. Calgary: Duhamel Historical Society, 1974.

Hamilton, J. Taylor. *A History of the Church Known as the Moravian Church or the Unitas Fratum or The Unity of the Brethren.* Bethlehem, PA: Times Publishing Co., 1900.

Hamerl, Arthur. *The Wild Exciting Years on the Battle River: 1920–1930.* Calgary: n.d.

Harrison, Tracey, *Place Names of Alberta, Vol. III Central Alberta.* Calgary: University of Calgary Press, 1994.

Hay Lakes History Book Committee. *Each Step Left Its Mark: A History of Hay Lakes and Surrounding Area.* Edmonton: Friesen, 1982.

Hedges, James B. *Building the Canadian West: The Land and Colonization Policies of the Canadian Pacific Railway.* New York: Macmillan, 1939.

Helgason, Gail. *The First Albertans: An Archaeological Search.* Edmonton: Lone Pine, 1987.

Hendrickson, James E., ed. *Pioneering in Alberta: Maurice Destrube's Story.* Introduction by L.G. Thomas. Calgary: Historical Society of Alberta, 1981.

Hendrickson, Magda, *This Land Is Our Land.* Calgary: Foothills Lutheran Press, 1972.

Henry, Alexander. *Travels and Adventures In Canada and the Indian Territories.* Edited by James Bain. Edmonton: M.G. Hurtig, 1969.

Hildebrandt, Walter and Brian Hubner. *The Cypress Hills: The Land and Its People.* 2nd ed. Calgary: Fifth House, 2007.

Hlady, Walter M. "Indian Migrations in Manitoba and the West." In *Historical and Scientific Society of Manitoba.* Papers, Series III, Nos. 17 and 18, 24–53. Winnipeg, 1964.

Horn, Michiel. *The Great Depression of the 1930s in Canada.* Ottawa: Canadian Historical Association, 1984.

Ironside, R.G. and E. Tomasky. "Development of Victoria Settlement." *Alberta History* 19, no. 2 (1971): 20–29.

Ironside, R.G., et al. *Frontier Settlement.* Studies in Geography. Monograph No. 1. Edmonton: University of Alberta, 1974.

Ise, John. *Our National Parks Policy: A Critical History.* Baltimore: Johns Hopkins Press, 1961.

Isenberg, Andrew C. *The Destruction of the Bison*. Cambridge: Cambridge University Press, 2000.

Irving, John A. *The Social Credit Movement in Alberta*. Toronto: University of Toronto Press, 1959.

Johnson, Alice M., ed. *Saskatchewan Journals and Correspondence, 1795–1802*. London: Hudson's Bay Record Society, 1967.

Keith, Lloyd B. "Early Notes on Wildlife from New Sarepta, Alberta." *Canadian Field Naturalist* 79 (1965): 29–34.

Keywan, Zonia. *Greater Than Kings: Ukrainian Pioneer Settlement in Canada*. Montreal: Harvest House, 1977.

Kidder, John. "Montana Miracle: It Saved The Buffalo." *Montana: The Magazine of Western History* (Spring 1965): 52–67.

Kooyman, Brian and Jane H. Kelley, eds. *Archaeology at the Edge: New Perspectives from the Northern Plains*. Calgary: University of Calgary Press, 2001.

Kostash, Myrna, *All of Baba's Children*. Edmonton: NeWest Press, 1992.

Krueger, Ralph. "The Disappearing Niagara Fruitbelt." In *Regional and Resource Planning in Canada*, ed. R. Krueger et al. Toronto: Holt, Rinehart and Winston, 1970.

Lamb, H.H. *Climate, History and the Modern World*. London: Methuen, 1982.

Lang, A.H. *Guide to the Geology of Elk Island National Park: The Origins of its Hills and other Scenery*. Geological Survey of Canada. Misc. Report No. 22. Ottawa: Energy Mines and Resources, 1974.

"The Last Stand of the Prairie Monarch," *Fort Saskatchewan Reporter*, June 6, 1907.

Leopold, Aldo. *Game Management*. New York: C. Scribner's, 1947.

Lister, Robert. *The Birds and Birders of Beaverhills Lake*. Edmonton: Edmonton Bird Club, 1979.

Lothian, W.F. *A History of Canada's National Parks*. 4 Vols. Ottawa: Parks Canada, 1976–81.

— 'Elk Island National Park' *Canadian Geographical Journal* 20, no. 1 (1940): 315–25.

Love, B.I. *Veterinarians of the North-West Territories and Alberta*. Edmonton: Alberta Veterinary Medical Association, 1965.

Lupul, David. "The Bobtail Land Surrender." *Alberta Historical Review* 26, no. 1 (1978): 29–39.

Lynch, Kevin. *Managing the Sense of Region.* Cambridge, MA: MIT Press, 1980.

Lysenko, Vera, *Men In Sheepskin Coats: A Study in Assimilation.* Toronto: Ryerson, 1947.

McClintock, Gray. *The Wolves at Cooking Lake and Other Stories.* Albany, NY: J. B. Lyon, 1932.

MacDonald, Graham A. *Where the Mountains Meet the Prairies: A History of Waterton Country.* Calgary: University of Calgary Press, 2000.

McGinnis, David P. "The Keynesian Revolution in Canada, 1929-1945." In *The Dirty Thirties in Prairie Canada,* ed. R.D. Francis and H. Ganzevoort, 46–63. Vancouver: Tantalus Research, 1980.

McGillivray, W. Bruce. "The Aspen Parkland: a Biological Perspective." In *Aspenland 1998: Local Knowledge and a Sense of Place,* ed. David J. Goa and David Ridley, 95–104. Red Deer, AB: Central Alberta Museums Network, 1998.

MacGregor, J.G. *The Battle River Valley.* Saskatoon: Western Producer Prairie Books, 1976.

— *Edmonton Trader: The Story of John A. McDougall.* Toronto: McClelland and Stewart, 1963.

— *John Rowand: Czar of the Prairies.* Saskatoon: Western Producer Prairie Books, 1978.

— *North-West of Sixteen.* Rutland: Charles Tuttle, 1968.

— *Senator Hardisty's Prairies: 1840–1889.* Saskatoon: Western Producer Prairie Books, 1978.

— *Vilni Zemli (Free Lands): The Ukrainian Settlement of Alberta.* Toronto: McClelland and Stewart, 1969.

MacKay, Douglas, *The Honourable Company.* Toronto: Musson Book Co., 1938.

Maclean, John. *Vanguards of Canada.* Toronto: The Missionary Society of the Methodist Church, 1918.

McMicking, Thomas. *Overland From Canada to British Columbia.* Edited by Joanne Leduc. Vancouver: University of British Columbia Press, 1981.

MacNab, John. "Carrying Capacity and Related Slippery Shibboleths." *Wildlife Society Bulletin* 13 (1985): 403–10.

MacPherson, C.B. *Democracy in Alberta: Social Credit and the Party System*. 2nd ed. Toronto: University of Toronto Press, 1962.

MacPherson, Ian. *The Co-operative Movement on the Prairies, 1900–1955*. Booklet No. 33. Ottawa: Canadian Historical Association. 1979.

Mah, Kim. "Alberta's Church Country," *Westworld Alberta* (Sept. 2000): 9.

Main, J.R.K. *Voyageurs of the Air: A History of Civil Aviation in Canada, 1858–1967*. Ottawa: Queen's Printer, 1967.

Makuch, Andry. *Hlus' Church: A Narrative History of the Ukrainian Catholic Church at Buczacz, Alberta*. Alberta Historic Sites Service. Occasional Paper No. 19. Edmonton: Alberta Culture, 1989.

Mann, William E. *Sect, Cult and Church in Alberta*. Toronto: University of Toronto Press, 1955.

Martin, Chester. *Dominion Lands Policy*. Edited by Lewis H. Thomas. Toronto: McClelland and Stewart, 1973.

Martynowych, Orest T. *The Ukrainian Bloc Settlement in East Central Alberta, 1890–1930: A History*. Historic Sites Service. Occasional Paper no. 10. Edmonton: Alberta Culture, 1985.

— *Ukrainians in Canada: The Formative Years, 1891–1924*. Edmonton: Canadian Institute of Ukrainian Studies/University of Alberta Press, 1991.

Mendelbaum, David. *The Plains Cree: An Ethnographic, Historical and Comparative Study*. Regina: Canadian Plains Research Center, 1979.

Miller, Bill, ed. *Our Home: A History of the Kikino Metis Settlement*. Edmonton: Alberta Federation of Métis Settlements, 1984.

Milloy, John S. *A National Crime: The Canadian Government and the Residential School System, 1879 to 1986*. Winnipeg: University of Manitoba Press, 1999.

— *The Plains Cree: Trade, Diplomacy and War, 1790 to 1870*. Winnipeg: University of Manitoba Press, 1988.

Mitchell, Elizabeth B. *In Western Canada Before the War: Impressions of Early Twentieth Century Prairie Communities*. Saskatoon: Western Prairie Producer Books, 1981.

Moodie, D.W. "Alberta Settlement Surveys." *Alberta History* 12, no. 4 (1964): 1–7.

Morrow, John. "The Blackfoot Stock Association." In *Land Among the Lakes: A History of the Deville and North Cooking Lake Area*, ed. Mildred Stefiszyn, 46–48. Edmonton: Deville-North Cooking Lake Historical Society, 1983.

— "The Deville Story." *Alberta Historical Review* 12, no. 4 (1964): 15–18.

Morton, W.L. *The Critical Years: The Union of British North America, 1857–1873.* Toronto: McClelland and Stewart, 1964.

— "Manitoba Schools and Canadian Nationality." In *Minorities, Schools and Politics*, ed. R. Craig Brown, 10–18. Toronto: University of Toronto Press, 1969.

Morton, A.S. *A History of Western Canada, 1870-71.* Rev. ed. Toronto, University of Toronto Press.

Morton, A.S., ed. *The Journal of Duncan M'Gillivray.* Toronto: MacMillan, 1929.

Mundare Historical Society. *Memories of Mundare.* Edmonton: Friesen, 1980.

Munro, K. Douglas, ed. *Fur Trade Letters of Willie Trail, 1864–1894.* Edmonton: University of Alberta Press, 2006.

Munro, Neil W.P. and J.H. Martin Willison, eds. *Linking Protected Areas with Working Landscapes Conserving Biodiversity.* Proceedings of the Third International Conference on Science and Management of Protected Areas. Wolfville, NS: Science and Management of Protected Areas Association, 1998.

Murphy, Peter. *History of Forest and Prairie Fire Control Policy in Alberta.* ENR Report No. T-77. Edmonton: Alberta Energy and Natural Resources, Forest Service, 1985.

Neatby, H. Blair, *The Politics of Chaos: Canada in the Thirties.* Toronto: Copp Clark, 1986.

Newton, B., et al. *Strathcona Site (FjPi-29): Excavations, 1978, 1979 and 1980.* Archaeological Survey of Alberta. Manuscript Series, Nos. 2, 3 and 4. Edmonton: Alberta Culture, Historic Resources Division, 1981.

Nix, James E. "John Chantler McDougall." *Dictionary of Canadian Biography.* Vol. 14. Toronto: University of Toronto Press, 1998.

Nix, John. "William Tomison," *Dictionary of Canadian Biography.* Vol. 6. Toronto: University of Toronto Press, 1987.

North West Mounted Police, Commissioners. *Opening Up The West: 1874–1881.* Introduction by W.L. Higgitt, Toronto: Coles, 1973.

Nyland, Edo, "Miquelon Lake." *Alberta Forests-Parks-Wildlife* 13, no. 1 (1970): 18–25.

— "This Dying Watershed," *Alberta Forests-Parks-Wildlife* 12, no. 3 (1969): 22–38.

Ogilvie, Sheilagh C. *The Park Buffalo*. Calgary: Calgary-Banff Chapter, National and Provincial Parks Association, 1979.

"Oldest Residence in National Parks System." *Elk Island Triangle*, Aug. 26, 1981.

Palmer, Howard. *Patterns of Prejudice: A History of Nativism in Alberta*. Toronto: McClelland and Stewart, 1982.

Palmer, Howard, ed. *The Settlement of the West*. Calgary: University of Calgary/ Comprint, 1977.

Palmer, Howard with Tamara Palmer. *Alberta: A New History*. Edmonton: Hurtig, 1990.

Palmer, Howard and Tamara Palmer, eds. *Peoples of Alberta: Portraits of Cultural Diversity*. Saskatoon: Western Producer Prairie Books, 1985.

Payment, Diane. *The Free People – Les Gens Libres: A History of the Métis Community of Batoche, Saskatchewan*. 2nd ed. Calgary: University of Calgary Press, 2008.

Payne, Michael, Donald Wetherell and Catherine Cavanaugh, eds. *Alberta Formed Alberta Transformed*. Edmonton/Calgary: University of Alberta, University of Calgary Press. 2006.

Peterson, Jacqueline and Jennifer S.H. Brown, eds. *The New Peoples: Being and Becoming Métis in North America*. Winnipeg: University of Manitoba Press, 1985.

Pettipas, Katherine. *Severing the Ties that Bind: Government Repression of Indigenous Religious Ceremonies on the Prairies*. Winnipeg: University of Manitoba Press, 1994.

Phillips, Grace A., ed. *Tales of Tofield*. Leduc: Tofield Historical Society. 1969.

Pielou, E.C. *After the Ice: The Return of Life to Glaciated North America*. Chicago: University of Chicago Press, 1991.

Piniuta, Harry. *Land of Pain, Land of Promise: First Person Accounts by Ukrainian Pioneers, 1891–1914*. Saskatoon: Western Producer Books, 1978.

Pollard, W.C. *Pioneering in the Prairie West*. Toronto: Thomas Nelson, 1926.

Pride in Progress. Chipman: Alberta Rose Historical Society, 1982.

Purich, Donald. *The Métis*. Toronto: James Lorimer, 1988.

Raisbeck, Tom. "Wilderness Park in the Suburbs." *Fish and Game Sportsman* 5, no. 1 (1973): 93–94.

Ray, Arthur J. "Diffusion of Diseases in the Western Interior of Canada, 1830–1850." In *People, Places, Patterns, Processes: Geographical Perspectives on the Canadian Past*, ed. Graeme Wynn, 68–87. Toronto: Copp Clark Pitman, 1990.

Ray, Arthur J., Jim Miller and Frank Tough. *Bounty and Benevolence: A History of Saskatchewan Treaties*. Montreal: McGill-Queens, 2000.

Ream, Peter T. *The Fort on the Saskatchewan*. 2nd ed. Fort Saskatchewan: Metropolitan Printing, 1974.

Redekop, Linda and Wilfred Gilchrist. *Strathcona County: A Brief History*. Edmonton: University of Alberta Printing Services, 1981.

Reeves, B.O.K. *Culture Change in the Northern Plains, 1,000 B.C.–A.D. 1000*. Archaeological Survey of Alberta, Occasional Paper No. 20. Edmonton: Alberta Culture, 1983.

Reid, Ida May. "Good Hope Days." *Alberta History* 9, no. 2 (1961): 22–24.

Reynolds, A. Bert. *'Siding 16': An Early History of Wetaskiwin to 1930*. Wetaskiwin: RCMP Centennial Committee, 1975.

Rich, E.E., ed. *Cumberland House Journals and Inland Journals, 1775–82*. Second Series, 1779–82. Introduction by Richard Glover. London: The Hudson's Bay Record Society, 1952.

Roe, Frank G. *The Indian and the Horse*. Norman: University of Oklahoma Press, 1955.

— *The North American Buffalo: A Critical Study of the Species in its Wild State*. 2nd ed. Toronto: University of Toronto Press, 1970.

Rowan, William. *The Riddle of Migration*. Baltimore: Williams and Wilkins, 1931.

— "Canada's Premier Problem of Animal Conservation: A Question of Cycles." *New Biology* 9 (1950): 38–57.

— "Some Effects of Settlement on Wildlife in Alberta." *Transactions of the Canadian Conservation Association* (1952): 31–39.

Ruggles, Richard I. *A Country So Interesting: The Hudson's Bay Company and Two Centuries of Mapping, 1670–1870*. Montreal/Kingston: McGill-Queen's University Press, 1991.

Russell, Dale R. *Eighteenth Century Western Cree and their Neighbours*. Archaeological Survey of Canada. Mercury Series Paper No. 143. Ottawa: Canadian Museum of Civilization, 1991.

Rye, Lawrence M. "Reminiscences of a Parry Sound Colonist." *Alberta Historical Review* 10, no. 4 (1962): 18–26.

Savoie, Donald, ed. *The Amerindians of the Canadian Northwest in the Nineteenth Century as seen by Emile Petitot. Vol. 2. The Loucheaux Indians*. MacKenzie Delta Research Project. Ottawa: DIAND, Northern Science Research Group, 1970.

Sawchuk, Joe, et al. *Métis Land Rights in Alberta: A Political History*. Edmonton: The Métis Association of Alberta, 1981.

Sessler, Jacob John. *Communal Pietism Among Early American Moravians*. New York: Henry Holt, 1933.

Silver, I.A. "French Canada and the Prairie Frontier, 1870–1890." *Canadian Historical Review* 50, no. 1 (1969): 11–36.

Silversides, Brock, *Fort de Prairies: The Story of Fort Edmonton*. Victoria: Heritage House, 2005.

Sissons, C.B. *Bilingual Schools in Canada*. Toronto: 1917.

Skwarok, J. *The Ukrainian Settlers in Canada and Their Schools, 1891–1921*. Toronto: Basilian Press, 1959.

Sloan, Robert W. "The Canadian West: Americanization or Canadianization?" *Alberta Historical Review* 16, no. 1 (1968): 1–7.

Smyth, David. "The Struggle for the Piegan Trade: The Saskatchewan Versus the Missouri." *Montana: The Magazine of Western History* 34, no. 2 (1984): 2–15.

Southesk, Earl of. *Saskatchewan and the Rocky Mountains*. Edinburgh: Edmonston and Douglas, 1875.

Spry, Irene M. *The Palliser Expedition*. Toronto: MacMillan, 1963.

Spry, Irene M., ed. *The Palliser Papers*. Toronto: Champlain Society, 1968.

Spry, Irene M. and Bennett McCardle. *The Records of the Department of the Interior and Research Concerning Canada's Western Frontier of Settlement*. Regina: Canadian Plains Research Center, 1993.

Stanley, G.F.G. *The Birth of Western Canada: A History of the Riel Rebellions*. Toronto: University of Toronto Press, 1961.

— "The Fur Trade Party." Parts I and II. *The Beaver* (Sept. and Dec. 1953): 35–39; 21–25.

— *A Short History of the Canadian Constitution*. Toronto: Ryerson Press, 1969.

Steen, Ragna, and Magna Hendrickson. *Pioneer Days in Bardo*. Tofield: Historical Society of Beaver Hills Lake, 1944.

The Story of New Sarepta Moravians in Commemoration of The Semi-Centennial of the Moravian Congregation, New Sarepta, Alberta, Canada 1904–1954. Privately Printed, 1954.

Sullivan, P.B. "Elk Park" *Edmonton Evening Bulletin*, Jan 20, 1917.

Syms, E. Leigh. "The Co-influence Sphere Model: A New Paradigm for Plains Developments and Plains-Parkland-Woodland Processural Interrelationships." In *Directions in Manitoba Prehistory; Papers in Honour of Chris Vickers*, ed. Leo Pettipas, 111–40. Winnipeg: Association of Manitoba Archaeologists and Manitoba Archaeological Society, 1980.

Thomas, Gregory. "Fire and the Fur Trade: The Saskatchewan District, 1790–1840." *The Beaver* 308, no. 2 (1977): 32–39.

Thomas, L.G. *The Liberal Party in Alberta: A History of Politics in the Province of Alberta, 1905–1921*. Toronto: University of Toronto Press, 1959.

Turner, Frederick Jackson. *The Frontier in American History*. New York: Dover, 1996.

Tyrrell, Henry G. "Down the Battle River." *Alberta History* 29, no. 3 (1981): 27–30.

Tyrrell, J.B. *Report on a Part of Northern Alberta and Portion of Adjacent Districts of Assiniboia and Saskatchewan*. Part E. Annual Report, 1886. Geological and Natural History Survey of Canada. Montreal: Dawson Bros., 1887.

Tyrrell, J.B., ed. *David Thompson's Narrative of his Explorations in Western America, 1784–1812*. Toronto: The Champlain Society, 1916.

Van Kirk, Sylvia. *"Many Tender Ties": Women in Fur Trade Society, 1670–1870*. Winnipeg: Watson and Dwyer, 1980.

Van Stone, James W. "The Isaac Cowie Collection of Plains Cree Material Culture from Central Alberta." *Fieldiana: Anthropology*, New Series No. 17 (Sept. 30, 1991): 1–56.

Vickers, J. Rod. *Alberta Plains Prehistory: A Review*. Archaeological Survey of Alberta. Occasional Paper No. 27. Edmonton: Alberta Culture, 1986.

Von Hauff, Donna, ed. *Alberta's Parks: Our Legacy*. Edmonton: Alberta Recreation, Parks and Wildlife Foundation. 1992.

Waddell, W.S. "Frank Oliver and the Bulletin." *Alberta History* 5, no. 3 (1957): 7–12.

Waiser, Bill. *Park Prisoners: The Untold Story of Western Canada's National Parks, 1915–1946*. Saskatoon: Fifth House, 1995.

Wackernagel, Mathis and William Rees. *Our Ecological Footprint: Reducing Human Impact on the Earth*. Gabriola Island: New Society Publishers, 1996.

Walker, Peter. "The Origins, Organization and Role of the Bison Hunt in the Red River Valley." *Manitoba Archaeological Quarterly* 6, no. 3 (1982): 62–68.

Warkentin, John. "The West of Canada in 1763: Imagination and Reality." *Canadian Geographer* 25, no. 4 (1971): 235–61.

Wilbur, Richard. *The Bennett Administration, 1930–35*. CHA Booklet No. 24. Ottawa. Canadian Historical Association, 1969.

Williams, Glyndwr, ed. *Hudson's Bay Miscellany, 1670–1870*. Winnipeg: Hudson's Bay Record Society, 1975.

Wonders, William C. "Scandinavian Settlement in Central Alberta." In *The New Provinces: Alberta and Saskatchewan, 1905–1980*, ed. Howard Palmer and Donald Smith, 131–71. Vancouver: Tantalus Research Ltd. 1980.

Woodcock, George and Ivan Avakkumovic. *The Doukhobors*. Toronto: Oxford University Press, 1968.

Woodsworth, J.S. *Strangers Within Our Gates*. Introduction by Marilyn Barber. Toronto: University of Toronto Press, 1972.

Yedlin, T., ed. *Germans from Russia in Alberta: Reminiscences*. n.p.: Central and East European Studies Society of Alberta, 1984.

York, G. "Ukraine fractured along ancient fault lines." *Globe and Mail* (June 22, 2001), A3.

Young, Jason E., G. Arturo Sanchez-Azofeifa, Susan J. Hannon and Ross Chapman. "Trends in land cover change and isolation of protected areas at the interface of the southern boreal mixedwood and aspen parkland in Alberta, Canada." *Forest Ecology and Management* 230 (2006): 151–61.

Young, Morley A.R. "The Buffalo at Elk Island Park." *Alberta Historical Review* 13, no. 1 (1965): 26–28.

Zimmerman, Larry J. *Peoples of Prehistoric South Dakota.* Lincoln: University of Nebraska Press, 1985.

Zoltai, S.C. *Southern Limit of Coniferous Trees on the Canadian Prairies.* Northern Forest Research Centre. Nor-X-128. Edmonton: Environment Canada, 1975.

Unpublished Reports

Alberta Environment. Conservation Authority. *Proceedings, Summary, Report and Recommendations: Public Hearings on Proposal to Restore Water Levels in Cooking and Hastings Lakes.* 3 vols. 1971.

Alberta Environment. Planning Division. *Cooking Lake Area Study.* 6 vols. 1976.

Alberta Culture. Ukrainian Cultural Heritage Village: Historical Development Proposal. 1981.

Blyth, C. and Hudson, R.J. Elk Island National Park: A Plan for Management of Vegetation and Ungulates. Elk Island National Park. Environment Canada Parks, 1991.

Canadian Wildlife Service. "A Program for the Control of Tuberculosis in the Wood Bison Herd at Elk Island National Park, Alberta." Report on File. Department of Indian Affairs. March 17, 1969.

"Correspondence with Old Timers, 1965–1969." Elk Island National Park. Warden's Office. 1969.

Edmonton Regional Planning Commission. *Edmonton Regional Plan.* 2 vols. 1978.

Elk Island National Park. *Park Management Plan Newsletter No. 1.* Canadian Parks Service. 1992.

Elk Island National Park. *Resource Description and Analysis.* Calgary: Natural Resource Conservation Division. 1989.

Elk Island National Park Visitor Guide. Parks Canada. 1999.

Emerson, Donald. "The Surficial Geology of the Cooking Lake Moraine, East Central Alberta." M.Sc. thesis, University of Alberta, 1977.

Ens, Gerhard. "Dispossession or Adaptation? Migration and Persistence of the Red River Métis, 1835–1890." Paper presented at the Canadian Historical Association, Annual Meeting, Windsor, 1988.

Getty, Ian L. "A History of Waterton Lakes National Park." Manuscript History. Ottawa: National Historic Sites Service. 1972.

Gilchrist, A.J. "Preliminary report on Miquelon Lake Provincial Park." Report. Edmonton: Alberta Department of Lands and Forests. Parks Division. n.d.

"History of the Cooking Lake Forest Reserve and Development of Elk Island National Park."

File Review. [Attachment to: J.I. Nicol, Director, National and Historic Parks Branch, Ottawa, to: R.G. Steele, Director of Forestry, Department of Lands and Forests, Edmonton, Alberta. Sept. 29, 1969]. Warden's Office. Elk Island National Park.

Holdsworth, W.N. "Interactions between moose, elk and buffalo in Elk Island National Park, Alberta." M.Sc. thesis, University of British Columbia, 1960.

Kjorlien, Monrad E. "A Review of historical information on fire history and vegetation description of Elk Island and the Beaver Hills." Paper on File, Warden's Office. Elk Island National Park. 1977.

Laycock, A. H. *Water Deficiency and Surplus Patterns in the Prairie Provinces*. Prairie Provinces Water Board. Report No. 13. Regina: Prairie Farm Rehabilitation Agency, 1967.

MacDonald, Graham A. *Science and History at Elk Island National Park: Conservation Work in a National Park, 1906-1994*. Parks Canada, MRS No. 525. Ottawa: Department of Canadian Heritage, 1994.

Murphy, Peter. *History of Forest and Prairie Fire Control Policy in Alberta*. ENR Report No. T-77. Edmonton: Alberta Energy and Natural Resources. Forest Service, 1985.

Reeves, B.O.K. *Cultural Resources Assessment: Elk Island National Park*. Report on File. Archaeological Research Unit. Calgary: Parks Canada, 1994.

— *Elk Island National Park Management Plan. Cultural Resources*. Report on File. Archaeological Research Unit. Calgary: Parks Canada, 1991.

Root, Judy, "Ethnobotany of some Plants of Elk Island National Park," Parks Canada 1977.

— "Native Man and the landscape." Interpretive Management Unit Plan. Elk Island National Park. 1978.

Scace, Robert C. *Elk Island National Park: A Cultural History.* Manuscript Report Series. Ottawa. National Historic Parks and Sites Branch. 1977. (Draft Report, 1975.)

Sumpter, Ian, *Report on Elk Island Park Archaeology.* Calgary: Parks Canada Regional Office. 1987.

Swinnerton, Guy S. "Beaver Hills Initiative: Applying the Protected Landscape Approach to Bioregional Planning." SRD-Integrated Land Management Workshop. Edmonton, Jan. 23, 2007.

Swinnerton, Guy S. and Otway, Stephen G. "Collaboration Across Boundaries, Research and Practice: Elk Island National Park and the Beaver Hills, Alberta." Typescript. University of Alberta. Faculty of Physical Education and Recreation. 2003.

Tway, Duane C. "The Influence of the Hudson's Bay Company Upon Canada, 1870–1879." Ph.D. dissertation, University of California, 1963.

Waddell, W.S. "The Honourable Frank Oliver." M.A. thesis, University of Alberta, 1950.

Wilson, Ian R. and Head, Thomas H. *Archaeology Inventory, Elk Island National Park.* Parks Canada. MR no. 318. (Calgary: Indian and Northern Affairs, 1978.

IMAGE SOURCES

The number references after the source indicate the page where the image or map appears in the present volume. Short title references are to listings in the main bibliography.

Maps

Alberta. *Atlas of Alberta* (1969): Glaciation, **10**

Beaver Hills Initiative: map based on source, **x**

Bruderheim Historical Committee, *From Bush to Bushels* (1983): Hoyler's Map, **87**

Canada. Department of the Interior: *Atlas* (1915), Aspen Parkland, **2**; Surveys Branch, Deville's Map, **77**; Forestry Division, Forestry Map of Beaver Hills, **82**

Edmonton Geological Society, *Edmonton Beneath our Feet* (1993): Decline of Ice, **11**

Manitoba Historical Society, *Atlas of Manitoba*, (1970): Norton, **4**

Spry, Irene M., ed. *Palliser Papers* (1968): Palliser's Map. (1860), **52**

Parks Canada: Elk Island Expansion, **151**

Redekop and Gilchrist, *Strathcona County* (1981): 'Trails' **viii** & **ix**

David Thompson, *Narrative* (1916): Map Detail, (1814), **40**

Pictures and Illustrations.

Memories of Mundare (1980): Store, **132**; Event in Hall, **134**

Mundare Museum: Wedding (1912), **130**

Moberly, H.J. *When Fur Was King* (1929): Travois, **29**

Parks Canada: Beaver Hills, p. **14**; Ungulate Populations, **164**; Residence, **101**; Pablo, **103**; Astotin Lake, **143**; Swans, **170**; Residence restored, **172**

Ream, P.T. *Fort on the Saskatchewan* (1974): Fort Saskatchewan (1905),

Ryley Ladies Auxiliary, Beaver Tales (1978): Lodge, **108**

Skwarok, J. *Ukrainian Settlers* (1959): **127**; Teaching Sister, **127**

Steen and Hendrickson, *Pioneer Days in Bardo* (1944): 'Spinning', **117**

Stefiszyn, ed. *Land Among the Lakes*, (1983): Simmons, **100, 105**; coyote hunters, **106**

Stephens, **109**; Kelly, **110**; seedlings, **111**; corral, **152**; Jack Gray, **157**

Umfreville, Edward. *Present State of Hudson Bay* (1790): Buffalo Pound, **36**

Ukrainian Heritage Cultural Village: 'structures' **173**

United Church of Canada. Alberta Conference Archives: George McDougall, **51**

University of Alberta Archives. Rowan Papers: Rowan with Raven. (69-16-793-2), **146**

INDEX